Natural Language Processing in the Real World

Natural Language Processing in the Real World is a practical guide for applying data science and machine learning to build Natural Language Processing (NLP) solutions. Where traditional, academic-taught NLP is often accompanied by a data source or dataset to aid solution building, this book is situated in the real world where there may not be an existing rich dataset.

This book covers the basic concepts behind NLP and text processing and discusses the applications across 15 industry verticals. From data sources and extraction to transformation and modeling, and classic Machine Learning to Deep Learning and Transformers, several popular applications of NLP are discussed and implemented.

This book provides a hands-on and holistic guide for anyone looking to build NLP solutions, from students of Computer/Data Science to those working as Data Science professionals.

CHAPMAN & HALL/CRC DATA SCIENCE SERIES

Reflecting the interdisciplinary nature of the field, this book series brings together researchers, practitioners, and instructors from statistics, computer science, machine learning, and analytics. The series will publish cutting-edge research, industry applications, and textbooks in data science.

The inclusion of concrete examples, applications, and methods is highly encouraged. The scope of the series includes titles in the areas of machine learning, pattern recognition, predictive analytics, business analytics, Big Data, visualization, programming, software, learning analytics, data wrangling, interactive graphics, and reproducible research.

Published Titles

Urban Informatics
Using Big Data to Understand and Serve Communities
Daniel T. O'Brien

Introduction to Environmental Data Science
Jerry Douglas Davis

Hands-On Data Science for Librarians
Sarah Lin and Dorris Scott

Geographic Data Science with R
Visualizing and Analyzing Environmental Change
Michael C. Wimberly

Practitioner's Guide to Data Science
Hui Lin and Ming Li

Data Science and Analytics Strategy
An Emergent Design Approach
Kailash Awati and Alexander Scriven

Telling Stories with Data
With Applications in R
Rohan Alexander

Data Science for Sensory and Consumer Scientists
Thierry Worch, Julien Delarue, Vanessa Rios De Souza and John Ennis

Big Data Analytics
A Guide to Data Science Practitioners Making the Transition to Big Data
Ulrich Matter

Data Science in Practice
Tom Alby

Natural Language Processing in the Real World
Text Processing, Analytics, and Classification
Jyotika Singh

For more information about this series, please visit: https://www.routledge.com/Chapman--HallCRC-Data-Science-Series/book-series/CHDSS

Natural Language Processing in the Real World

Text Processing, Analytics, and Classification

Jyotika Singh

CRC Press
Taylor & Francis Group
Boca Raton London New York

CRC Press is an imprint of the
Taylor & Francis Group, an **informa** business

A CHAPMAN & HALL BOOK

First edition published 2023
by CRC Press
6000 Broken Sound Parkway NW, Suite 300, Boca Raton, FL 33487-2742

and by CRC Press
4 Park Square, Milton Park, Abingdon, Oxon, OX14 4RN

CRC Press is an imprint of Taylor & Francis Group, LLC

© 2023 Jyotika Singh

Library of Congress Cataloging-in-Publication Data

Names: Singh, Jyotika, author.
Title: Natural language processing in the real-world : text processing, analytics, and classification / Jyotika Singh.
Description: First edition. | Boca Raton, FL : CRC Press, 2023. | Includes bibliographical references and index. | Summary: "This book introduces the basic concepts of Natural Language Processing (NLP) along with a wide variety of applications of NLP across 15 industry verticals. Practical examples containing tools, techniques and Python code are included alongside the basic concepts for a hands-on experience. The book includes applications from recruiting, social media and entertainment, finance, marketing and advertising, research and education, medical and healthcare, travel and hospitality, gaming, oil and gas, supply chain, writing, retail, real estate, insurance and telecommunications. It also includes implementation and code examples around advanced NLP utilizations, as well as popular industrial products"-- Provided by publisher.
Identifiers: LCCN 2022060257 (print) | LCCN 2022060258 (ebook) | ISBN 9781032195339 (hbk) | ISBN 9781032207032 (pbk) | ISBN 9781003264774 (ebk)
Subjects: LCSH: Natural language processing (Computer science) | Data mining.
Classification: LCC QA76.9.N38 S526 2023 (print) | LCC QA76.9.N38 (ebook) | DDC 006.3/5--dc23/eng/20230123
LC record available at https://lccn.loc.gov/2022060257
LC ebook record available at https://lccn.loc.gov/2022060258

ISBN: 978-1-032-19533-9 (hbk)
ISBN: 978-1-032-20703-2 (pbk)
ISBN: 978-1-003-26477-4 (ebk)

DOI: 10.1201/9781003264774

Typeset in LM Roman
by KnowledgeWorks Global Ltd.

Publisher's note: This book has been prepared from camera-ready copy provided by the authors.

To my late grandfather, Sardar Sardul Singh. He was a passionate reader and would have been very happy seeing a book published by his youngest granddaughter. Thank you for your wisdom and love.

Contents

List of Figures

List of Tables

Preface

In the modern day, data digitization has scaled and there are means to store every interaction happening across the world. Text data is heavily generated across the globe. Some common sources of text data include social media data, consumer interaction, reviews, articles, documents, emails, and others. More and more businesses have started leveraging machine learning, and a large majority have some type of text data available to them. Over the last decade, several businesses have explored and been successful in getting intelligence out of text data generated by them or publicly available from the web. While many are on that path, many want to get on that path and exploit the potential of building data-driven offerings. Thus, knowing about NLP and how you can use it is prime in today's time.

Natural language processing (NLP) is a hot topic with a lot of applications and an increasing amount of research across the globe. NLP refers to a machine's process to understand language. With the immense amount of text data generated today, there is an increase in the scope for leveraging NLP to build intelligent solutions. Google Trends suggests a 112% increase in searches on the topic of natural language processing in the past seven years. Many businesses today offer products and services powered by NLP. Common examples include Amazon Alexa, Gmail sentence auto-completion, and Google Translate for language translation. With the increasing demand for NLP-based products and services, there is a strong need for a workforce that is able to understand and implement NLP solutions.

I started working in the industry as a Data Scientist after finishing grad school. At the time, I didn't have any guidance in my field at the company I was working at. I was faced with tasks that seemed impossible to solve given my grad school background. In an educational setting, you are working on defined problems. In the real world, you need to define these problems yourself given the knowledge of the business objective. In an educational setting, you have data available. You're either working on publicly available datasets or one available at your educational institution. In the real world, you may not have labeled data, you may not have enough data, and you may not even have any data at all. Having faced these obstacles, I learned several lessons that over time helped me to excel at my work. I would often share my learnings and findings with the Python and Data Science community in the form of talks and presentations at conferences across the globe. After accumulating close to a decade of experience in working with language data and building NLP solutions in the real world, I wrote this book.

What does this book contain?

This book starts by introducing NLP, underlying concepts, and popular tools. Then, the book dives into everything around data – data curation, data extraction, and data storage. The data needs to be cleaned and converted to a language that a machine can understand. The book implements several data preprocessing methods, data transformation methods, distance metrics, machine learning, deep learning, and transformers. In a practical sense, businesses make use of the technique that best solves their use case, including classic/traditional models and state-of-the-art models. This book covers them all through a practical lens. With the knowledge about data and models, you are ready to put it together to build NLP applications. But what are these NLP applications, who uses them, and for what? This book dives into NLP applications across 15 industry verticals. Then, we pick the most commonly used applications and implement them in many different ways using Python and various open-source tools. Then, this book describes NLP projects in the real world, in an actual business setting. Why do you decide to build an NLP-based project? How do you measure success? Where does it fit into your company's goals? How is the model then consumed by other users and applications? All these aspects are discussed, and these NLP projects are implemented using Python and the knowledge gained from the previous sections of the book. https://github.com/jsingh811/NLP-in-the-real-world contains all the code used in this book. This book is structured as shown below.

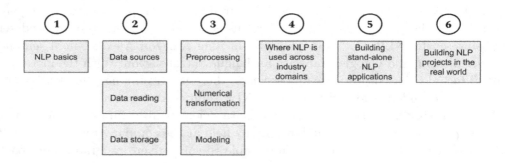

Who this book is for?

This book is an ideal resource for those seeking to expand their knowledge of NLP and develop practical NLP solutions. Whether you are new to NLP, seeking to deepen your understanding, or exploring NLP for a specific use case, this book caters to all levels of expertise. By emphasizing practical applications of NLP and providing insights into how more than 15 industry verticals leverage NLP, this book offers valuable guidance for those looking to develop their own solutions using text data.

But how would you go about it? What sets this book apart is its focus on implementation. With numerous real-world NLP applications and projects using open-source tools and the Python programming language, readers will gain hands-on experience and be able to apply the solutions in your work. Readers will be able to learn the concepts and refer back to the book any time they need to brush up on their understanding of NLP usage and applications across industry verticals.

Assuming the reader has a basic understanding of machine learning and programming in Python, this book focuses on practical aspects of NLP, covering the basic concepts from a practical perspective, rather than diving into detailed architectures. As such, this book is set to be a valuable resource for anyone looking to develop practical NLP solutions.

The solutions we build involve using classic machine learning approaches, deep learning models, and transformers, covering everything from the basics to the state-of-the-art solutions that are used by companies for building real-world applications. The reader will:

- Gain knowledge about necessary concepts and methods to build NLP solutions.

- Curate, extract, process, transform, and model text data for various use cases.

- Learn about how several industries solve NLP problems and apply the learnings to new and unseen NLP tasks.

- Experience hands-on practical examples to build NLP applications and projects of the real world using classic as well as cutting-edge algorithms.

- Implement real-world NLP projects to get real-world experience.

- Learn to use open-source Python tools for quick NLP implementations.

- Get practical tips throughout the book around different scenarios with data, processing, and modeling.

Author Bio

For nearly a decade, Jyotika has focused her career on Machine Learning (ML) and Natural Language Processing (NLP) across various industry verticals, using practical real-world datasets to develop innovative solutions. Her work has resulted in multiple patents that have been utilized by well-known tech companies for their advancements in NLP and ML. Jyotika's expertise in the subject has made her a highly sought-after public speaker, having presented at more than 20 conferences and events around the world.

Her work on building proprietary NLP solutions for ICX Media, a previous employer, resulted in unique business propositions that played a pivotal role in securing multi-million dollar business and the successful acquisition by Salient Global. Jyotika currently holds the position of Director of Data Science at Placemakr, a leading technology-enabled hospitality company in the USA. Moreover, Jyotika is the creator and maintainer of open-source Python libraries, such as pyAudioProcessing, that have been downloaded over 24,000 times.

Jyotika's commitment to promoting diversity in STEM is evident through her active support of women and underrepresented communities. She provides early-career mentorship to build a diverse talent pool and volunteers as a mentor at Data Science Nigeria, where she engages in mentorship sessions with young Nigerians aspiring for a career in data and technology. Furthermore, Jyotika serves as a mentor at Women Impact Tech, US, supporting women in technology, product, and engineering.

Jyotika has received numerous awards for her contributions to the field, including being recognized as one of the top 50 Women of Impact in 2023 and being named one of the top 100 most Influential people in Data 2022 by DataIQ. Additionally, Jyotika has been honored with the Data Science Leadership award in 2022, Leadership Excellence in Technology award in 2021, and other accolades.

Acknowledgments

Writing this book would not have been possible without the plethora of excellent resources, such as papers, articles, open-source code, conferences, and online tools. I am thankful to the Python, machine learning, and natural language processing community for their efforts and contributions toward knowledge sharing. Along my journey, I have asked a lot of individuals I do not personally know a lot of questions about this topic and the book publishing process. Thank you all for selflessly taking the time to answer my questions. Thank you to all the companies and publishers that have permitted me to use their figures to aid the material of my book. I am grateful for your contributions to this field and your prompt responses.

I am grateful to everyone who has reviewed sections and chapters of this book. Thank you Shubham Khandelwal, Manvir Singh Walia, Neeru, Jed Divina, Rebecca Bilbro, Steven McCord, Neha Tiwari, Sumanik Singh, Joey McCord, Daniel Jolicoeur, Rekha, and Devesh for taking the time and sharing all your helpful suggestions along my writing journey. Your feedback helped shape this book into what it is today, and I could not have completed it without your input and support. It has been a pleasure knowing each one of you and being able to count on your support.

The team at Taylor and Francis has been incredibly helpful throughout this process. Your prompt responses and incredible input into this book are huge contributors. Thank you, Randi (Cohen) Slack, for being a part of this journey.

I am grateful to my employer, Placemakr, for always encouraging and supporting my book-writing journey. Thank you for sharing my excitement and supporting me with everything I needed to be able to write this book.

On a personal note, I want to thank my family, the Walias and the Khandelwals, for motivating me throughout this process. I wrote this book alongside my full-time job responsibilities, volunteer mentorship work, and other life struggles. It has involved a lot of late nights and weekends to get this book completed. My husband and my parents have been tremendously helpful in taking care of everything else so I got to focus on this book. Thank you Shubham, Mumma, and Papa. Your support means the world to me. I want to especially acknowledge my late grandparents, Sardar Sardul Singh and Raminder Kaur, and my husband's grandmother, Radhadevi Khandelwal. I have received nothing but love, support, and blessings from you all. Thank you for being a part of my life.

I

NLP Concepts

In this section, we will go over some basic concepts that lead up to natural language processing (NLP). Believe it or not, each one of us has at some point interacted with a technology that uses NLP. Yes, it is that common! We will describe NLP and share some examples of where you may have seen a product or technology powered by NLP.

We will dive into where it all starts from and is centered around, i.e., language. We will follow it with a brief introduction to concepts of linguistics that form the basis for many NLP tasks. Often when thinking of how to implement a method for a machine to do a task that humans perform well, it is useful to consider the perspective – how would I (human) solve this? The answer often inspires mathematical modeling and computer implementation for the task. Thus, we will spend some time in this section on how the human-based understanding of language influences NLP tasks.

Language data needs preparation before a machine can find meaning from it. Have you ever received a text message from a friend with a term you didn't understand that you had to look up on the Internet? Have you ever needed to translate a sentence from one language to another to understand its meaning? Machines can require similar and various additional types of preprocessing before they can make sense of the language input. In general, language is not numeric (not represented as numbers), whereas a machine understands data in only binary numbers – 1's and 0's. We'll introduce the basic concepts of converting language into numeric features before diving into further details in the later chapters.

To build successful NLP solutions, it is important to note challenges in NLP and why they arise. There are many challenges, some that remain challenging, and some that can be fully or partially solved by using certain techniques. We will introduce NLP challenges and potential solution options.

Finally, we will list setup requirements and introduce popular tools that we will use in the rest of the book.

This section entails the following topics:

- Natural language processing

- Language concepts

- Using language as data

- NLP challenges

- Setup

- Tools

## CHAPTER 1

NLP Basics

1.1 NATURAL LANGUAGE PROCESSING

Language is a way that humans have been using for communicating with one another since the beginning of time. The term 'natural language' refers to language that has naturally evolved over time due to repeated use by humans. In essence, natural language is referred to as the language humans use to communicate with one another.

Natural language processing, often abbreviated as NLP, refers to the field of programming computers to allow the processing and analysis of natural language. From something as basic as a computer program to count the number of words in a piece of text, to something more complex such as a program that can serve replies to questions asked by humans or translate between languages, all qualify as NLP. Essentially, regardless of the difficulty level, any task that involves a computer dealing with language through a program qualifies as natural language processing.

Knowing about the range of applications helps us understand the impact of NLP. Consider the following example. You are cooking in the kitchen and want your voice assistants, such as Alexa or Google Home, to turn on your TV.

DOI: 10.1201/9781003264774-1

You: **Turn on the Living Room TV**

TV turns on

You: **Play the soccer match on NBC Sports 11.**

Match starts playing on your TV

You: **Pause TV**

TV pauses your video

You: **At what temperature should I bake vegetables?**

'400 degrees Fahrenheit is the perfect temperature for most vegetables for a crispy exterior and a tender interior.'

You: **Play TV**

TV resumes your paused video

Conversation as the above in these voice assistants is powered by NLP. Furthermore, you may have noticed the auto-correct and word recommendation features on your cell phone. Have you noticed how most spam email successfully makes it to the Spam or Junk folder? What about the times when you are purchasing a product online and need to contact customer service regarding an issue? Have you noticed how in many online retailers the chat service starts with an automatic reply service that tries to get you what you need without, or before, having to connect to a customer service representative? Examples include assistance with returns, order status, and product information. All these are instances of how humans interact with NLP systems regularly where the machine can understand what you type or what you speak.

There exist popular applications that are built using NLP across several different industry verticals. Some of these remain common across the board, while some applications remain specific to particular industries. We'll be looking at how and where several industries utilize or explore NLP in Section IV of this book. These industry verticals include Social Media, Real Estate, Finance, Medical and Healthcare, E-commerce, Travel and Hospitality, Marketing, Oil and Gas, Supply chain, Insurance, Gaming, Law, Telecommunication, Automotive, Education and Research, and others.

Often, implementations of NLP form a part of a larger product. For instance, is Alexa all NLP? No, but NLP is a part of making Alexa a successful product. We'll be diving into the popular NLP applications in Section V that often help in contributing to larger products across different industry verticals. We'll also dive into industrial projects that make use of the different NLP applications in Section VI.

NLP applications

The advanced applications of NLP that are discussed and implemented in Section V include the following.

1. Named-entity recognition: Named entity recognition (NER) is a form of natural language processing and is also known as entity extraction, entity identification, or entity chunking. This technique identifies segments of key information within a piece of text and categorizes the segments into predefined categories such as person name, location, date, timestamp, organization name, percentages, codes, numbers, and more. See Figure 1.1 for an example.

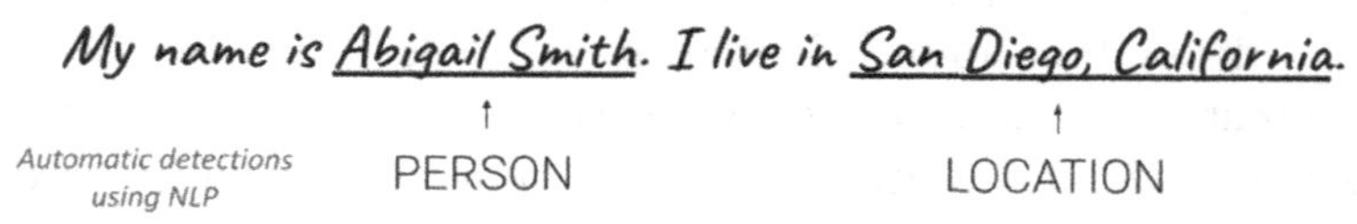

My name is _Abigail Smith_. I live in _San Diego, California._

Automatic detections using NLP   PERSON   LOCATION

FIGURE 1.1   An example of named-entity recognition.

2. Keyphrase extraction: Key-phrase extraction is a textual information processing task concerned with the automatic extraction of representative and characteristic phrases from a document that express all the key aspects of its content. Keyphrases aim to represent a succinct conceptual summary of a text document. They find use in various applications such as digital information management systems for semantic indexing, faceted search, document clustering, and classification [129]. See Figure 1.2 for an example.

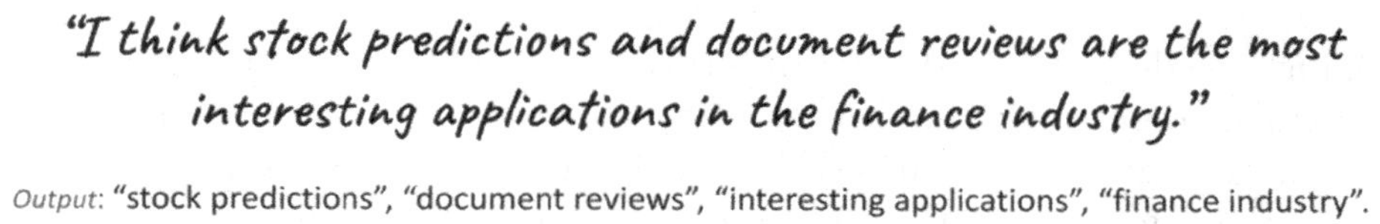

"I think stock predictions and document reviews are the most interesting applications in the finance industry."

Output: "stock predictions", "document reviews", "interesting applications", "finance industry".

FIGURE 1.2   An example of keyphrase extraction.

3. Topic modeling: Topic modeling is the process of identifying different topics from a set of documents by detecting patterns of words and phrases within them as seen in Figure 1.3. Topic modeling finds applications in document clustering, text organization, information retrieval from unstructured text, and feature selection [24].

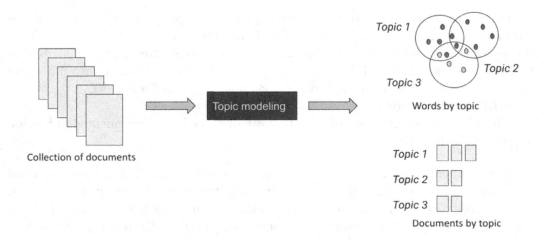

FIGURE 1.3 Topic modeling.

4. Text similarity: Text similarity is a popular NLP application that finds use in systems that depend on finding documents with close affinities. A popular example is content recommendations seen on social media platforms. Ever noticed that when you search for a particular topic, your next-to-watch recommended list gets flooded with very similar content? Credit goes to text similarity algorithms, among some other data points that help inform user interest and ranking.

5. Text classification: Text classification refers to classifying text into user-defined categories. This can be something as basic as binary labels to hundreds and thousands of categories. Examples include categorizing social media content into topics and consumer complaint categorization in customer service.

6. Text summarization: Long blobs of text such as articles, papers, or documents are condensed into a summary that aims to retain vital information using text summarization techniques. Google News[1], the Inshorts app[2], and various other news aggregator apps take advantage of text summarization algorithms.

7. Language detection and translation: Detection of language from text refers to language detection. The process of translating text from one language to another is language translation. There exist many pre-trained models for numerous language tasks that can be used right out of the box by practitioners. Most models are trained on a particular text language. Such models don't perform as well if used on text of a different language. In such cases, practitioners often resort to language detection and translation techniques. Such techniques also find use in language translation tools to help people communicate in non-native languages.

---

[1]https://news.google.com/
[2]https://www.inshorts.com/

8. Sentiment analysis: Sentiment analysis is the work of a model that is built to gauge human sentiment in a sentence. This application is a part of many analytics-powered organizations that rely on understanding consumer sentiment toward a product or content.

NLP industry projects

Some popular NLP projects used across various industries that are discussed and implemented in Section VI include the following.

1. Chatbots: Chatbots, also called chatterbots, are bots or artificial intelligence systems that are able to chat with humans, often customers of a business. Chatbots can handle tasks from understanding the customer's question to giving replies and answers. This tool often adds a convenient way for apps and businesses to provide their customers with a human-like interaction experience while keeping the costs involved low.

2. Customer review analysis: Customer reviews are important to understand the feedback for a product or business. However, customer comments are often not categorized and thus do not enable quick analysis. Analyzing customer feedback and sentiment, and creating relevant classification models finds use in many industry domains.

3. Recommendation systems: Many industries deploy products based on recommendation algorithms. Examples include ads that are recommended to you by advertisers and marketers, product recommendations on e-commerce websites, and social media post recommendations.

4. Faster documentation services: Next word prediction models aid in implementing an industry-specific or topic-specific auto-complete service to enable faster documentation processes.

While natural language is not only text but also other forms of communication, such as speech or gestures, the methods and implementation in this book are focused primarily on text data. Here are a few reasons for that.

- A lot of popular products using speech as input often first transcribe speech to text and then process the text data for further analysis. The resultant text is converted to speech after analysis for applications using a speech output.

- Speech processing is a large field of its own. On the other hand, gesture detections fall under the realm of image processing and computer vision, which is also a large field of its own. These fields are different, rich, diverse, and call for a massive write-up like an entire book pertaining to these individual topics to do them justice. For reference, a brief introduction, some resources, and open-source Python tools are listed below that you might find useful if interested in diving further into language processing for speech or gestures.

Speech

Introduction

Speech is a form of audio that humans use to communicate with one another. Speaking is the exercise where forced air is passed through the vocal cords, and depending on the pressure areas and amount, certain sounds are produced. Reading speech using a Python program, speech signals are seen as time-series events where the amplitude of one's speech varies at different points. Often in speech processing, frequency is of massive interest. Any sound contains underlying frequencies of its component sounds. Frequency can be defined as the number of waves that pass a fixed place in a given amount of time. These frequencies convey a great deal of information about speech and the frequency domain representation is called the spectrum. Derived from the spectrum is another domain of speech, called cepstrum. Common features used from speech signals for machine learning applications include spectral features, cepstral features, and temporal (time-domain) features.

Challenges

Common challenges in this field include the quality and diversity of data. Speech in the presence of different background noises forms challenges for a machine to interpret the signals and distinguish between the main speech versus the background sounds. Basic techniques such as spectral subtraction [186], and more sophisticated and actively researched noise removal models are used. There is scope for speech recognition to be made available for more languages and cover wider topics [164].

Tools

Some popular tools help extract features from speech and audio and build machine learning models [154]. Examples of such open-source tools include `pyAudioProcessing`[3] [156], `pyAudioAnalysis`,[4] `pydub`,[5] and `librosa`.[6]

Gestures

Introduction

Gestures form an important type of language. Many individuals rely on gestures as their primary source of communication. Building systems that understand gestures and smart machines that can interact with gestures is a prime application vertical. Other applications include programming a system to understand specific gestures and programming smart devices to optionally take an action based on the gesture, e.g., turn off a room light, play music, etc. For gesture analysis, there has been ongoing research in improving and creating gesture detection and recognition systems [79].

Challenges

Some of the main issues have been around image quality and dataset sizes. Training a model to recognize images from a clean/fixed dataset may seem simpler. But in a more realistic setting, the image quality is not always homogeneous or clean, and training a model to recognize images that it hasn't seen before in real-time can be challenging. Data augmentation techniques to artificially add noise to clean sam-

---

[3]https://github.com/jsingh811/pyAudioProcessing
[4]https://pypi.org/project/pyAudioAnalysis/
[5]https://pypi.org/project/pydub/
[6]https://librosa.org/doc/latest/index.html

ples have been popularly implemented in this area to build a model that is able to circumvent the noise.

Tools

Popular libraries include OpenCV[7], scikit-image[8], SciPy[9] and PIL[10]. Artificial neural networks have been popular in image processing. [79] walks through a simple model to understand gestures. Here's another guide to developing a gesture recognition model using convolutional neural networks (CNN) [36].

We have visited several applications and products powered by NLP. How does a machine make sense of language? A lot of the inspiration comes from how humans understand language. Before diving further into machine processes, let's discuss how humans understand language and some basic linguistic concepts.

1.2 LANGUAGE CONCEPTS

1.2.1 Understanding language

Humans can understand and decipher language with the help of their brains. Let's learn a bit more about how this happens.

The brain has certain areas responsible for forming, expressing, and processing language. To summarize, the brain receives signals from the inner ear at different frequencies and deciphers the words being spoken based on its understanding of language. Similarly, the image an eye sees, reflecting different pixel values, excites certain neurons and the text is interpreted based on the ability of the human being to associate meaning with the structure of the way the words are written. Signs are interpreted in the same way and are interpreted by the brain based on the understanding of the meaning of gestures. Further details on the works of biology can be found below.

Ears

Per Sound Relief Healing Center [43], the human ear is fully developed at birth and responds to sounds that are very faint as well as very loud sounds. Even before birth, infants respond to sound. Three parts in the human ear help relay signals to the brain; the outer ear, middle ear, and inner ear. The outer ear canal collects sounds and causes the eardrum to vibrate. The eardrum is connected to three bones called ossicles. These tiny bones are connected to the inner ear at the other end. Vibrations from the eardrum cause the ossicles to vibrate which, in turn, creates movement of the fluid in the inner ear. The movement of the fluid in the inner ear, or cochlea, causes changes in tiny structures called hair cells that sends electric signals from the inner ear up the auditory nerve to the brain. The brain then interprets these electrical signals as sound.

---

[7]https://opencv.org/
[8]https://scikit-image.org/
[9]https://scipy.org/
[10]https://pillow.readthedocs.io/en/stable/

Eyes

An article in Scientific Journal on 'The Reading Brain in the Digital Age: The Science of Paper versus Screens' [88] yields insights on how the eyes help in reading. Regarding reading text or understanding gestures, the part of the brain that processes visual information comes into play, the visual cortex. Reading is essentially object detection done by the brain. Just as we learn that certain features—roundness, a twiggy stem, smooth skin—characterize an apple, we learn to recognize each letter by its particular arrangement of lines, curves, and hollow spaces. Some of the earliest forms of writing, such as Sumerian cuneiform, began as characters shaped like the objects they represented—a person's head, an ear of barley, or a fish. Some researchers see traces of these origins in modern alphabets: C as a crescent moon, S as a snake. Especially intricate characters—such as Chinese hanzi and Japanese kanji—activate motor regions in the brain involved in forming those characters on paper: The brain goes through the motions of writing when reading, even if the hands are empty.

How we make sense of these signals as a language that conveys meaning comes from our existing knowledge about language rules and different components of language including form, semantics, and pragmatics. Even though some language rules apply, because of the different ways people can communicate, often there are no regular patterns or syntax that natural language follows. The brain relies on an individual's understanding of language and context that lies outside of linguistic rules.

Whether we are consciously aware of it or not, any external sound, gesture, or written text is converted to signals that the brain can operate with. To perform the same tasks using a machine, language needs to be converted to signals that a computer can interpret and understand. The processing required to do so is referred to as Natural Language Processing (See Figure 1.4).

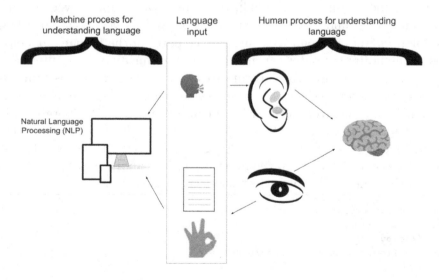

FIGURE 1.4 Understand language - humans versus machines.

1.2.2 Components of language

Let's consider the language of the form of speech and text. Humans can understand each other's language when it is of the form that a person has been exposed to in the past. For instance, an English speaker born in the US will be able to understand the language of an English speaker born in the UK. A non-native individual with a different first language, who still knows the English language will also be able to understand other English speakers. How does the exposure help in the understanding of language? Language is governed by certain rules that apply to characters, the usage of characters to form words, and the usage of words to form phrases and sentences. People who are aware of these rules are also able to understand the language.

In this book, the primary focus will be on the English language.

There are three major components of language – form, semantics, and pragmatics. There are three types of forms, namely phonology, morphology, and syntax [22]. Let's see what each of these means.

1. Form

    (a) Phonology: Phonology is the study of individual sound units within a language and the combination of these units to create larger language units. Each unit of sound is called a phoneme. Examples include \s\, \f\. The use of different phonemes can alter the meaning of words such as – 'sit' and 'fit'. There are a total of about 40 phonemes in the English language which can be vowels or consonants.

    (b) Morphology: Morphemes are the smallest unit of language that conveys a meaning. Examples include 'car' and 'teach'. Prefixes and suffixes when attached to these words may change the meaning – 'teach' -> 'teacher'.

    (c) Syntax: Syntax is the study of rules by which words are organized into phrases or sentences. When combining two or more words to form a sentence, following the language's grammar rules, or syntax, makes it understandable. For instance, 'I tied my shoes' conveys meaning, whereas 'my tied I shoes' does not.

2. Semantics: Semantics relates to the meaning of the language which is formed by the use of words together to convey a meaning. This includes objects, actions, events, or relationships between different objects, actions, and/or events. It is not just the syntax that conveys all the meaning, but also our understanding of figurative language. The understanding of semantics is what helps us understand that the popular phrase 'getting cold feet' does not literally convey information about the temperature of one's feet.

3. Pragmatics: Pragmatics is the use of language for communication in a social or interactive environment. The language used to convey a variety of intentions

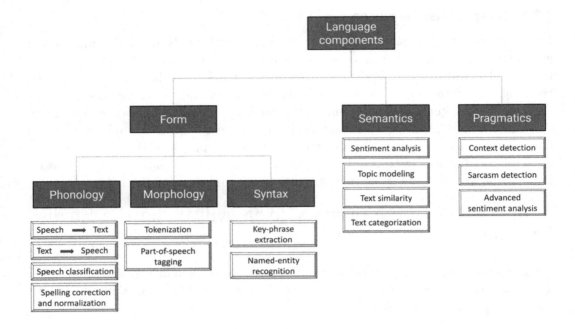

FIGURE 1.5 Some popular applications of NLP that leverage different language components.

such as requesting, asserting, or questioning falls under this category. Furthermore, the way a person speaks with their toddler is completely different from the way the same individual may speak with a co-worker or a friend. The understanding of the difference between such communication styles, and when to use which style is the essence of pragmatics.

Each component described above forms a basis for how we, as humans, interpret the meaning of speech or text. It also forms the basis for many language features that are used popularly in NLP to understand language. Figure 1.5 shows popular NLP applications that make use of the different language components discussed above. Tokenization refers to breaking down sentences into words, and words into the base form. Part-of-speech tagging marks words in the text as parts of speech such as nouns, verbs, etc.

1.3 USING LANGUAGE AS DATA

Using language as data needs specific types of processing that a machine can understand and make sense of. Parsing language is one thing for a human, but language data for a machine is unstructured. Unstructured data is data that does not conform to a predefined data model, such as rows and columns with defined relationships. Thus, it is not a ready-to-be-analyzed type of data. While language may be usually unstructured, it is not completely random. Language is governed by linguistic rules that make it interpretable by humans. For a machine to be able to learn the context, it requires to have seen such data and its usage patterns before and learn the language rules that humans are likely to follow. This section lists some methods and factors that are important when thinking of using language as data.

1.3.1 Look-up

> *TIP*
>
> It is a popular thought that when an NLP task needs to be performed, it must entail some sort of complex modeling. That is not always true. It can be a very fruitful exercise to start by thinking of the most basic solutions first. See the example below.

Consider a task where you need to find all the entries in a dataset of sentences where the entry contains content about the movie – Ghostbusters. What solutions come to mind? Curate training data, manually label some samples, and train a model that predicts – Ghostbusters versus **not-**Ghostbusters?

Let's look at a much easier and much faster solution. Why not look up the presence of the string 'ghostbusters' in each data sample? If it is present, mark it as Ghostbusters, else not-Ghostbusters.

Limitations?

Some samples may mention 'ecto-1' which is the vehicle name in the movie and not the term 'ghostbusters'. Such a sample would be missed by our approach. Solution – how about using multiple relevant keywords to search the samples with, including popular actor names, character names, director names, and popular movie elements such as the vehicle name? The results may not be all-encompassing but would certainly return an easy and fast solution and could serve as a great first approach before a complex solution needs to be scoped out. Furthermore, this method can form a first step for curating data labels for your dataset that can come in handy for future model building.

Look-ups and similarly other basic approaches to NLP tasks such as using word counts work as a great starting point for simpler tasks and result in simple yet effective solutions.

1.3.2 Linguistics

Let's look at the following sentence where the task is to identify location names from text:

Arizona Smith uses a car in New York.

How could we solve this problem? One simple solution might be to have a list of all location names and search for their presence in the sentence. While it is not an incorrect solution and would work perfectly for many use cases, there are certain limitations.

Arizona (location) Smith uses a car in New York (location).

The look-up approach would detect 'Arizona' and 'New York' as location names. We, as humans, know that Arizona is a location name, but based on the sentence above, it refers to a person and not the location.

There are advanced techniques that can distinguish between Arizona and New York in the above example. The process of being able to recognize such entities is called named-entity recognition, information extraction, or information retrieval and leverages the syntax rules of language. How does it work? The process includes tagging the text, detecting the boundaries of the sentence, and capitalization rules. You can use a collection of data sets containing terms, and their relationships or use a deep learning approach using word embeddings to understand the semantic and syntactic relationship between various words. Don't worry if this sounds unfamiliar. We'll dive further into it in Section III and Section V. The best part is that there are existing tools that offer models that do a reasonable job for such tasks. Using the spaCy library `en_core_web_sm` trained model, the below results can be accomplished:

Arizona Smith *(name) uses a car in* ***New York*** *(location).*

With the knowledge of linguistics and the relationship between terms, the machine can accomplish the detection of location names from a challenging sentence.

Many other NLP tasks can be solved using the knowledge of linguistics as seen previously in Figure 1.5.

1.3.3 Data quantity and relevance

Linguistic rules seem to have importance. Look-up methods are also a good option for some simple NLP tasks. What else do we need to know about using language as data? A good quantity of data and relevant data are some of the most important requirements. For instance, consider the following fill-in-the-blank scenario:

David is going out for a __ with his spouse.

Humans may guess 'meal', 'game', 'date', 'movie', 'vacation', or 'holiday'. Given enough text samples, a machine could guess the same answers. The guesses can only be as good as the data it has seen before. If all our training dataset contains is a few samples of someone going out for a 'movie' with their spouse, then that's the best prediction we can get. But if the dataset is more representative, we could have the machine capture many other possible answers, such as 'date', 'game', 'meal', 'vacation', 'grocery run', and even the less common events that every human may not be able to guess. Why may that be? We as humans meet several people in our lives, watch TV and movies, text our friends, read, and perform many such activities that open our imagination to different degrees. Let's consider a person named Emma. Emma is unmarried and has very few married friends. She may not able to guess where one may go out with their spouse. This is because Emma hasn't seen many examples of such an event. However, a machine has the capacity to learn from a lot more data than what a human brain can process and remember. Having large enough datasets can not only represent Emma's imagination of what David may be going out with his spouse for, but also represent the imagination of several such individuals, and thus make guesses that a single individual may not think of.

> *TIP*
>
> Does it mean the bigger the dataset, the better? Not necessarily. The dataset needs to be big enough for the task at hand. One way to measure it would be to evaluate your model's performance while incrementally increasing the size of the data and observe at what data size the model stops improving considerably. At that point, you probably have a good enough amount of data!

Now we know that data quantity matters, let's consider something a bit more ambiguous now. Let's say we want to infer which sentence is related to Art:

Fry onions in Safflower oil.
I use Safflower oil to slow the drying of my oil paints.

While 'safflower oil' is used in both examples, the topic of the first is completely different from the second. This is known to humans because when we see the word 'fry' or 'onions' used with 'oil', it becomes apparent that it is likely not about art. Similarly, 'oil paints' and 'safflower oil' used together seem likely to be about art. We are able to make that inference because we know what food is and what paints are.

To make a machine understand the same, it is important to feed in relevant training data so it can make similar inferences based on prior knowledge. If the machine has never seen food items used in a sentence or has not seen it enough, it would be an easy mistake to mark the first sentence as art if it has seen enough samples of 'safflower oil' usage in art.

To successfully build an art/not-art classifier, we not only need a representative, relevant, and good quantity of training dataset, but also preprocessing and cleaning of data, a machine learning model, and numerical features constructed from the text that can help the model learn.

1.3.4 Preprocessing

Data preprocessing refers to the process of passing the data through certain cleaning and modification methods before analyzing or converting it into numerical representation for modeling. Depending on the source of data, the text can contain certain noises that may make it hard for the machine to interpret.

For instance, consider a task where you have a list of text documents that were written by people regarding a private review of a product. The product owners have permission to display these reviews selectively on their websites. Now let's talk about constraints. The program that needs these reviews as input to display on the website cannot parse language other than English. So as a preprocessing step, you'll remove any non-English language content. Furthermore, the product managers desire to not display any reviews having less than 10 characters of text on the website. Thus, you'll further apply a filtering step where you only pass the documents that have a length of more than 10. But when you further look at the data samples resulting after the filters are applied, you find some reviews contain meaningless information in the form of random URLs and non-alphabets. Thus, for a cleaner output, you may pass the data through further steps, such as removing URLs, checking for the presence of alphabets, stripping leading and trailing spaces to get the relevant text lengths, etc. All these steps count as preprocessing and are very tailored towards the goal.

> *TIP*
>
> For any text processing, it is valuable to first assess your data for the types of noise it contains before analyzing it for the final goal, whether that's something like simply displaying the text, or passing the data ahead for numerical feature extraction. Your final NLP application is only ever as good as your data!

Popular data preprocessing techniques are discussed in further detail in Chapter 3 (Section 3.1) and include data segmentation, cleaning, and standardization techniques.

1.3.5 Numerical representation

There are several numerical representations of text that are known to convey meaningful information. These are also referred to as features in machine learning. Whichever way we obtain and prepare the text, to build a machine learning model we need to have numerical vectors. This can be achieved by passing the text through numerical transformations for the machine to make sense of it. This is also called feature formation. Often, the data needs to go through preprocessing before the features can be formed to remove noise and pass a cleaner input into the feature formation techniques. Some popular numerical transformation methods include encoding, term frequency-based vectorizers, co-occurrence matrix, and word embedding models. These will be discussed in further detail in Chapter 3 (Section 3.4).

Once features are formed, they can be used as input to build machine learning models. Machine learning models aim to make sense of the data that is fed in. Examples include sentiment analysis model, text classification model, and language translation model. We'll dive further into modeling including classic machine learning, deep learning, and transformers in Section III (Chapter 4) along with model evaluation. We'll also visit text visualization using Python and data augmentation techniques in Section III (Chapter 3, Section 3.2 and 3.3).

1.4 NLP CHALLENGES

All the applications of NLP that we have looked at thus far seem very useful. Since practitioners have implemented some NLP applications before, are there existing solutions available that one can leverage? Will an existing and already solved solution fit any new or different NLP needs? Humans interpret language based on context and understanding that the brain has picked up over the years of existence and experiences. What does that mean for a machine?

Now that you know what NLP is, it is important to learn about the challenges of building good NLP solutions. For instance, in machine learning, concept drift and data drift are principles that relate to changes in data or data distribution requiring model re-training and other cautionary considerations. The same applies to language data as well. Below, we describe the challenges that occur due to language diversity, language evolution, context awareness, and utilizing existing solutions.

1.4.1 Language diversity

The nature of natural language is diverse. People use completely different words while describing different topics. People express themselves differently. While some basic grammar rules exist in different languages, each individual writes and speaks in a style that is unique to them. This variety in writing styles and language further adds to the complexity of building NLP solutions.

1.4.1.1 Writing styles

Some sources of text data such as formal language articles and documents are less likely to have a large variety in grammar usage, whereas platforms such as social media allow users to use any language, abbreviations, emojis, emoticons, punctuation, or a combination thereof. Thus, a perfectly built text category classifier trained on journal articles may not work as well when applied to social media data, given the differences in language style.

The difference in abbreviation usage, writing styles, and industry-specific jargon usage can further bring massive differences in how training data is interpreted. Here is an example of the same sentence that is written in different styles.

I am honored to be awarded the president's award at tomorrow's graduation event.
Im honored 2 b awarded d presidents award @ 2mrws grad event.

It is often found useful to communicate to the machine that 'grad' and 'graduation' mean the same, and words with or without apostrophes can be considered the same for a dataset as such. There are techniques to achieve normalization as such, such as stemming, lemmatizing, ensuring diverse dataset representation, and creating custom maps for word normalizations. This will be further discussed in detail in Chapter 3 (Section 3.1).

Additionally, different geographical locations can represent different accents and usage of words. Not only is the way of saying the same word different for the same language across the world, but what they mean at times changes with geography. For instance, biscuit in the USA refers to a quick bread that is typically unsweetened. In the UK, a biscuit is a hard, flat item. A British biscuit is an American cookie, an American biscuit is a British scone, and an American scone is something else entirely [123]. Sometimes challenging for humans to understand, such differences certainly pose challenges for a machine meant to understand language globally. Having a well-represented dataset for your use case becomes very important in solving such challenges.

1.4.1.2 Sentence ambiguities

Many times, it is not the writing styles or grammar usage that leads to language diversity. Another type of ambiguity that exists in a language is called sentence ambiguity. There are many types of sentence ambiguities. Let's see a few examples.

Semantic ambiguity
Semantic ambiguity results when words that are spelled the same have different meanings.

> *I went out in the forest and found a bat.*

Was it a bat, the animal? Or a baseball, cricket, or table tennis bat? The word 'bat' is a homonym, which means it can have multiple meanings but reads and sounds the same. This forms a simple example of semantic ambiguity.

Syntactic ambiguity
Syntactic ambiguity is also called structural or grammatical ambiguity and occurs when the structure of the sentence leads to multiple possible meanings.

> *The end . . . ?*

There's an ambiguous ending in the American science fiction horror film The Blob (1958). The film ends with parachutes bearing the monstrous creature on a pallet down to an Arctic ice field with the superimposed words 'The End' morphing into a question mark [196]. The question mark at the end leaves a possibility that the monster is not dead or may resurface. A classic ending for a horror film.

Narrative ambiguity
Narrative ambiguity arises when the intent of the text is unclear. If someone aims a stone at a person and hits the target, it may count as a good shot, but not necessarily a good deed. At such an event, commenting 'that was good' without the context of what exactly the commenter found good is an example of narrative ambiguity.
Consider the following example:

> *Sarah gave a bath to her dog wearing a pink t-shirt.*

Ambiguity: Is the dog wearing the pink t-shirt or is Sarah wearing a pink t-shirt?
Sometimes it is tricky even for humans to depict the intended meaning of an ambiguous sentence. The same holds true for a machine.

FIGURE 1.6 Word cloud of top 100 most spoken languages across the world.

1.4.1.3 *Different languages*

There are over 7000 languages in the world today [104]. Figure 1.6 represents the top most spoken languages (source [214]) across the globe, where the size of the language names represents a scaled version of the population that speaks the languages. This type of representation is called a word cloud [126], which is a popular form of word and phrase visualization (code implementation for creating word clouds is shared in Section III).

Each language has its own set of linguistic rules around form, semantics, and morphology. This makes porting over NLP models built for one language difficult for other languages. Many researchers and practitioners actively research NLP for various languages and develop methods that work well. There is still some transfer learning that can help develop techniques between different languages. Some recent papers published at Natural Language Processing and Chinese Computing (NLPCC) suggest that a lot of the latest research takes inspiration from methods that work for a different language by developing an analogous algorithm for the language at hand.

Another methodology that practitioners apply is to use language translation to convert between languages and then apply the NLP model to the translated version.

Translation has the capacity to lose certain information, as goes with the popular phrase – 'lost in translation'. Nonetheless, it works well for many applications.

1.4.2 Language evolution

The language humans use to communicate evolves and changes over time. The acknowledged ways of structuring a sentence, grammar, abbreviations, figures of speech, and accents not only differ with location but also change with time.

Let's consider an example. Usage of abbreviations such as 'lol', 'brb', and 'ttyl', got popular only in the twenty-first century. We asked a group of 20 people born between 1950 and 1970 if they knew or used any such abbreviations in their 20s–30s and if they remembered recognizing these terms or their meanings. The answer was no. Even emojis were not invented before the 1990s. In the late 1990s, a Japanese artist named Shigetaka Kurita created the first emoji. Instagram has always supported emojis but did not see wide adoption until iOS and Android emoji keyboards were launched. In 2011, the iOS emoji keyword was launched while emoji usage remained around 1% of comments and captions on Instagram. By 2013, the Android stack emoji keyboard was launched and the overall emoji usage increased up to 20% of comments and captions [117].

1.4.3 Context awareness

As humans, we have context for things going on around us. This context helps us determine when there is a typing error in a piece of text, what the text means even in presence of major grammatical errors, identify sarcasm, and identify errors in the information that the text contains. A machine may not be able to infer the same context as easily. Let's consider an example:

Handyman repaired the fridge.
Fridge repaired the handyman.

We can tell that the second sentence is likely erroneous because the probability of an object like the fridge fixing a human, i.e., the handyman, is very low. A machine may not be able to tell when it encounters erroneous sentences. Bad or incorrect data as such can impact the performance of your NLP model. Identifying and eliminating incorrect samples and outliers can help with such data problems.

While removing outliers and bad data samples can help many applications, cases like sarcasm detection remain challenging. The language concept of pragmatics plays a role in humans detecting sarcasm. For a machine, many times in sentiment or emotion classification tasks, the use of sarcasm is observed along with non-sarcastic sentences. If sarcasm is known to occur in conjunction with certain topics, then building a model to detect that can be reasonably successful. Many practitioners have developed models to help detect sarcasm. There continues to be research in the area and this kind of problem is an example of one that remains challenging today [201].

1.4.4 Not always a one-size-fits-all

While building applications in language, there is often not a one-size-fits-all solution. This can also stem from data diversity and evolution.

Imagine a task where you need to identify if someone is happy based on their text messages.

As seen in Figure 1.7, when Arthur is happy, he uses non-standard vocabulary to express his excitement. But when Beatrice is happy, she uses multitudes of emojis. Going with a completely different expression, Charan directly elicits his emotion by writing – *I'm happy*. This is an example of language diversity based on communication styles.

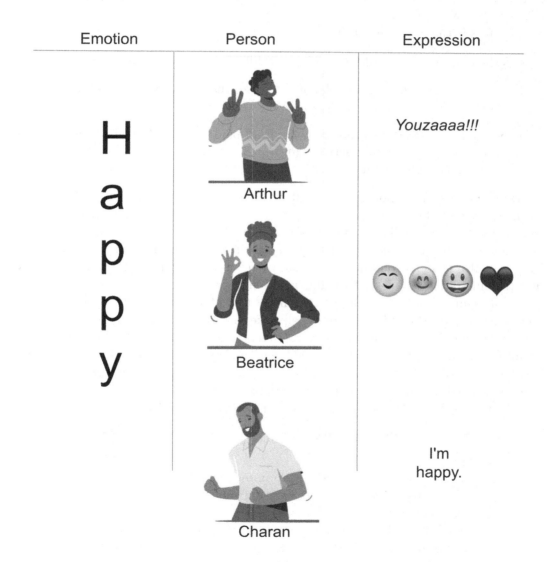

FIGURE 1.7 Happiness expressions of individuals representing diversity in styles of communication.

Every individual can describe a similar emotion in innumerable ways. One would need to know various expressions of happy emotion to build a model that successfully infers the happiness state of an individual based on text. If our model was only built on the happy expressions of Charan, we would not be able to guess when Beatrice or Arthur is happy.

As another example, let's say we have a pre-trained category classifier. The classifier was trained on social media data from 2008 and has historically given an 80% accuracy. It does not work as well on social media data from 2022 and gives a 65% accuracy. Why? Because the way people communicate changes over time along with the topics that people talk about. This is an example of language evolution and data drift and can present a lower accuracy of classification if training data differs from the data you want to classify.

When is it that you can't use a pre-trained model?

1. When you need to build a model with different classes/parameters.

2. When you are running a model on a dataset that is so vastly different from the training data that the model fails to do well.

3. Sometimes, pre-trained models come from paid services. Certain organizations do not want to use paid services and/or many times want to build something they can call proprietary.

Does that mean no model works well if built on a different dataset? No! Transfer learning refers to the process of learning from one data source and applying it to data from a different source. This works very well in many cases. If any existing models do not work for you, they can still form a good baseline that you can refer to. Sometimes, they may also form as good inputs to your model and might require you to need less new training data. This is further illustrated in Figure 1.8.

While some of these challenges are difficult to find a way around by both humans and machines, several NLP techniques help take care of the most commonly seen noise and challenges. Examples include cleaning techniques to strip off URLs and emojis, spelling correction, language translation, stemming and lemmatization, data quantity and quality considerations, and more. We will be discussing data preprocessing and cleaning techniques in further detail in Chapter 3 (Section 3.1).

We started this section with a few questions. Let's summarize their answers below.

> *TIP*
>
> Since practitioners have implemented some NLP applications before, are there existing solutions available that one can leverage?
>
> Sometimes. If an existing solution serves your purpose, more often than not it is the industry practitioner's preference to go with it. Depending on the use case, existing solutions can also be leveraged to partially solve the problem.

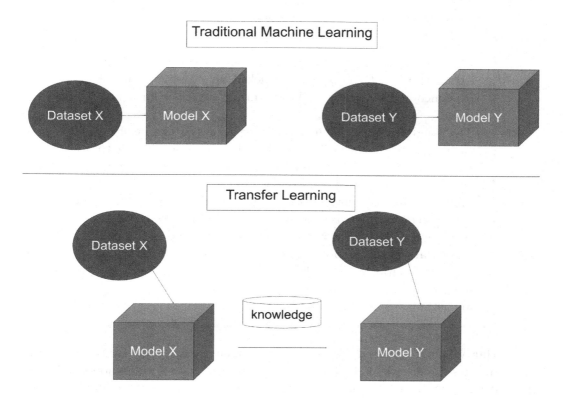

FIGURE 1.8 Transfer learning versus traditional machine learning.

TIP

Will an existing and already solved solution fit any new or different NLP needs?

Not always. Your needs in any industry vertical can be very specific to datasets from that industry, containing jargon and industry-specific language styles. The needs can also be very focused on a specific problem rather than a generic problem. Thus, it is common that an existing solution does not fit new and different NLP needs entirely. Nonetheless, it is always worth exploring available solutions first.

> *TIP*
>
> Humans interpret language based on context and understanding that the brain has picked up over the years of existence and experiences. What does that mean for a machine?
>
> The language goes through preprocessing and is converted to numerical representation so that it means something to the machine, and it is then able to process and interpret it. There are several challenges associated with processing and understanding language from the perspective of a machine that we covered in this section. We need to process the data to make it clean and provide enough quantity and good quality of data samples to the machine so it can learn from the data. It is vital to mix a human-level understanding of the data and its state (clean/noisy) with the machine's powerful algorithms for the best results.

Thus far, we have discussed NLP examples, language concepts, NLP concepts, and NLP challenges. Before we wrap up this chapter, we will go over setup notes and some popular tools that we will be using for the remaining chapters while implementing NLP using Python.

1.5 SETUP

First, you will need Python >=3.7, pip >=3.0, and Jupyter [99] installed on your machine. If you don't already have these, follow[11] to download Python,[12] for installing pip on MAC and[13] on Windows, and[14] for installing Jupyter on MAC and[15] on Windows. Another option is to install Anaconda[16], which comes with pre-installed Jupyter. You can then install many libraries using `conda` instead of `pip`. Both `pip` and `conda` are package managers that facilitate installation, upgrade, and uninstallation of Python packages.

We'll also be showing some examples using bash in this book. Bash is pre-installed on MAC machines (known as Terminal). Follow[17] to install bash on Windows.

You can launch a Jupyter notebook by typing the following bash command.

```
jupyter notebook
```

To install a library in Python, pip [198] can be used as follows using bash.

---

[11]https://www.python.org/downloads/

[12]https://www.geeksforgeeks.org/how-to-install-pip-in-macos/

[13]https://www.geeksforgeeks.org/how-to-install-pip-on-windows/

[14]https://www.geeksforgeeks.org/how-to-install-jupyter-notebook-on-macos/

[15]https://www.geeksforgeeks.org/how-to-install-jupyter-notebook-in-windows/

[16]https://www.anaconda.com/

[17]https://itsfoss.com/install-bash-on-windows/

```
pip install <library>
```

When working with Jupyter notebooks, you can do this from within the notebook itself as follows.

```
! pip install <library>
```

To install a particular version of a library, you can specify it as follows. The below example installs NLTK version 3.6.5.

```
! pip install nltk==3.6.5
```

To install the latest version of a library, the following can be run.

```
! pip install --upgrade nltk
```

For this book, most demonstrated Python code was written in Jupyter notebooks. You will find Jupyter notebook notation for library installs throughout the book unless otherwise specified.

Some libraries may require you to install using Homebrew.[18] Follow the instructions in the URL for installing Homebrew. Homebrew is MacOS-only command line installer application and it does not exist for Windows. The Windows alternative is Chocolatey.[19]

1.6 TOOLS

There are several open-source libraries in Python to help us leverage existing implementations of various NLP methods. The below list introduces some of the popular Python libraries used for text NLP. We'll find ourselves leveraging these and some others for many implementations in Sections II, III, V, and VI.

1. NLTK[20]: NLTK stands for natural language toolkit and provides easy-to-use interfaces to over 50 corpora and lexical resources such as WordNet[21] (large lexical database for English), along with a suite of text-processing libraries for classification, tokenization, stemming, tagging, parsing, and semantic reasoning, wrappers for industrial-strength NLP libraries, and an active discussion forum [34].

   NLTK can be installed as follows.

   ```
   ! pip install nltk
   ```

2. spaCy[22]: spaCy is a library for advanced NLP in Python and Cython. spaCy comes with pre-trained pipelines and currently supports tokenization and training for 60+ languages. It features state-of-the-art speed and neural network models for tagging, parsing, named entity recognition (NER), text classification, and multi-task learning with pre-trained transformers like BERT, as well

---

[18]https://brew.sh/
[19]https://chocolatey.org/
[20]NLTK https://www.nltk.org/
[21]https://wordnet.princeton.edu/
[22]spaCy https://spacy.io/

as a production-ready training system and easy model packaging, deployment, and workflow management. [80].

spaCy can be installed as follows.

```
! pip install spaCy
```

3. Genism[23]: `Gensim` is an open-source Python library for representing documents as semantic vectors efficiently and painlessly. The algorithms in `Gensim`, such as Word2Vec, FastText, Latent Semantic Indexing (LSI, LSA, and LsiModel), Latent Dirichlet Allocation (LDA and LdaModel), etc., automatically discover the semantic structure of documents by examining statistical co-occurrence patterns within a corpus of training documents [140].

`Gensim` can be installed as follows.

```
! pip install gensim
```

4. Scikit-learn[24]: `Scikit-learn` (or `sklearn`) is a free software machine learning library in Python. It features various classification, regression, and clustering algorithms, and is designed to interoperate with the Python numerical and scientific libraries `NumPy` and `SciPy` [130].

`Sklearn` can be installed as follows.

```
! pip install scikit-learn
```

5. TensorFlow[25]: `TensorFlow` is a free and open-source software library for machine learning. It can be used across a range of tasks but has a particular focus on training and inference of deep neural networks [179].

`Tensorflow` can be installed as follows.

```
! pip install tensorflow
```

6. Keras[26]: `Keras` is an open-source software library that provides a Python interface for neural networks and is an interface for the `TensorFlow` library. `Keras` supports multiple backends, including `TensorFlow`, `Microsoft Cognitive Toolkit`, `Theano`, and `PlaidML`.

`Keras` can be installed as follows.

```
! pip install keras
```

7. PyTorch[27]: `PyTorch` is an open-source machine learning framework based on the `Torch` library. It was developed by Meta AI.

`PyTorch` can be installed as follows.

---

[23]Gensim `https://radimrehurek.com/gensim/`
[24]Scikit-learn `https://scikit-learn.org/stable/getting_started.html`
[25]TensorFlow `https://www.tensorflow.org/learn`
[26]Keras `https://keras.io/`
[27]PyTorch `https://pytorch.org`

```
! pip install torch torchvision
```

8. Hugging Face transformers[28]: The Hugging Face **transformers** package is a popular Python library that provides several pre-trained models for a variety of natural language processing (NLP) tasks. It supports PyTorch, Tensorflow, and JAX.[29]

   Transformers can be installed as follows.

```
! pip install transformers

# For CPU-support only, you can install transformers and a deep
    learning library in one line.
# PyTorch
! pip install transformers[torch]
# TensorFlow 2.0
! pip install transformers[tf-cpu]
# Flax (neural network library for JAX)
! pip install transformers[flax]
```

For code demonstrated in this book, we have used the following versions of these libraries. We have specified if any different versions were used for any application. Other details can be found in the Jupyter notebooks containing the code using different libraries. All the code used in this book can be found at https://github.com/jsingh811/NLP-in-the-real-world and can be downloaded from there.

- NLTK 3.6.5

- spaCy 3.2.3

- Gensim 4.2.0

- scikit-learn 1.1.3

- Tensorflow 2.11.0

- Keras 2.11.0

- Torch 1.13.0

- Torchvision 0.14.0

- Transformers 4.17.0

---

[28]Hugging Face transformers https://huggingface.co/docs/transformers/main/en/index
[29]JAX https://jax.readthedocs.io/en/latest/notebooks/quickstart.html

Windup

We discussed language, natural language processing, examples of applications and products, the challenges associated with building successful NLP solutions, and the consideration factors and how language can be used as data that machines can understand. There is a significant amount of preprocessing that is prime, along with feature-building techniques, machine learning, and neural networks. For many language tasks, your end goal may be around the analysis of text rather than building a model. Preprocessing text followed by data visualization can come in handy for such applications. Before diving into those stages in Section III, let's talk about the one thing NLP is not possible without– the data! Where can you get text data from? How can you read text from different types of data sources? Where can you store text? The next section will answer all these questions and further dive into popular data sources, text extraction with code examples of reading text from common sources and formats, popular storage considerations and options with code samples, and data maintenance.

II

Data Curation

In this section, our focus will surround data curation - where from, how, where to, and other consideration factors. First, we will dive into the various sources which text is commonly curated from. We will list publicly available data sources, as well as common sources of data found within organizations. We'll then dive into data extraction and how data can be read from commonly used formats for storing text, such as CSV, PDF, Word documents, images, APIs (Application Programming Interface), and other structured and unstructured formats using Python and open-source libraries. Finally, with all the text data at hand, data storage becomes prime. Sometimes saving the data on your machine in different files suffices. Other times, a database management system serves as a more practical solution. We'll discuss some popular databases that are used widely for text data. Each database comes with ways to query and perform operations on text. We'll implement some of these operations. Finally, we will introduce the concept of data maintenance and discuss some useful tips and tricks to prevent the data from corruption.

This section includes the following topics:

- Sources of data

- Data extraction

- Data storage

All the code demonstrated in this section can be found of section 2 folder of the GitHub repository (https://github.com/jsingh811/NLP-in-the-real-world).

## CHAPTER 2

Data Sources and Extraction

2.1 SOURCES OF DATA

2.1.1 Generated by businesses

The most common source of text data is the data generated by the business's operations and is dependent on what the business does. For example, in real estate, sources of text data include property listing descriptions, agent comments, legal documents, and customer interaction data. For some other industry verticals, the source of text data can include social media posts, product descriptions, articles, web documents, chat data, or a combination thereof. When there is an absence of owned (first-party) data, organizations leverage data from different vendors and clients. Overall, from a business's standpoint, the commonly seen text data is of the following types.

1. Customer reviews/comments

    User comments are a very common source of text, especially from social media, e-commerce, and hospitality businesses that collect product reviews. For instance, Google and Yelp collect reviews across brands as well as small and large businesses.

2. Social media/blog posts

    Social media posts and blogs find presence in most types of businesses. In today's world, social media reaches more people globally than any other form of media. Whether or not a business is directly associated with social media, there's often social media presence of businesses, products, service promotions, articles, or more. On the other hand, there are many businesses offering a product/service for analyzing the social media presence of other businesses. Whether one is gathering one's own media data or on behalf of a client, there's a rich volume of text associated which makes this a popular text data source that spans many industry verticals.

3. Chat data

    E-commerce, banking, and many other industries leverage chat data. Chat data is essentially the chat history of messages exchanged between a business and its client or customer. This is a common source of text data in industries and is useful for monitoring user sentiment, improving customer experience, and creating smart chatbots where computers respond to customer messages, thereby reducing human labor.

4. Product descriptions

Text descriptions are attached to most products or services being sold to people or businesses. For instance, when you check any product on Amazon, you will find a detailed product description section that helps you get more information. Descriptive and categorical data associated with a product and service is yet another common text data source in the industry.

5. News

News is used very popularly across finance and real estate industries to predict stock and property prices. For many other industry verticals, what's in the news impacts their businesses, and ingesting news and articles can be beneficial. Thus, it is common for organizations to have analytical engines built specifically for curating and classifying news and article headlines on the Internet.

6. Documents

Resumes, legal documents, research publications, contracts, and internal documents are examples of document-type data sources. Across industries, several resume filtering and searching algorithms are put in place to sift through the hundreds of applications received for an open job position. In law and banking, as well as many other industries, legal and contractual documents are present in bulk and need to be sifted through for an important compliance term or detail. In physics, NLP plays an important role in automatically sifting through bulk volumes of research publications to find relevant material for drawing inspiration, using as a guide, or referencing.

7. Entry-based data

Feedback and survey forms are another source of text data in the enterprise. As an example, SurveyMonkey and Google Forms allow creation of custom forms with categorical, select one, select many, or free-form text entry options. Parsing free-form text fields manually, especially if they are present in large volumes, can be a time-consuming effort. Building tools to parse the relevant information for analysis is a common solution.

8. Search-based data

The searches that a customer or a client performs on a website is an example of search-based data. This type of data consists of free-form text searches along with categorical selects and timestamps. One popular application for such data is to understand consumer interest and intent, design customer experience, and recommend relevant items.

2.1.2 Openly accessible

For the times you do not have an existing dataset, open-source datasets can come in handy to kick-start research, test, or build prototypes. There are many such datasets available that form a great resource for just practicing machine learning and NLP skills or using it for a real-world problem that you might be trying to solve as an industry practitioner. Some popular text datasets are listed in Table 2.1.

TABLE 2.1 Publicly available text datasets.

UCI (66 text datasets) [67][1]	Amazon Reviews [107][2]	Wikipedia [159, 194][3]
Standford Sentiment Treebank [162][4]	Twitter US Airlines Reviews [93][5]	Project Gutenberg[6]
Enron Dataset [51][7]	The Blog Authorship Corpus[8]	SMS Spam Collection[9]
Recommender Systems Datasets[10]	WordNet[11]	Dictionaries for Movies and Finance[12]
Sentiment 140[13]	Multi-domain Sentiment Analysis Dataset[14]	Yelp Reviews: Restaurant rankings and reviews[15]
20 Newsgroups[16]	The WikiQA Corpus[17]	European Parliament ProceedingsParallel Corpus[18]
OpinRank Dataset[19]	Legal Case Reports Dataset[20]	Stanford Question Answering Dataset (SQuAD)[21]
TIMIT[22]	IMDB datasets (unpaid version)[23]	Jeopardy! Questions in a JSON file[24]

[1]https://archive.ics.uci.edu/ml/datasets.php
[2]https://snap.stanford.edu/data/web-Amazon.html
[3]https://dumps.wikimedia.org/
[4]https://nlp.stanford.edu/sentiment/index.html
[5]https://www.kaggle.com/datasets/crowdflower/twitter-airline-sentiment
[6]https://paperswithcode.com/dataset/standardized-project-gutenberg-corpus
[7]https://www.cs.cmu.edu/~enron/
[8]https://www.kaggle.com/rtatman/blog-authorship-corpus
[9]https://archive.ics.uci.edu/ml/datasets/SMS+Spam+Collection
[10]https://cseweb.ucsd.edu/~jmcauley/datasets.html
[11]https://wordnet.princeton.edu/download
[12]https://github.com/nproellochs/SentimentDictionaries
[13]http://help.sentiment140.com/for-students/
[14]https://www.cs.jhu.edu/~mdredze/datasets/sentiment/
[15]https://www.yelp.com/dataset
[16]http://qwone.com/~jason/20Newsgroups/
[17]https://www.microsoft.com/en-us/download/details.aspx?id=52419
[18]https://www.statmt.org/europarl/
[19]http://kavita-ganesan.com/entity-ranking-data/#.Yw1NsuzMKXj
[20]https://archive.ics.uci.edu/ml/datasets/Legal+Case+Reports
[21]https://rajpurkar.github.io/SQuAD-explorer/
[22]https://catalog.ldc.upenn.edu/LDC93s1
[23]https://www.imdb.com/interfaces/
[24]https://www.reddit.com/r/datasets/comments/1uyd0t/200000_jeopardy_questions_in_a_json_file/

2.1.3 Conditionally available

There are certain sources of text data that are not openly accessible but also not completely inaccessible. Such data sources may require agreeing to certain terms and conditions, payment plans, or following the source's guidelines for access. There exist many businesses that source different types of data and sell it to other businesses.

An example of conditionally available data sources includes social media APIs (Application Programming Interfaces). They often have a certain version that is free and another version that charges a fee for expanded usage. With some social media APIs, you can get a lot of publicly available data, and with some others, you can only get data for the social media channels you own or are permitted to access by the data owners/creators. Let's look at some popular ones below.

1. YouTube

   YouTube has multiple APIs, some that allow you to access publicly available data and some that allow you to access data that you own on YouTube or that you have been given permission to access by the content owners. YouTube Data API [204] allows you to gather public data from YouTube. This includes YouTube channel title, channel description, channel statistics such as video count and subscriber count, video title, video description, video tags, video statistics (number of likes, dislikes, views, and comments), comments, user public subscriptions, and more. The openness of the API is subject to change and is based on YouTube's developer terms. To access this API, you will need to register your account and generate your API tokens. There are daily rate limits associated with each account, which sets a limit on how many requests you can make in a 24-hour window [205]. More on accessing data using YouTube data API is discussed in Section 2.2.7.

2. Twitter

   Twitter has multiple APIs. Most of the APIs that offer advanced data metrics require payment. Further details on Twitter data and APIs are linked here [184]. Common types of data you can fetch for free includes tweets, users, followers, and friends. Your friends on Twitter refer to the users you follow as per the API's term definitions. The free API comes with a rate limit that refreshes every 15 minutes. More on accessing data using Twitter API is discussed in Section 2.2.7.

3. Reddit

   Reddit offers some freely accessible data. Post data, subreddits, and user data are available with the Reddit API. Their developer terms are linked here [139].

4. LinkedIn

   LinkedIn API offers user, company, and post data [111]. Requests can be made for a particular user or company to access the posts. Client authentication/permissions is a requirement for gathering more details.

5. IMDb datasets (paid and unpaid versions)

   IMDb offers some free datasets[25] that represent a small sample of the large data pool they store. They offer a much richer dataset in their paid contractual versions that contains data on movies, tv shows, actors and actresses, directors, and crew. Usage of data requires compliance with their terms and services [84].

6. Facebook

   Facebook [119] and Instagram [120] data can be accessed using the Graph API. The amount of data accessible via the API for these platforms is limited. Certain Facebook page data can be publicly accessed. For a richer data dimension, authentication is required so you are only able to gather either your own data or the data of a client that has authorized you to do so on their behalf.

7. Twitch

   Twitch allows you to ingest comments and details of a known and active streaming event, along with the user names of individuals making the comments. Terms and services, and details of the data available can be found here [183].

Note of caution

One caveat is to ensure to **not** use openly accessible data to commercialize a product if the data source forbids it. This is often ignored by most practitioners but forms an important part of abiding by open-source ethics and staying clear of potential legal issues. Consider the following example.

You want to build a project that returns movies that an actor has appeared in with maximum positive ratings vs least positive ratings. IMDB provides publicly available datasets here[a]. You can freely use this dataset to build your project. Now let's say you got a brilliant idea and wanted to convert your project into a product that sells this information to other businesses or users. That would be problematic because this data resource does not permit use for commercial purposes. How to ensure you are cognizant of such terms? Always get the data from the original source and refer to the document that provides download links to the datasets. While the same IMDB dataset can be found in multiple users' GitHub repositories, and Kaggle competitions, the original source remains the URL noted above and specifies the following.

Subsets of IMDb data are available for access to customers for personal and non-commercial use. You can hold local copies of this data, and it is subject to our terms and conditions. Please refer to the Non-Commercial Licensing and copyright/license and verify compliance.

Some other data sources do not object to using for the commercialization and some others require proper citation of the resource. Following the guidelines will certainly save you time and effort at a later stage while ensuring good ethical standing and compliance.

---
[a]https://www.imdb.com/interfaces/

---
[25]https://www.imdb.com/interfaces/

2.2   DATA EXTRACTION

Let's look at examples of parsing data stored in different types of formats using Python. The code used can also be found in section2/data-extraction-file-formats.ipynb on GitHub.

2.2.1   Reading from a PDF

In many scenarios, there is information embedded inside PDF files that you may want to extract and process as you would any other string variable in code. The easiest way to read PDFs using Python is using the pyPDF2 library.

The below Python snippet highlights a basic way of using this library for PDF reading.

Step 1:
Install the library. We have used the version 2.11.1.

```
! pip install PyPDF2==2.11.1
```

Step 2:
Let's read a sample PDF file in Python. You can download any PDF from the web. Name it *sample.pdf* and place it in your code directory.

```
# Imports
from PyPDF2 import PdfFileReader

with open("sample.pdf", "rb") as pdf:
    # Creating pdf reader object
    pdf_reader = PdfFileReader(pdf)

    # Fetching number of pages in the PDF
    num_pages = pdf_reader.numPages
    print(
        "Total no. of pages: {}".format(num_pages)
    )
    if num_pages > 0:
        # Creating a page object for the 1st page
        # Replace 0 with 1 to access the 2nd page,
        # and so on
        page = pdf_reader.getPage(0)
        # Extracting text from the page
        text = page.extractText()
        print("Contents of the first page:\n")
        print(text)
```

You can also do the above without using the 'with' clause. In that case, remember to close your file towards the end using `file.close()` to avoid unintentional and excess memory usage.

One limitation of this approach is that it does not work for scanned files saved as PDFs. Next, we'll look into an approach that works for extracting text from scanned documents.

2.2.2 Reading from a scanned document

Scanned documents are a challenging and common source of text. Optical Character Recognition, or OCR, refers to the process of extracting text from scanned documents [197]. Let's see a code sample below.

Step 1:

Install the libraries.

```
! pip install pytesseract==0.3.9
! pip install opencv-python==4.6.0.66
```

Step 2:

Read a sample scanned PNG (source [132]) with Python.

```
# Imports
import cv2
from pytesseract import image_to_string

filename = "20220629_131726.jpg"
img = cv2.imread(filename)
text = image_to_string(img, lang='eng')
print(text)
```

While using mac OS, several users have reported errors as follows.

`FileNotFoundError: [Errno 2] No such file or directory: 'tesseract': 'tesseract'`

To resolve, run the below install using **Homebrew** and try the Step 2 code again. Homebrew is a missing package manager. Don't have Homebrew installed? Follow this installation guide[26].

```
brew install tesseract
```

The results can differ depending on the quality of the scanned document. Thus, passing the image through certain filters can help get better results [207]. Examples of such filters can be seen below.

```
import numpy as np
import cv2

def get_grayscale(image):
  return cv2.cvtColor(
    image, cv2.COLOR_BGR2GRAY
  )

def thresholding(image):
  return cv2.threshold(
    image, 0, 255, cv2.THRESH_BINARY + cv2.THRESH_OTSU
  )[1]

def opening(image):
  return cv2.morphologyEx(
    image, cv2.MORPH_OPEN, np.ones((5,5),np.uint8)
  )
```

---

[26]https://docs.brew.sh/Installation

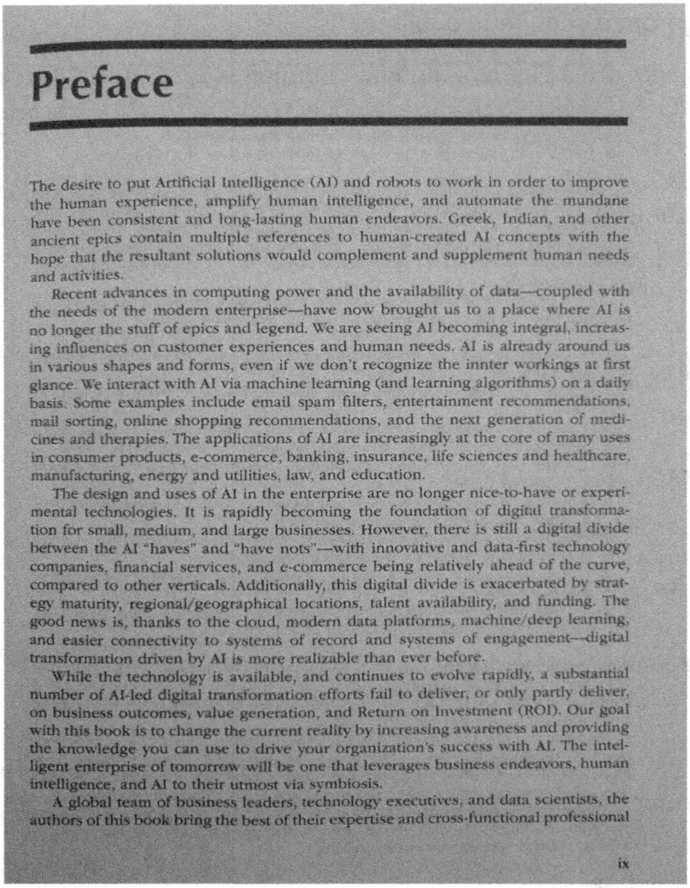

FIGURE 2.1 Image of a page in a book [132] scanned from a smart phone.

```
gray = get_grayscale(img)
thresh = thresholding(gray)
openn = opening(gray)

text_filt = image_to_string(thresh, lang="eng")
```

For a sample scanned PDF shown in Figure 2.1, the results can be seen in Figure 2.2. The code used can be found in section2/ocr-book-page-image.ipynb.

You can also build models that perform OCR using open-source libraries[27].

Like all methods, there are expected to be certain drawbacks in terms of false detections based on the quality of the scanned file and the limitations of the underlying algorithm. There is a chance that your output may contain spelling errors and other data noise issues. We'll talk about data cleaning and preprocessing in Chapter 3

---

[27]https://pyimagesearch.com/2020/08/24/ocr-handwriting-recognition-with-opencv-keras-and-tensorflow/

a a a ae ae a ER ee

Preface

a a Ee ee a Ee a ee Sd

The desire to put Artificial Intelligence (AI) and robots to work in order to improve the human experience, amplify human intelligence, and automate the mundane have been consistent and long-lasting human endeavors. Greek, Indian, and other ancient epics contain multiple references to human-created AI concepts with the hope that the resultant solutions would complement and supplement human needs and activities.

Recent advances in computing power and the availability of data—coupled with the needs of the modern enterprise—have now brought us to a place where AI is no longer the stuff of epics and legend. We are seeing AI becoming integral, increasing influences on customer experiences and human needs. AI is already around us in various shapes and forms, even if we don't recognize the innter workings at first glance. We interact with AI via machine learning (and learning algorithms) on a daily basis. Some examples include email spam filters, entertainment recommendations, mail sorting, online shopping recommendations, and the next generation of medicines and therapies. The applications of AI are increasingly at the core of many uses in consumer products, e-commerce, banking, insurance, life sciences and healthcare, manufacturing, energy and utilities, law, and education.

The design and uses of AI in the enterprise are no longer nice-to-have or experimental technologies. It is rapidly becoming the foundation of digital transformation for small, medium, and large businesses. However, there is still a digital divide between the AI "haves" and "have nots"—with innovative and data-first technology companies, financial services, and e-commerce being relatively ahead of the curve, compared to other verticals. Additionally, this digital divide is exacerbated by strategy maturity, regional/geographical locations, talent availability, and funding. The good news is, thanks to the cloud, modern data platforms, machine/deep learning, and easier connectivity to systems of record and systems of engagement—digital transformation driven by AI is more realizable than ever before.

While the technology is available, and continues to evolve rapidly, a substantial number of AI-led digital transformation efforts fail to deliver, or only partly deliver, on business outcomes, value generation, and Return on Investment (ROD. Our goal with this book is to change the current reality by increasing awareness and providing the knowledge you can use to drive your organization's success with AI. The intelligent enterprise of tomorrow will be one that leverages business endeavors, human intelligence, and AI to their utmost via symbiosis.

A global team of business leaders, technology executives, and data scientists, the authors of this book bring the best of their expertise and cross-functional professional

ix

Oe

Preface

OO

The desire to put Artificial Intelligence (AI) and robots to work in order to improve the human experience, amplify human intelligence, and automate the mundane have been consistent and long-lasting human endeavors. Greek, Indian, and other ancient epics contain multiple references to human-created AI concepts with the hope that the resultant solutions would complement and supplement human needs and activities.

Recent advances in computing power and the availability of data—coupled with the needs of the modern enterprise—have now brought us to a place where AI is no longer the stuff of epics and legend. We are seeing AI becoming integral, increasing influences on customer experiences and human needs. AI is already around us in various shapes and forms, even if we don't recognize the innter workings at first glance. We interact with AI via machine learning (and learning algorithms) on a daily basis. Some examples include email spam filters, entertainment recommendations, mail sorting, online shopping recommendations, and the next generation of medicines and therapies. The applications of AI are increasingly at the core of many uses in consumer products, e-commerce, banking, insurance, life sciences and healthcare, manufacturing, energy and utilities, law, and education.

The design and uses of AI in the enterprise are no longer nice-to-have or experimental technologies. It is rapidly becoming the foundation of digital transformation for small, medium, and large businesses. However, there is still a digital divide between the AI "haves" and "have nots"—with innovative and data-first technology companies, financial services, and e-commerce being relatively ahead of the curve, compared to other verticals. Additionally, this digital divide is exacerbated by strategy maturity, regional/geographical locations, talent availability, and funding. The good news is, thanks to the cloud, modern data platforms, machine/deep learning, and easier connectivity to systems of record and systems of engagement—digital transformation driven by AI is more realizable than ever before.

While the technology is available, and continues to evolve rapidly, a substantial number of AI-led digital transformation efforts fail to deliver, or only partly deliver, on business outcomes, value generation, and Return on Investment (ROD. Our goal with this book is to change the current reality by increasing awareness and providing the knowledge you can use to drive your organization's success with AI. The intelligent enterprise of tomorrow will be one that leverages business endeavors, human intelligence, and AI to their utmost via symbiosis.

A global team of business leaders, technology executives, and data scientists, the authors of this book bring the best of their expertise and cross-functional professional

ix

FIGURE 2.2 Results of OCR on Figure 2.1. On the left, results are produced without any image filtering. On the right, results are produced with the thresholding filter applied to the image. The errors are highlighted in grey.

(Section 3.1) which will highlight spelling correction techniques and cleanup methods that can handle some of such data inconsistencies.

2.2.3 Reading from a JSON

JSON stands for JavaScript Object Notation. It is an open standard file format that is a popular storage format commonly used to store Python dictionary objects. The easiest way to read JSON into Python is using the inbuilt json library. The below Python snippet highlights a basic way of using this library for JSON reading.

```
# Imports
import json

# Writing a sample dict to json file
sample = {
  "Mathew": ["mathematics", "chemistry"],
  "Perry": ["biology", "arts"]
}
with open("sample.json", "w") as f:
  json.dump(sample, f)
```

```
# Reading the json file back
with open("sample.json", "r") as f:
    read_sample = json.load(f)

# Printing
print("Sample written to json file: {}".format(sample))
print("Sample read from json file: {}".format(read_sample))
```

2.2.4 Reading from a CSV

CSV stands for Comma Separated Values. It is a simple and popular way to store data in tabular form as plain text. In a CSV file, the comma in each row separates the different values from each other as separate columns or cells. There are multiple ways of reading a CSV with Python. Let's look at a few below.

Using inbuilt module csv

Reading a CSV is made easy using Python's inbuilt module called csv using the csv.reader object.

```
# Imports
import csv

# Creating csv reader object
with open("sample_csv.csv", "r") as file:
    csvreader = csv.reader(file)

    # If your file has a head, then
    header = next(csvreader)
    print(header)
    # get rows in a list
    rows = [row for row in csvreader]
    print(rows)
```

Using readlines

```
file = open('sample_csv.csv')
content = file.readlines()

# If the first row is the header
header = content[:1]

# Fetching the rows
rows = content[1:]

# Printing header and rows
print(header)
print(rows)

# Close the file
file.close()
```

Using Pandas library
Step 1:
Install the library.

```
! pip install pandas
```

Step 2:
Let's read a sample CSV file in Python with the file in your working directory.

```
# Imports
import pandas as pd

# Load the data into a pandas dataframe
data = pd.read_csv("sample_csv.csv")

# print column names
print(data.columns)

# print data
print(data)
```

2.2.5   Reading from HTML page (web scraping)

When the data of interest is on a particular website that does not have related datasets or an API of data source offering, web scraping is one way to capture the data. It is important to be aware of any terms of usage of the website to avoid legal violations.

Any website that we see has a lot of information, where we may only be interested in grabbing certain text. HTML parsing is a popular way to scrape the web. We can leverage libraries such as beautifulsoup to do so.

Let's consider a task where you want to fetch answers to common questions about natural language processing in Python to help new students or employees quickly look up answers. The first step is to look at the website you want to extract text from. Here, we'll consider Stack Overflow (stackoverflow.com)[28] and select the most up-voted answer as the best answer. Looking at a Stack Overflow page, you can see that their text fields are tagged in a particular way. The tags associated with the different fields keep changing, so it is advisable to right-click on the page of interest to *inspect* the site's HTML structure. You can check which div or class in the HTML contains the relevant information by performing a search of the text seen on the website that you want to get the tags for. After that, something like the one below would work to extract the top answer.

Step 1:

```
! pip install beautifulsoup4 ==2.2.1
```

Step 2:

```
# Imports
from bs4 import BeautifulSoup
from urllib.request import urlopen

# URL to questions
myurl = "https://stackoverflow.com/questions/19410018/how-to-count-
    the-number-of-words-in-a-sentence-ignoring-numbers-punctuation-an"

html = urlopen(myurl).read()
```

---

[28]https://stackoverflow.com

```
soup = BeautifulSoup(html, "html.parser")
question = soup.find("div", {"class": "question"})

# Print top 1000 characters of question to find relevant tag
ques_text = question.find(
  "div", {"class": "s-prose js-post-body"}
)
print("Question: \n", ques_text.get_text().strip())

answers = soup.find("div", {"class": "answer"})
# print to check the correct class tag.

ans_text = answers.find(
  "div", {"class": "s-prose js-post-body"}
)
print("Top answer: \n", ans_text.get_text().strip())
```

An example of another library that can help with HTML parsing is **scrappy**[29].

2.2.6   Reading from a Word document

Reading a Word document using Python can be performed using the library `docx`.

Step 1:

Install the library.

```
! pip install python-docx==0.8.11
```

Step 2:

Let's read a sample Word file in Python with the name sample_word.docx in your working directory.

```
# Imports
from docx import Document

doc = open("sample_word.docx", "rb")
document = Document(doc)

# Placeholder for text
doc_text = ""
for para in document.paragraphs:
  doc_text += para.text

# Print the final output
print(doc_text)

# Close the file
doc.close()
```

2.2.7   Reading from APIs

Several data houses have APIs (Application Programming Interfaces) that are developed to fetch underlying data with the help of functions and queries. We'll look at

---

[29]https://scrapy.org/

two social media APIs - YouTube Data API and Twitter API. Both require you to register an app and generate tokens before you can start making requests to their APIs.

YouTube API

Step 1: Registration and token generation

The first two steps include registering a project and enabling it[30]. The API key produced as a result can be used to make requests to the YouTube API.

Step 2: Making requests using Python

YouTube API has great documentation[31] and guides on accessing it using Python. Below is an example of searching for videos using a keyword on YouTube, grabbing video tags and statistics, reading video comments, and fetching commenter subscriptions.

Note that it is a good practice to **not** keep any API keys and secrets in your Python scripts for security reasons. A common practice is to keep these defined as local environment variables or fetch these from a secure location at runtime.

```
! pip install google-api-python-client==2.66.0
! pip install google-auth-httplib2==0.1.0
! pip install google-auth-oauthlib==0.7.1
```

```
# Imports
from googleapiclient.discovery import build
from googleapiclient.errors import HttpError

# Set DEVELOPER_KEY to the API key value
# from the APIs & auth > Registered apps tab of
#    https://cloud.google.com/console
# Please ensure that you have enabled
# the YouTube Data API for your project.
DEVELOPER_KEY = 'REPLACE_ME'
YOUTUBE_API_SERVICE_NAME = 'youtube'
YOUTUBE_API_VERSION = 'v3'

youtube = build(
  YOUTUBE_API_SERVICE_NAME,
  YOUTUBE_API_VERSION,
  developerKey=DEVELOPER_KEY
)
```

Searching for videos.

```
# Call the search.list method to retrieve results that
# match the specified query term.
# (here we use "natural language processing"
# as an example query term)
video_search_response = youtube.search().list(
  q="natural language processing",
  part='id,snippet',
  maxResults=50,
```

---

[30]https://developers.google.com/youtube/v3/getting-started
[31]https://developers.google.com/youtube/v3/docs

```
    type='video'
).execute()

# Let's store IDs for videos returned,
# and then get their tags and stats
# tags come as a part of 'snippet',
# stats come as a part of 'statistics'
video_ids = [
    i['id']['videoId']
    for i in video_search_response.get('items', [])
]

# At a time only 50 video IDs can be queried.
# Iterate trough pages with the help of the
# API documentation. Here we limit to 50 videos only.
video_details = youtube.videos().list(
    id=video_ids,
    part='statistics,snippet',
    maxResults=50
).execute()

print(video_details["items"][0]["snippet"]["title"])
print(video_details["items"][0]["statistics"])
```

Getting comments.

```
# Get comments for one video
comment_details = youtube.commentThreads().list(
    videoId=video_ids[0],
    part='snippet',
    maxResults=50
).execute()
first_cmnt = comment_details["items"][0]
top_level_data = first_cmnt["snippet"]["topLevelComment"]
print(
    top_level_data["snippet"]["textDisplay"],
    top_level_data["snippet"]["authorDisplayName"]
)
```

Getting subscriptions.

```
# Get commenting user IDs
commeters = [
    i['snippet']['topLevelComment']['snippet']\
    ['authorChannelId']['value']
    for i in comment_details.get('items', [])
]

# Get subscriptions of commenters
subs = {}
for com_id in commeters[0:5]:
    try:
        subs[com_id] = youtube.subscriptions().list(
            channelId=com_id,
            part='snippet',
            # Get 50 subscriptions per commenter
            maxResults=50
```

```
      ).execute()
  except HttpError as err:
    print("""Could not get subscriptions
    for channel ID {}.\n {}""".format(
      com_id, err
    )
  )
print('Videos: {}'.format(video_details))
print('Comments: {}'.format(comment_details))
print('Subscriptions: {}'.format(subs))
```

The notebook section2/youtube-api.ipynb contains the output of the above code. The YouTube API keys come with a limit on the daily number of available units to spend on making data requests. Each request costs a certain number of units which is listed here[32]. The limit is usually on the total number of units per day which refreshes every 24 hours at midnight Pacific Time. Currently, the standard daily limit is 10,000 units. This limit is subject to change based on YouTube's developer terms. If you are making a massive number of requests and want to avoid premature termination of your code, you can either include a `time.sleep()` in your code or terminate the script with proper logging so you are able to resume the next day.

Twitter API

Step 1: Registration and token generation

To use the Twitter API, you will need to create an app[33]. The form leads to a few questions that you will need to answer. Once the app is created, you should be able to generate API tokens - consumer key, consumer secret, API token, and API secret. There are standard limits associated with your application and tokens that determine how many requests you can make to the Twitter API in a given time frame. The limits are different for different requests and can be found here[34]. There are packages offered by Twitter to businesses that would like higher limits at different costs. This can be determined by reaching out to a Twitter API contact.

Step 2: Making requests using Python

You can make requests to the Twitter API using the library `tweepy`. An example for searching for users, tweets, and fetching followers and friends can be found below. For more code samples, `tweepy`'s API guide is a great resource[35].

```
! pip install tweepy==4.12.1

# Imports
import tweepy
from tweepy import OAuthHandler

# Globals
CONSUMER_KEY = 'REPLACE_ME'
CONSUMER_SECRET = 'REPLACE_ME'
ACCESS_TOKEN = 'REPLACE_ME'
ACCESS_SECRET = 'REPLACE_ME'
```

---

[32]https://developers.google.com/youtube/v3/determine_quota_cost
[33]https://developer.twitter.com/en/apps
[34]https://developer.twitter.com/en/docs/twitter-api/v1/rate-limits
[35]https://docs.tweepy.org/en/stable/api.html

```
# Set connection
auth = OAuthHandler(CONSUMER_KEY, CONSUMER_SECRET)
auth.set_access_token(ACCESS_TOKEN, ACCESS_SECRET)
query = tweepy.API(auth)
```

The below code snippet gets user details when the screen name or Twitter ID of the desired user is known.

```
screen_names = ['CNN']
users = query.lookup_users(screen_name=screen_names)
for user in users:
    print(user._json)
```

If the screen name or ID is not known, you can also search for users using free-form text as seen in the following code snippet.

```
search_term = "natural language processing"
users = query.search_users(search_term)
for user in users:
  print(user._json)
```

To get followers or friends of a known screen name or Twitter ID, the following code can be used.

```
screen_name = "PyConAU"

followers = query.get_followers(screen_name=screen_name)
for fol in followers:
  print(fol._json)

friends = query.get_friends(screen_name=screen_name)
for fr in friends:
  print(fr._json)

# To get only IDs rather than detailed data for each follower/friend,
#   the below can be used instead

follower_ids = query.get_follower_ids(screen_name=screen_name)
print(follower_ids)

friend_ids = query.get_friend_ids(screen_name=screen_name)
print(friend_ids)
```

To iterate through result pages, use `tweepy.Cursor`.

```
cursor = tweepy.Cursor(
  query.get_followers, screen_name=screen_name, count=200
).pages()

followers = []
for _, page in enumerate(cursor):
  followers += [itm._json for itm in page]

print("No. of follower details", len(followers))
print(followers[0])
```

The below code snippet gets tweets for a twitter screen name @PyConAU.

```
screen_name = "PyConAU"
alltweets = []
# make initial request for most recent tweets
# (200 is the maximum allowed count)
new_tweets = query.user_timeline(
  screen_name=screen_name,
  count=200
)
# save most recent tweets
alltweets.extend(new_tweets)

# To get more tweets,
# save the id of the oldest tweet less one
oldest = alltweets[-1].id - 1
# Grab tweets until there are no tweets left to fetch
while len(new_tweets) > 0:
  # all subsiquent requests
  # use the max_id param to prevent duplicates
  new_tweets = query.user_timeline(
    screen_name=screen_name,
    count=200,
    max_id=oldest
  )
  # save most recent tweets
  alltweets.extend(new_tweets)
  # update the id of the oldest tweet less one
  oldest = alltweets[-1].id - 1
  print("{} tweets downloaded\n".format(len(alltweets)))

# transform the tweepy tweets into a 2D array
all_tweets = [tweet._json for tweet in alltweets]

# Print
print("Total count", len(all_tweets))
print(all_tweets[0])
```

If the followers are more than a certain amount, the code for getting followers using Cursor can terminate before getting all the results. Same applies to requesting tweets.

One important thing to note here is the influence of the limitations of your API tokens. Twitter API tokens allow you to make a certain number of each type of request per 15-minute window. Integrating logic to handle these limits can help avoid premature termination of the code. Below is an example of introducing a 15-minute wait for allowing a reset of the token before making further requests using library tweepy.

```
# Add the query variables  as below
query = tweepy.API(
  auth,
  wait_on_rate_limit=True
)
```

Now you can run the request for getting tweets and followers using Cursor without errors. The runtime might be long because of the 15-minute sleeps. The output of the above code can be found in the notebook twitter-api.ipynb on GitHub.

2.2.8 Closing thoughts

Data extraction needs are commonly encountered while reading and storing text data. At times, we may not want to extract all the data from these sources, but just a few entities like names, dates, or email addresses. Not storing unwanted data helps save space and reduces data complexity. In structured data formats with different fields corresponding to different information, it is trivial to just read the fields of interest. At other times, entities of interest may be embedded in a single piece of text. There are ways to extract such data from text using Python using information extraction. Preprocessing will be discussed further in Chapter 3 (Section 3.1) and information extraction in Chapter 7 (Section 7.1).

2.3 DATA STORAGE

Storage of data becomes a prime question, especially when you are no longer only dealing with text that can fit into a local variable or a few files saved on your computer. When you need to store your data more stably, using a file system or database is beneficial.

A database is simply an organized collection of data. Technically, if you take 10 CSV files and put them in a folder, that is considered a database. There are times when that is not a feasible option due to scaling difficulties or the time it takes to access data. While it may be feasible to manage 10 CSV files on a local system, the same will not hold if the number of files increases to 10,000.

> TIP
>
> Let's assume you need a database. With so many options available, how do you make the choice?
>
> There are a few points to consider while making a database choice.
>
> 1. Evaluate your current needs with the data. Also, evaluate your future needs with the data.
>
> 2. Evaluate your data structure. Are you going to store data that is structured or unstructured?
>
>   (a) Example of structured data includes categorical data, numbers, and other predefined data types.
>
>   (b) Example of unstructured data includes text data, image data, and video data.
>
> 3. The volume of data you want to store.
>
> 4. Performance requirements (reading and writing data).

Since you may not only have text data to think about, but also timestamps, numbers, and other kinds of data, it is important to evaluate your needs accordingly. The solution you pick should fit all your data needs and formats.

There are several database options in general, including relational, non-relational, cloud, columnar, wide column, object-oriented, key-value, document, hierarchical, and graph databases.[36] contains further information about each. For our scope, specifically for use cases around text data, the database types that are popularly used include relational, non-relational, and document databases.

A relational database is a structure that recognizes relationships between stored items. Most of such databases use Structured Query Language (SQL) as their underlying query language. A non-relational database does not rely on known relationships and use a storage model that is optimized for the type of data being stored. They are also referred to as NoSQL, or not only SQL. A document database is a type of a non-relational database suitable for document-oriented information.

An often preferred and easy solution is to store your data in a relational database if you can set expectations of which data can be added to a table in the future. The queries are easy and the data schema can be standardized. However, when you don't have set fields and field types that a data table can contain, and want the flexibility for adding new and unknown field types to your data tables at any time, non-relational databases are a better choice. Next, let's assume you have a collection of white papers or resumes that you want to store. If you know how to extract the relevant pieces of information within those documents, it can be a good idea to transform the data into

---

[36]https://www.geeksforgeeks.org/types-of-databases

the fields needed first and then store them in a structured format. However, if the intention is to perform full-text searches of the documents, then choosing a document database will be suitable.

Popular databases that work well with text data include Elasticsearch, and MongoDB if you have larger documents to store. We'll also explore Google Cloud Platform's (GCP) BigQuery and a simple flat file system. Next, let's look at the capabilities and some query samples for each.

2.3.1 Flat-file database

For many NLP tasks, there are popular Python libraries that can run operations and methods on a JSON or CSV format, such as `pandas`. A CSV file format is easy to open, evaluate, learn, parse, serialize, filter, and includes different encodings and languages. CSV is also easy to share and works well when you need the ability to share data via email. This is particularly a common choice in academia. With the presence of libraries such as `pandas` in Python, such data is easy to manipulate, explore, filter, and reorganize.

In cases where the issue involves small-scale data that needs to be easily shared without investment in any database setup, a CSV, JSON, or another text file format can be a great choice.

A collection of flat files is considered a flat-file database. There is no linkage between records. Maintaining files may not be convenient when you need to add and/or refresh your dataset periodically or are dealing with a larger scale of data that is making your code run slow and inefficiently. Considering a database management system is a good choice in such cases and is a popular choice for industry practitioners. Practitioners still often take a smaller segment of their data and store it in local files when they want to dig into the data and experiment with NLP tasks. It gives you a way to view, and slice and dice what you need on your local machine without putting unnecessary load on your in-memory storage.

2.3.2 Elasticsearch

Elasticsearch is a NoSQL, distributed document-oriented database. It serves as a full-text search engine designed to store, access, and manage structured, semi-structured, and unstructured data of different types. Elasticsearch uses a data structure called an inverted index. This data structure lists each word appearing in a document and is then able to easily return documents where a word has occurred, thus supporting fast full-text searches. These capabilities offered with Elasticsearch make it a popular choice for text. Elasticsearch is also a popular choice for numeric and geospatial data types[37].

With Elasticsearch, you can get documents matching other documents using TF-IDF (discussed further in Chapter 3 (Section 3.4)), along with other simpler operations such as finding documents that contain or don't contain a word/phrase as an exact field value or within a text field, or a combination thereof. Every record

---

[37]`https://www.javatpoint.com/elasticsearch-vs-mongodb`

returned has an attached score that represents the closeness to your search criteria. Elasticsearch is a great choice when you need fast searches from your database and supports fast filtering and aggregation.

For text fields, Elasticsearch offers two types – *text* and *keyword*. Type *keyword* arguments are optimized for filtering operations. Type *text* arguments are better suited for performing searches within the strings. A field can also be made as both *keyword* and *text* if desired.

An *index* in Elasticsearch can be set up to expect documents containing fields with certain names and types. Let's consider the following example. You want to create a new index in Elasticsearch and add data to it. This can be done as follows using Python with the library `elasticsearch`.

```
! python -m pip install elasticsearch==8.5.0
```

We start by defining data mappings as follows.

```
mappings = {
  "users": """{
    "mappings" : {
      "entity" : {
        "properties" : {
          "name" : {
            "type" : "text",
            "fields" : {"keyword" : {
                "type" : "keyword", "ignore_above" : 256
            }}
          },
          "userId" : {
            "type" : "text",
            "fields" : {"raw" : {"type" : "long"}}
          }
        }
      }
    }
  }"""
}
```

Then, we can create an index as follows.

```
from elasticsearch import Elasticsearch

conn = Elasticsearch(
  [{"host": <host>, "port": <port>}],
  http_auth=(<username>, <password>),
  timeout=60,
  max_retries=5,
  retry_on_timeout=True,
  maxsize=25,
)

for index_name in mappings:
  conn.indices.create(
    index=index_name, ignore=400,
    body=mappings[index_name]
  )
```

Finally, we can add data as follows.

```
# Add data
conn.index(
  index=index_name, doc_type="entity", id=1,
  body={"name": "mandatory payment", "userId": 1}
)

conn.index(
  index=index_name, doc_type="entity", id=2,
  body={"name": "herman woman", "userId": 2}
)
```

Let's assume your host and port is 'elastic.org.com:9200'.

Now `http://elastic.org.com:9200/users?pretty` will show you the data that you just inserted.

```
{
  "took" : 53,
  "timed_out" : false,
  "_shards" : {
    "total" : 5,
    "successful" : 5,
    "failed" : 0
  },
  "hits" : {
    "total" : 2,
    "max_score" : 1.0,
    "hits" : [
      {
        "_index" : "users",
        "_type" : "entity",
        "_id" : "1",
        "_score" : 1.0,
        "_source" : {
          "name" : "mandatory payment",
          "userId" : "1"
        }
      },
      {
        "_index" : "users",
        "_type" : "entity",
        "_id" : "2",
        "_score" : 1.0,
        "_source" : {
          "name" : "herman woman",
          "userId" : "2"
        }
      }
    ]
  }
}
```

There are multiple ways to query data in Elasticsearch. Kibana[38] is a great data exploration tool that works on top of Elasticsearch.

---

[38]https://www.elastic.co/kibana

Here, we'll look at a few bash and Python examples of querying Elasticsearch.

2.3.2.1 Query examples

Let's look at some query samples below using the command line and Python.

Basic data filtering query

```
curl -X GET
"elastic.org.com:9200/users/_search?size=10000&pretty"
-H 'Content-Type: application/json' -d'
{
  "query": {
    "bool": {
      "filter": {"terms": {"name": ["herman woman"]}}
    }
  }
}'
```

This will return your record with _id 2.

Searching for documents with a term present in a particular field.

```
curl -XGET 'elastic.org.com:9200/channel/_search?pretty'
-H 'Content-Type: application/json' -d'
{
  "query": {
    "bool": {
      "must": [{
        "match": {
          "name": "*man*"
        }
      }]
    }
  }
}' -o /Users/xyz/Desktop/temp.txt
```

This will return your record with _id 1 and 2 as "man" is present in both the *records* in the *name* field and save the results in the specified temp.txt file.

Using Python

```
from elasticsearch import Elasticsearch
es_master = "elastic.orgname.com"
es_port   = "9200"
es = Elasticsearch([{'host':es_master, 'port':es_port}])

# This query will return only userId field both both
# document _id 1 and 2
query = { "_source": ["userId"],
  "query": {
    "bool": {
      "must": [
      {"match": {"name": "*man*"}}
      ]
    }
  }
}
```

```
res = es.search(
  index="user",
  body=query,
  size=10000,
  request_timeout=30
)

hits = res['hits']['hits']
print("no. of users: ", len(hits))
```

Searching for a query term anywhere in the documents

```
curl -XGET 'elastic.org.com:9200/users/_search?q=herman&scroll=1m&
    pretty' -H 'Content-Type: application/json' -d'
{"size" : 10000}' -o /Users/xyz/Desktop/temp1.txt
```

This will return your record with _id 2.

Finally, query to find similar records based on TF-IDF. Let's assume you added some new text fields in your *users* index, and 100 more records. Now you want to find all records that are similar to records with _id 1 and 2.

```
{
  "query": {
    "bool": {
      "must": [
      {"range": {"_id": {"gte":0}}},
      { "match": {"name":"herman woman"}},
      {
        "more_like_this": {
          "fields":[ "name", "title",  "description"],
          "like" :[
          {"_index": "source", "_type": "entity", "_id": "1"},
          {"_index": "source", "_type": "entity", "_id": "2"}
          ],
          "min_term_freq": 1,
          "min_doc_freq": 3,
          "max_query_terms": 25,
          "max_word_length": 15,
          "min_word_length": 3,
          "minimum_should_match": "7",
          "stop_words": ["myself", "our", "ours"]
        }
      }
      ]
    }
  }
}
```

2.3.3 MongoDB

MongoDB is a NoSQL document-oriented database. It is a popular choice for storing text data. The DB supports query operations for performing a search on text.

Let's consider an example dataset using the MongoDB Shell, mongosh, which is a fully functional JavaScript and Node.js 14.x REPL environment for interacting with MongoDB deployments. You can use the MongoDB Shell to test queries and operations directly with your database. `mongosh` is available as a standalone package in the MongoDB download center.[39]

```
db.stores.insert(
  [
    { _id: 1, name: "Java Hut",
      description: "Coffee and cakes" },
    { _id: 2, name: "Burger Buns",
      description: "Gourmet hamburgers" },
    { _id: 3, name: "Coffee Shop",
      description: "Just coffee" },
    { _id: 4, name: "Clothes Clothes Clothes",
      description: "Discount clothing" },
    { _id: 5, name: "Java Shopping",
      description: "Indonesian goods" }
  ]
)
```

MongoDB uses a text index and $text operator to perform text searches.

2.3.3.1 Query samples

Text index

Text index in MongoDB is for supporting text search queries. Text index can include any field with a string value or array of string values. It is required to have a text index on your collection if you want to perform text search queries. A collection is allowed to have only one text search index. The text search index can itself cover multiple fields.

The text index can be created as follows.

```
db.stores.createIndex( { name: "text", description: "text" } )
```

This will allow you to perform text search on fields *name* and *description*.

$Text operator

The $text query operator can be used for performing text searches on a collection with a text index. $text tokenizes the text using whitespace and common punctuation as delimiters. For matching the field with a string, this operator performs a logical OR with all tokens in the text field.

For instance, the following query can be used to find matches with any of these terms - 'coffee', 'shop', and 'java'.

```
db.stores.find( { $text: { $search: "java coffee shop" } } )
```

An exact phrase match can also be searched for by wrapping the string in double quotes. The following finds all documents containing *coffee shop*.

```
db.stores.find( { $text: { $search: "\"coffee shop\"" } } )
```

---

[39]https://docs.mongodb.com/mongodb-shell/

Furthermore, if you want to search for the presence of certain words, but also the absence of a word, you can exclude a word by prepending a – character. For instance, the following finds stores containing 'java' or 'shop', but not 'coffee'.

```
db.stores.find( { $text: { $search: "java shop -coffee" } } )
```

MongoDB returns the results without any sorting applied as the default. Text search queries compute a relevance score for every document. This score is the measure of how well a document matches the query of the user. It is possible to specify a sorting order within the query. This can be done as follows.

```
db.stores.find(
   { $text: { $search: "java coffee shop" } },
   { score: { $meta: "textScore" } }
).sort( { score: { $meta: "textScore" } })
```

Text search can also be performed in the aggregation pipeline. The following aggregation searches for the term 'cake' in the $match stage and calculates the total views for the matching documents in the $group stage.[40]

```
db.articles.aggregate(
   [
     { $match: { $text: { $search: "cake" } } },
     { $group: { _id: null, views: { $sum: "$views" } } }
   ]
)
```

How to query MongoDB using Python?
This can be done using the Python client for MongoDB - pymongo[41].

```
! python -m pip install pymongo==4.3.3

from pymongo import MongoClient

# Note: Change connection string as needed
client = MongoClient("mongodb://localhost:27017/")

# Database Name
db = client["database"]

# Collection Name
collection = db["your collection name"]

# to find one record
one_result = collection.find_one()

# To perfrom text search as discussed above
result = collection.find(
   {"$text": {"$search": "cake"}}
)
```

---

[40]https://docs.mongodb.com/manual/text-search/
[41]https://www.mongodb.com/blog/post/getting-started-with-python-and-mongodb

Language support

In addition to the English language, MongoDB supports text search for various other languages. These include Danish, Dutch, Finnish, French, German, Hungarian, Italian, Norwegian, Portuguese, Romanian, Russian, Spanish, Swedish, and Turkish.

Other examples of document databases include RethinkDB[42] and OrientDB.[43]

2.3.4 Google BigQuery

BigQuery is a data warehouse and fully managed serverless data storage solution. You can make standard SQL queries with data in BigQuery, and leverage regex functions to manipulate text fields.

BigQuery supports a range of regular expression (regex) and string query functions for a convenient way to perform a text search across string fields using queries. As a drawback, there is a limit of 64k per row for any field in a BigQuery record, so storing large unlimited-size text documents for text searching would not be suitable.

Regex

Regular expression functions are listed below[44].

REGEXP_MATCH('str', 'reg_exp') returns true if str matches the regular expression. For string matching without regular expressions, use CONTAINS instead of REGEXP_MATCH.

REGEXP_EXTRACT('str', 'reg_exp') returns the portion of str that matches the capturing group within the regular expression.

REGEXP_REPLACE('orig_str', 'reg_exp', 'replace_str') returns a string where any substring of orig_str that matches reg_exp is replaced with replace_str. For example, REGEXP_REPLACE ('Hello', 'lo', 'p') returns Help.

String functions

Several string functions exist in BigQuery that operate on string data.[45] Table 2.2 contains the function and their descriptions.

2.3.4.1 Query examples

Below are some query examples to do various kinds of text searches using BigQuery.

Let's assume we have a dataset in BigQuery with the field *title*. Here are all the rows for the field *title*.

---

[42]https://rethinkdb.com/
[43]https://orientdb.org/
[44]https://developers.google.com/bigquery/docs/query-reference#regularexpressionfunctions
[45]https://developers.google.com/bigquery/docs/query-reference#stringfunctions

TABLE 2.2 BigQuery string functions.

String function	Description
CONCAT()	Returns the concatenation of two or more strings
expr CONTAINS 'str'	Returns true if expr contains the specified string argument
INSTR()	Returns the one-based index of the first occurrence of a string
LEFT()	Returns the leftmost characters of a string
LENGTH()	Returns length of the string
LOWER()	Lowercasing the string
LPAD()	Inserts characters to the left side of a string
LTRIM()	Removes characters from the left of the string
REPLACE()	Replaces all occurrences of a sub-string
RIGHT()	Returns the rightmost characters of a string
RPAD()	Inserts characters to the right side of a string
RTRIM()	Removes trailing characters from the right side of a string
SPLIT()	Splitting string into repeated sub-strings
SUBSTR()	Returns a substring
UPPER()	Uppercasing all string characters

Amazing SpiderMan
I am a woman
I am a Man
I am HUMAN
Commander
mandatory
man

Let's say our task is to find all rows where the *title* contains the term 'man'. Let's see the solution a few different ways.

Presence of the search term 'man' anywhere in the string matching the case specified.

```
SELECT title
FROM sample_project.sample_table
WHERE title LIKE '%man%'
```

This will result in titles containing 'man', and would also work for words such as 'woman' or 'commander', that contain the search string within. This particular search will only return rows that match the case with our search term. In this case, it would be the lowercase word 'man'. The following titles will be returned.

I am a woman
Commander
mandatory
man

Presence of the search term 'man' only at the start of the string field, matching the case specified.

```
SELECT title
FROM project.sample_table
WHERE title LIKE 'man%'
```

The above query returns the below rows.

mandatory
man

Similarly, to get an exact match, the % sign from the right can be removed. To get string fields ending with 'man', the % sign can be placed on the left and removed from the right.

Presence of the search term 'man' with case insensitivity.

In this case, we want to return all rows that have the presence of the search term 'man' in any case - upper, lower, or mixed.

```
SELECT title
FROM project.sample_table
WHERE LOWER(title) LIKE '%man%'
```

The above query returns the following rows.

Amazing SpiderMan
I am a woman
I am a Man
I am HUMAN
Commander
mandatory
man

Finding all rows that contain the search term 'man' as a separate word/phrase with case insensitivity.

This use case differs from the search criteria perspective. Until now, we were searching for the presence of a term within a string. Now, we want to detect rows where the search string is present as a word/independently occurring phrase of its own. We can leverage regex_contains for a use case as such.

```
SELECT title
FROM project.sample_table
WHERE REGEXP_CONTAINS(
  title, "(?i)(?:^|\\W)man(?:$|\\W)"
)
```

The above query returns the following rows.

I am a Man
man

This expression can be used for a phrase as well.

```
SELECT title
FROM project.sample_table
WHERE REGEXP_CONTAINS(
  title, "(?i)(?:^|\\W)a man(?:$|\\W)"
)
```

The above query returns the following rows.

I am a Man

How to query BigQuery using Python?

This can be done using the BigQuery Python client – `google-cloud-bigquery`[46].

```
! pip install google-cloud-bigquery==3.4.0

from google.cloud import bigquery

# Construct a BigQuery client object.
client = bigquery.Client()

query = """
  SELECT title
  FROM project.sample_table
"""
# Make an API request.
query_job = client.query(query=query)

results = query_job.result()
```

> **TIP**
>
> There are ways to optimize your database query performance. One of them is the way you partition your data in your database. Be sure to pay attention to data partitioning based on how you plan to query your data. For example, if your data records include a timestamp, and you plan to make queries for before or after certain dates, then making timestamp a partition field would help improve query performance and return results faster. Partitioning applies to most databases.

---

[46]https://cloud.google.com/bigquery/docs/reference/libraries#client-libraries-install-python

Data maintenance

Now that you have made a call on how to store your data, an important follow-up is considerations around maintaining your data. This includes the following.

1. Backup strategy

   One of the unfortunate events that happen at different scales to most of us at some point in our life is 'accidental deletions!'. It is important to take or schedule regular data backups. This is also useful when your data is getting constantly updated. It will help restore a previous version if the recent data updates introduced unwanted data or other noise.

2. Maintaining data quality

   When storing data in a database, it is a popular practice to store ingestion timestamps along with every record to retain the knowledge of when something was inserted or changed. This helps in partitioning manual quality checks on your data, so you do not need to re-check data you have checked before, but only the new additions/changes.

3. Monitoring

   Establishing processes and systems for monitoring data is an important practice for maintaining data quality and identifying issues in a timely manner. Set alerts to get notified of errors or data changes. Datadog[a] is an example of a tool that offers monitoring and analysis of the health and performance of your databases.

---

[a]https://docs.datadoghq.com/getting_started/database_monitoring/

Windup

In this section, we discussed several sources of text data, including first-party data (a business's own asset), public sources, and conditionally available data sources such as social media APIs. We shared how you can extract text from different document formats using Python and open-source tools. We also shared code samples for reading text from different APIs. Once you have text data, exploring data storage solutions is the next step. We have investigated data storage options that can help you stably keep your data around, update it, and query it as per the need. We also shared several query samples for performing text operations in different databases.

It is vital to note that some APIs change their supported methods with different versions without backwards compatibility. For example, `tweepy 3.10` versus `tweepy 4.12` have different method names for getting followers (`followers` versus `get_followers`).

We also discussed the importance of data maintenance and tips and tricks to ensure the data retains quality. Now you know the basics of NLP and where the data comes from, how you can extract it, and where you can store your data. In the next section, we will discuss data preprocessing, modeling, visualization, and augmentation.

Previously, we discussed several reasons why NLP is challenging. That included language diversity, language evolution, and context awareness, among others. These challenges impact how the text data looks. What does that mean? Text data can be curated from multiple resources. The data's nature itself can vary in quality and quantity. Let's consider an corpus curated from Research Gate that contains research papers. How would you expect the text would look like from this corpus? Perhaps long, formal language, field-specific jargon usage. Now consider a text corpus curated from YouTube that contains comments on a gaming video. How would you expect this corpus to look in comparison to the Research Gate corpus? Perhaps shorter length documents, informal language, gaming-specific abbreviations, and term usage. What if we were fetching comments from unpopular videos? Now another variation may be the total number of documents in the corpus. We can see how changing the source completely changes certain properties of the text documents within a corpus.

The below lists the most common text document varieties that are commonly dealt with.

1. Amount of data: Variation in quantity depends on the data source. Popular topics can have a large number of documents, whereas less popular subjects can have a very small number of documents available.

2. Language style: The style of language usage in the corpus can be formal, informal, semi-formal, or a combination thereof.

3. Text length: The length of text documents within a corpus can be short, long, or a combination thereof.

4. Language of communication: Even if you expect to deal with only one language of content, let's say English, you can still have documents containing other languages.

5. Jargons/context-specific terms: Based on the topic of content within the corpus, certain different jargon usages can be popularly found in some text corpora versus others.

Why do we care about the variety found within text data? It is important to know your data, and how it may be different from other text data that you are trying to learn from or may have worked on in the past. The nature of the data is a useful consideration factor for deciding between storage options and maintenance logic. It also informs whether certain cleaning algorithms need to be applied to your dataset prior to any processing. We will look at different data cleaning and preprocessing, and data augmentation methods in Chapter 3.

III

Data Processing and Modeling

What you do once you have the data depends on the task you are trying to accomplish. For data scientists, there are two common possibilities.

1. The task at hand requires data analysis and aggregations to draw insights for a business use case.

2. The task at hand requires you to build models using machine learning (ML).

Figure 2.3 summarizes the chain of events most commonly expected in a Data Scientist's work. In this section, we will discuss all the phases - data, modeling, and evaluation.

To begin with, we will dive into the data phase. We already discussed data sources and curation in Section II. In this section, we will dive into data cleaning and preprocessing techniques that eliminate unwanted elements from text and prepare the data for numerical transformations and modeling. We'll look at Python implementations for removing commonly observed noise in the different varieties of data, including lowercasing, stop word removal, spelling corrections, URL removal, punctuation removal, and more. We'll also discuss stemming, lemmatization, and other standardization techniques. Before further processing, a text document often needs to be segmented into its component sentences, words, or phrases. We'll implement different data segmentation techniques.

Once the data is clean, the next step includes data transformations to convert the text into numerical representations. We'll look at data transformation techniques that include text encoding, frequency-based vectorization, co-occurrence matrix, and several word embedding models (word embedding models convert words into numeric

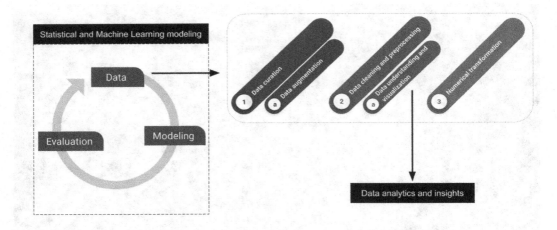

FIGURE 2.3   Data Science project phases.

representation by using machine learning techniques) along with their implementations.

Once we have numerical representations, we can proceed on to creating models for our applications. These models can be statistical algorithms such as distance measures to find similar words or sentences, or machine learning algorithms that attempt to find patterns or classify your data into categories. We'll discuss some popular algorithms for text data and spotlight open-source tools to build these models. We'll look at classic machine-learning algorithms that do well on several tasks and a variety of dataset sizes including smaller datasets, and deep-learning neural networks models that do better on larger datasets including transformers that do well on tasks where word order in a sentence plays a critical role while handling long-term relationships in a sentence.

Model evaluation is an important phase of the data science cycle. Each model comes with certain parameters that you can set that alter the outcome of the models. These are also called hyperparameters. Model evaluation helps you choose the right model and tune the hyperparameters appropriately. This step also informs any changes that need to happen in the data or modeling phase for getting to the desired results.

Going back to the data phase, in Figure 2.3, notice that the goal can sometimes be to understand your data so you can draw insights. Such scenarios may not need you to always build models. Visualizations enable understanding and analyzing data. We will look at popular visualizations for text data and share implementation examples.

When there is a lack of data, increasing the number of samples can be critical. One popular way to get some samples is to self-label data or create new samples which can be a highly manual and slow process requiring resources. To ease the process of the generation of new samples, certain techniques can be leveraged to quickly create thousands of samples. We will discuss data augmentation which explores techniques to create new data samples when your existing number of samples is lacking.

To summarize, this section includes the following.

- Data cleaning and preprocessing

- Visualization

- Data augmentation

- Data transformation

- Distance metrics

- Modeling

- Model evaluation

The reader is assumed to have an understanding of machine learning models and how they work. Thus, in this section, we will not go deep into every model's architecture but cover the basic concepts and principles that a model is based on and share implementation guides. Resources are linked and cited for readers that want to learn more about a model's inner workings. The section 3 folder in https://github.com/jsingh811/NLP-in-the-real-world contains the code used in this section.

## CHAPTER 3

Data Preprocessing and Transformation

3.1 DATA CLEANING

In most scenarios, there are several steps you will run your data through before you create models or visualizations. These include cleaning steps to remove noisy elements from your data. Noisy elements are elements in your text that are not relevant to your applications. For instance, in order to extract topics from a sentence, the URLs, special characters, and words like 'is' and 'my' are not relevant in the sentence '13@# My Ford car is https://tinyurl....'. A cleaned-up version may look like 'ford car'. Furthermore, it is a common practice to standardize the words in your text, e.g., car and cars both fall under the vehicles category. Thus if you are building a categorizer as such, stemming and/or lemmatizing can improve your model results.

We'll dive into common cleaning and standardization techniques below. Then, we'll look at an example scenario and implement all relevant cleaning steps for it.

DOI: 10.1201/9781003264774-3

> *TIP*
>
> Select what you want to remove from your data based on the application. For instance, to create a sentiment classification model, you would not expect elements such as URLs to convey meaning.
>
> The anticipated noise can also vary with language style and data source. For instance, the language used on social media can have excessive punctuations, emojis, and typing errors. For some applications, retaining punctuation might be necessary, while for others it might not be useful or could also be detrimental to your model. For instance, if you are creating a classifier model using the count of words in the text as features, you may want to map 'great' , 'great' , and 'GREAT!' , to the single word 'great' . In this example, you will need to remove punctuation from your data and lowercase before extracting word frequencies. On the contrary, most named entity recognition (NER) models rely on punctuation and case to identify entities in the text, such as a person's name. For example, below we run two sentences through spaCy's NER using the `en_web_core_sm` pre-trained model.
>
> 'hi my name is jane songh i work at apple' -> no entities detected
> 'Hi. My name is Jane Songh. I work at Apple.' -> Jane Songh (PERSON), Apple(ORG)
>
> We'll look at code implementations for NER using spaCy and some other tools in Chapter 7 (Section 7.1).

3.1.1 Segmentation

Sentence segmentation

A long document can be split into multiple component sentences using sentence segmentation. This can be accomplished using many Python libraries. Let's see an example below using spaCy.

```
! pip install spacy

import spacy

nlp = spacy.load("en_core_web_sm")
doc = nlp(u"Hi!. I like NLP. Do you??")

for sent in doc.sents:
  print(sent)
# >> Hi!.
# >> I like NLP.
# >> Do you??
```

You can also perform sentence segmentation using the `NLTK` library, or write your own regex function depending on how you want to split the text. We'll look at an example of the latter in Chapter 10 (Section 10.1.3).

> What is regex?
> Regex stands for regular expression. A regular expression is a sequence of characters that specifies a pattern for searching text.

The implementation of sentence segmentation with `NLTK` is as follows.

```
! pip install nltk

from nltk import sent_tokenize

sentences = sent_tokenize("I like it. Did you like it too?")
print(sentences)
# >> ['I like it.', 'Did you like it too?']
```

Word tokenization

Text tokenization refers to the splitting of text into meaningful tokens or units. You can use `text.split()` (split() is a python inbuilt string function) to break the text down into smaller units as well, however, that does not treat punctuation as a separate unit from words. It can still work well for your data if you remove punctuation before splitting the text, but fail to differentiate between regular period usage versus something like 'U.K.', which should be one token.

Libraries such as TextBlob, `NLTK`, and `spaCy` can be used to tokenize text. Here are a few implementations.

```
! pip install textblob==0.17.1

from textblob import TextBlob

text = "Hi! I like NLP. Do you?? Do you live in the U.K.?"
tokens = TextBlob(text).words
# >> WordList(['Hi', 'I', 'like', 'NLP', 'Do', 'you', 'Do', 'you', '
    live', 'in', 'the', 'U.K'])

! pip install nltk

from nltk import word_tokenize

text = "Hi! I like NLP. Do you?? Do you live in the U.K.?"
tokens = word_tokenize(text)
# >> ['Hi', '!', 'I', 'like', 'NLP', '.', 'Do', 'you', '?', '?', 'Do
    ', 'you', 'live', 'in', 'the', 'U.K.', '?']

! pip install spacy

import spacy

nlp = spacy.load("en_core_web_sm")
# spaCy offers many pre-trained models that you can choose from

text = "Hi! I like NLP. Do you?? Do you live in the U.K.?"
```

```
doc = nlp(text)
print([token for token in doc])
# >> [Hi, !, I, like, NLP, ., Do, you, ?, ?, Do, you, live, in, the,
    U.K., ?]
```

Part-of-speech tagging

Part-of-speech tagging is also called POS tagging. Sometimes, it might be desired to retain only certain parts of speech, such as nouns. The use cases can be cleaning data before creating a word-counts (bag-of-words) model or further processing that depends on parts of speech, such as named entity recognition (where two nouns occurring together are likely first and last names of a person) and keyphrase extraction. This can be implemented in Python as follows.

```
from nltk import word_tokenize, pos_tag

tokens = word_tokenize(
  "Can you please buy me an Arizona Ice Tea? It's $0.57."
)
pos = pos_tag(tokens)

print(pos)
# >> [('Can', 'MD'), ('you', 'PRP'), ('please', 'VB'), ('buy', 'VB'),
    ('me', 'PRP'), ('an', 'DT'), ('Arizona', 'NNP'), ('Ice', 'NNP'),
    ('Tea', 'NNP'), ('?', '.'), ('It', 'PRP'), ("'s", 'VBZ'), ('$', '$
    '), ('0.57', 'CD'), ('.', '.')]
```

N-grams

N-grams are a contiguous sequence of N elements. For instance, 'natural', 'language', and 'processing' are unigrams, 'natural language' and 'language processing' are bigrams, and 'natural language processing' is the trigram of the string 'natural language processing'.

In many NLP feature generation methods, each word in a sentence is used as an independent unit (token) while encoding data. Instead, getting multi-word pairs from a sentence can be beneficial for certain applications that contain multi-word keywords or sentiment analysis. For example, 'not happy' bigram versus 'happy' unigram can convey different sentiments for the sentence 'James is not happy."

```
! pip install textblob

from textblob import TextBlob

text = "natural language processing"

TextBlob(text).ngrams(2)
# >> [WordList(['natural', 'language']), WordList(['language', '
    processing'])]
```

3.1.2 Cleaning

Punctuation removal

For many applications such as category classification and word visualizations, the words used in the text matter and the punctuation does not have relevance to the application. Punctuation can be removed using a regex expression.

In regex, \n matches a newline character. \w is a word character that matches any single letter, number, or underscore (same as [a-zA-Z0-9_]). \s is for matching whitespaces. ^ is for matching with everything except the pattern specified. A pattern such as the below would remove everything other than word characters and spaces from text.

```
import re

text = "Hi. I like NLP, do you?"

# .sub substitutes all matches with empty string below
punc_cleaned = re.sub(r'[^\w\s]', '', text)
# >> Hi I like NLP do you
```

URL removal

In language documents, removing URLs can be beneficial in reducing overall text length and removing information that does not convey meaning for your application.

In regex, \s matches all white-space characters and \S matches with all non white-spaced characters. | stands for OR and can be used when you want to match multiple patterns with the OR logic. An example can be seen below for removing URLs from text.

```
import re

text = """
  Check it out on https://google.com or www.google.com for more
    information.
  Reach out to abc@xyz.com for inquiries.
"""

url_cleaned = re.sub(r"https?://\S+|www\.\S+", "", text)
# >> Check it out on  or  for more information.
# >> Reach out to abc@xyz.com for inquiries.'
```

Emoji removal

Unicode is an international standard that maintains a mapping of individual characters and a unique number across devices and programs. Each character is represented as a code point. These code points are encoded to bytes and can be decoded back to code points. UTF-8 is an encoding system for Unicode. UTF-8 uses 1, 2, 3 or 4 bytes to encode every code point.

In the unicode standard, each emoji is represented as a code. For instance, \U0001F600i s the combination that triggers a grinning face across all devices across the world in UTF-8. Thus, regex patterns can be used to remove emojis from the text.

For the sentence 'What does 😵 emoji mean?', the following code replaces the emoji with and empty string.

```
import re

emoji_cleaned = re.sub(
  r'[\U00010000-\U0010ffff]', '' , text, flags=re.UNICODE
)
# >> 'What does  emoji mean?'
```

Spelling corrections

Sometimes the data consists of a lot of typing errors or intentional misspellings that fail to get recognized as intended by our models, especially if our models have been trained on cleaner data. In such cases, algorithmically correcting typos can come in handy. Libraries such as pySpellChecker, TextBlob, and pyEnchant can be used to accomplish spelling corrections.

For spelling corrections, common underlying approaches use character-based differences. We'll go over some character-based distance metrics later in Chapter 4 (Section 4.1.1).

Let's look at the library pySpellChecker. The library has some drawbacks in recognizing typos containing more than 2 consecutively repeated alphabets, e.g., 'craazy' -> 'crazy' , but 'craaazy' x> 'crazy'. If relevant to your data, consider limiting consecutive occurrences of any alphabet to a maximum of 2 times before passing the text through pySpellChecker for getting more accurate spelling corrections. This operation can take a long time depending on the length of the text.

> **Methodology behind pySpellChecker**
> pySpellChecker uses Levenshtein distance (discussed in Section 4.1.1) based logic to find permutations within an edit distance of two from the original word. It compares different permutations (insertions, deletions, replacements, and transpositions) to known words in a word-frequency list. Words that are found more often in the frequency list are returned as the result.

```
! pip install pyspellchecker==0.7.0

from spellchecker import SpellChecker

spell = SpellChecker()

# List the words that might be misspelled
misspelled = spell.unknown(
    ['mispell', 'craazy', 'craaaazy']
)

for word in misspelled:
    # Get the one `most likely` answer
    print(f"{word} -> {spell.correction(word)}")
# >> craazy -> crazy
# >> craaaazy -> craaaazy
# >> mispell -> misspell
```

The library TextBlob also does not always handle well more than two consecutive repeated alphabets. You can also train a model on your own custom corpus using TextBlob.

```
! pip install textblob

from textblob import TextBlob

data = "Are yu suuree about your decisiion?"
```

```
output = TextBlob(data).correct()
print(output)
# >> Are you sure about your decision?

data = "Are yu suuuree about your decisiion?"
output = TextBlob(data).correct()
print(output)
# >> Are you suture about your decision?
```

And lastly, the library `pyenchant` helps accomplish spelling corrections with similar issues as seen in the other tools.

```
! pip install pyenchant==3.2.2

# if you get errors, try "brew install enchant"
# Don't have homebrew? Visit https://brew.sh/

from enchant.checker import SpellChecker

# Creating the SpellChecker object
chkr = SpellChecker("en_US")

# Spelling error detection
chkr.set_text("This is sme sample txt with erors.")

for err in chkr:
  corrections = chkr.suggest(err.word)
  if len(corrections) > 0:
    # Get top likely correction
    correction = corrections[0]
    print("ERROR:", err.word, "Correction:", correction)
```

In many use cases where the terms are expected to be specific to an industry, custom spelling checker tools can be built using available and relevant datasets.

Stop words removal

Stop words refer to the commonly occurring words that help connect important key terms in a sentence to make it meaningful. However, for many NLP applications, they do not represent much meaning by themselves. Examples include 'this', 'it', 'are', etc. This is especially useful in applications using word occurrence-based features. There are libraries and data sources containing common stop words that you can use as a reference look-up list to remove those words from your text. In practice, it is common to append to an existing stop words list the words specific to your dataset that are expected to occur very commonly but don't convey important information. For example, if you are dealing with YouTube data, then the word 'video' may commonly occur without conveying a unique meaning across text documents since all of them come from a video source.

Here's how to use the `NLTK` library to remove stop words.

```
! pip install nltk

import nltk
nltk.download()
```

```
from nltk.corpus import stopwords

sw = stopwords.words('english')

text = "Hi I like NLP, do you?"

# Get token from text using word tokenizers
# described in the previous section
from nltk import word_tokenize

tokens = word_tokenize(text)

stop_cleaned = [
  w for w in tokens if w.lower() not in sw
]
# instead, you can also lowercase the text before tokenizing,
# unless retaining case is required for your application

print(stop_cleaned)
# >> ['Hi', 'like', 'NLP', ',', '?']
```

3.1.3 Standardization

Lowercasing

For applications where 'Natural Language Processing', 'natural language processing', and 'NATURAL LANGUAGE PROCESSING' convey the same meaning, you can lowercase your text as follows.

```
text = "NATURAL LANGUAGE PROCESSING"
lower_cleaned = text.lower()
# >> natural language processing
```

`text.upper()` can be used to convert text to uppercase. Lowercasing is a more popular choice among practitioners to standardize text.

Stemming

Stemming is the process of producing morphological (described in Chapter 1 (Section 1.2.2) variants of a root word. These methods help convert a word into its base form, called the stem.

For example, 'scanned' -> 'scan'.

Stemming is not only helpful in reducing redundancies in the text as a preprocessing step, but is also used in search engine applications and domain analysis for determining domain vocabularies.

Did you know that Google search adopted a word stemming in 2003? Previously, a search for 'fish' would not have returned 'fishing' or 'fishes'.

Porter's stemming method is a rule-based approach introduced by Martin Porter in 1980. Like any method, this method has some failure points, for example, 'computer'-> 'comput'; 'computation' -> 'comput'.

There are many other stemming methods available with NLTK, such as Snowball-Stemmer and ARLSTem[1].

---

[1]https://www.nltk.org/howto/stem.html

```
! pip install nltk

from nltk.stem import PorterStemmer

tokens = [
  "cars", "car", "fabric", "fabrication", "computation", "computer"
]
st = PorterStemmer()
stemmed = " ".join([st.stem(word) for word in tokens])

print(stemmed)
# >> car car fabric fabric comput comput
```

Lemmatization

Lemmatization is the process of extracting the root word by considering the various words in a vocabulary that convey a similar meaning. Lemmatization involves morphological (described in Section I) analysis of words that remove inflectional endings only to return a base word called the lemma. For example, lemmatizing the word 'caring' would result in 'care', whereas stemming the word would result in 'car'.

There are many tools you can use for lemmatization. NLTK, TextBlob, spaCy, and Gensim are some popular choices. Let's look at a few implementation examples below.

```
! pip install textblob

from textblob import Word

tokens = [
  "fabric", "fabrication", "car", "cars", "computation", "computer"
]
lemmatized = " ".join(
  [Word(word).lemmatize() for word in tokens]
)

print(lemmatized)
# >> fabric fabrication car car computation computer

! pip install spacy

import spacy
nlp = spacy.load('en_core_web_sm')

# Create a Doc object
doc = nlp(u'the bats saw the cats')

# Lemmatize each token
lemmatized = " ".join([token.lemma_ for token in doc])
print(lemmatized)
# >> the bat see the cat

! pip install nltk
```

```
import nltk
nltk.download('wordnet')
from nltk.stem import WordNetLemmatizer

wnl = WordNetLemmatizer()
lemmatized = " ".join(
  [wnl.lemmatize(word) for word in tokens]
)
```

Computationally, stemming is less complex than lemmatizing.

Other standardization techniques

Standardization can be helpful when you have important elements in your text that can be written in multiple ways but all map to one keyword such as acronyms and short-forms. An example includes standardizing location names in your text. USA, US, United States of America, all map to one location and you can have a location name lookup dictionary to convert all occurrences of these in the text to one name.

3.1.4 Example scenario

Cleaning is customized based on noise observed or expected in the data. Let's say you have your text from social media. So it has a lot of punctuation, URLs, and special characters. You want to build a content category classification model based on word occurrence counts. Thus, all you need for your application is words, and maybe numbers. To do so, let's clean the text by removing everything except alphabets and numbers. Ordering your preprocessing steps correctly is important. Hence before we remove non-alpha-numeric characters, we'll remove URLs. If we don't order the steps this way, the URLs will get stripped off their usual expected format that contains punctuation, and hence identifying URLs using the regex we wrote will not work. Additionally, we'll remove stop words. All these steps together will prepare your data for numerical transformation (feature extraction) steps.

```
! pip install nltk
```

```
import re
from nltk.corpus import stopwords
from nltk import word_tokenize

text = """
  Hi all! I saw there was a big snake at https://xyz.he.com.
  Come check out the big python snake video!!!!
"""
stop_words = stopwords.words("english")

url_cleaned = re.sub(r"https?://\S+|www\.\S+", "", text)

cleaned = re.sub(r"[^a-zA-Z\s+]+", " ", url_cleaned).lower()

tokens = word_tokenize(cleaned)
```

```
stop_removed = [
  word
  for word in tokens
  if word not in stop_words
]

print(stop_removed)
# >> ['hi', 'saw', 'big', 'snake', 'come',
# >> 'check', 'big', 'python', 'snake', 'video']
```

You can further remove common words in your dataset associated with greetings that do not convey meaning for your application. All the code used in this section can be found in the notebook section3/preprocessing.ipynb in the GitHub location.

Applying data cleaning and preprocessing also reduces the size of the data samples by retaining only the meaningful components. This in-turn reduces the vector size during numerical transformations of your data, which we will discuss next.

3.2 VISUALIZATION

The most popular library in Python for representing text is `wordcloud` [127]. Word cloud allows you to generate visualizations on a body of text, where the frequency of words/phrases is correlated with the size of the word/phrase on the plot along with its opacity. Figure 3.1 shows an example of the word cloud visualization. You can install this library using the following install command in a Jupyter notebook. You will also need `matplotlib` for creating word cloud visualizations.

```
! pip install wordcloud
! pip install matplotlib
```

Here is some sample code.

```
from wordcloud import WordCloud
from matplotlib import pyplot as plt

wc = WordCloud(
  mode = "RGBA",
  collocations = False,
  background_color = None,
  width=1500, height=1000
)

word_cloud = wc.generate(text)
plt.figure(figsize=(30,20))
plt.imshow(word_cloud, interpolation='bilinear')
plt.axis("off")
plt.show()
```

We'll be generating word clouds as a part of building an application with code in Chapter 10 (Section 10.1.2).

Another useful Python library is `ScatterText` [96] that allows you to extract terms in a body of text and visualize as an interactive HTML display. Figure 3.2

FIGURE 3.1   An example of a word cloud visual.

FIGURE 3.2   ScatterText sample output.

shows an example outcome of using this tool. You can install this library using the following command.

```
! pip install scattertext
```

Here is some sample code.

```
from scattertext import (
    SampleCorpora,
    CorpusFromParsedDocuments,
    produce_scattertext_explorer,
    whitespace_nlp_with_sentences,
    AssociationCompactor,
    Scalers
)

df = SampleCorpora.ConventionData2012.get_data().assign(
    parse=lambda df: df.text.apply(
        whitespace_nlp_with_sentences
    )
)
corpus = CorpusFromParsedDocuments(
    df,
    category_col='party',
    parsed_col='parse'
).build().get_unigram_corpus().compact(
    AssociationCompactor(2000)
)

html = produce_scattertext_explorer(
    corpus,
    category='democrat',
    category_name='Democratic',
    not_category_name='Republican',
    minimum_term_frequency=0,
    pmi_threshold_coefficient=0,
    width_in_pixels=1000,
    metadata=corpus.get_df()['speaker'],
    transform=Scalers.dense_rank
)
open('./demo_compact.html', 'w').write(html)
```

Then you can open demo_compact.html in your browser.

Other libraries such as `matplotlib` and `searborn` can be used for other visualization needs in Python for creating common types of graphs and charts.

The code used for visualizations can be found in the notebook section3/visualization.ipynb.

3.3 DATA AUGMENTATION

When the available data does not suffice for the task, there are a few ways to increase the dataset size. Hand curating more samples, accessing similar public datasets, or purchasing relevant data from data vendors are some common ways. However, in many situations with resource constraints or unavailability of other data sources, these options may not be feasible. Another way to increase the size of your text dataset is using some text manipulation hacks.

Data augmentation refers to artificially synthesizing data samples based on the samples present.

Data augmentation is a popularly used technique for images. For images, simply rotating an image, replacing colors, adding blurs/noise, and such simple modifications help generate new data samples. For text, the problem is a bit more challenging. Popular techniques include word replacements in the text. However, replacing certain words can at times completely change the context of a sentence. Furthermore, not every word is replaceable by another or has a synonym. Nonetheless, it serves as a popular technique to augment text data and works well for many cases.

A quick note before we dive into data augmentation techniques. The approaches discussed here have solved problems that many individuals have faced while trying to augment the text. While a technique may work for someone, it may not apply to the data you are dealing with. It is recommended to tailor a data augmentation approach based on the data available and your understanding of it.

The Python libraries `pyAugmentText`[2], `nlpaug`[3], and `TextAugment`[4] contain implementations for many data augmentation methods. Below are a few techniques that have been adopted for data augmentation on text.

1. Word replacement using a thesaurus

   Leveraging a thesaurus can help generate a lot of text data very quickly. A common approach is to select n random words that are not stop words, and then replace them with a synonym. The synonyms code shown below can also be found in section3/synonyms.ipynb.

   ```
   from nltk.corpus import wordnet

   synonyms = []

   for syn in wordnet.synsets("good"):
     for l in syn.lemmas():
       synonyms.append(l.name())

   synonyms = set(synonyms)
   # >> {'beneficial', 'well', 'dependable', ...}
   ```

2. Word replacement using word embeddings

   You can also leverage word embeddings to find the closest/most similar words and replace them to create new data samples.

3. Entity replacement

   Replacing entities with different values is a useful technique for augmentation. For example, replace a location name with another location, a person's name with another person's name, etc. This can help generate different looking sentences. 'Paul Benes went to Paris.' -> 'Taylor Frank went to Belgium.', 'Noah

---

[2]https://github.com/jsingh811/pyAugmentText
[3]https://github.com/makcedward/nlpaug
[4]https://github.com/dsfsi/textaugment

FIGURE 3.3 Translation from English to Hindi, and back to English.

Kohler went to Zurich.', etc. Code samples on extracting such entities are discussed in Chapter 7 (Section 7.1).

4. Back translation

Back translation refers to translating text to another language and then translating it back to the original language. The results produced can give you a different way of writing the same sentence that can be used as a new sample. Language translation libraries are discussed in Section V with code samples. Figure 3.3 shows an example of how the sentence changes using Google Translate.

5. Adding intentional noise

This can be done by replacing target words with close but different spellings. Introducing changes in spelling based on the keys next to each other on a QWERTY keyboard are common practices.

Other advanced techniques include active learning [1], snorkel [10], and easy data augmentation (EDA) [192]. [113] is a good further reading material on data augmentation.

3.4   DATA TRANSFORMATION

Once you have preprocessed your text, there are several options to represent the data numerically that a machine can comprehend and perform operations on, such as the training of a machine learning model. Numerical representations are also called numerical features or features.

> You will come across the term *vector* several times. Let's quickly summarize what a vector is before we proceed.
>
> Vectors are a foundational element of linear algebra. Vectors are used throughout the field of machine learning. A vector can be understood as being a list of numbers. There are multiple ways to interpret what this list of numbers is. One way to think of the vector is as being a point in a space (we'll call this the vector space). Then this list of numbers is a way of identifying that point in space, where each value in the vector represents a dimension. For example, in 2-dimensions (or 2-D), a value on the x-axis and a value on the y-axis gives us a point in the 2-D space. Similarly, a 300-length vector will have 300 dimensions, which is hard to visualize.

Let's look at some ways to numerically transform text.

3.4.1 Encoding

Label encoding

Label encoding is a method to represent categorical features as numeric labels. Each of the categories is assigned a unique label.

name	grade
..	A
..	B
..	C

After encoding with mapping - A=1, B=2, C=3,

name	grade
..	1
..	2
..	3

In Python, you can use **sklearn**'s LabelEncoder to implement this.

```
! pip install scikit-learn

from sklearn.preprocessing import LabelEncoder

lenc = LabelEncoder()
x = ["A", "B", "C", "B", "A"]
x_enc = lenc.fit_transform(x)

print(lenc.classes_)
# >> ['A' 'B' 'C']
print(x_enc)
# >> [0 1 2 1 0]
```

One hot encoding

One hot encoding generates a vector of length equal to the number of categories. Each entry in the vector represents a category as 1 or 0, 1 if the category is present for a row of features, and 0 is not.

artist	record	genre
..	..	pop
..	..	rock
..	..	pop, rock

After encoding 'genre',

artist	record	genre_pop	genre_rock
..	..	1	0
..	..	0	1
..	..	1	1

In order to perform one hot encoding in Python, you can use the OneHotEncoder from `sklearn`.

```
from sklearn.preprocessing import OneHotEncoder

x = [["Pop"], ["Rock"], ["Rock"]]
oenc = OneHotEncoder()
x_enc = oenc.fit_transform(x)

print(oenc.categories_)
# >> [array(['Pop', 'Rock'], dtype=object)]
print(x_enc.toarray())
# >> [[1. 0.] [0. 1.] [0. 1.]]
```

> **TIP**
>
> When to use label encoding and when to use one hot encoding?
>
> If the label encoding preserves the hierarchy of the original feature, then label encoding can be a good choice. However, when your data does not represent any hierarchy, e.g., categories of content like 'music' and 'sports', then label encoding may not be as meaningful. One hot encoding is a better choice in such scenarios. Look at the example below.

Let's assume you have a simple linear model (weight * input -> output) where a weight multiplied by your input is used to select a threshold for the possible outputs. Let's consider school grades for two subjects as the input, and the output as 'pass' or 'fail'. For simplicity, let's assume that the weights are 1 for both subjects. Let's label encode the grades to convert data to numeric form.

$1 * A + 1 * C$ = pass
$1 * B + 1 * D$ = pass
$1 * E + 1 * E$ = fail
$1 * D + 1 * E$ = pass
$1 * F + 1 * D$ = fail
$1 * F + 1 * F$ = fail

Representing grades as labels A, B, C, D, E, F = 1, 2, 3, 4, 5, 6 yields equations as follows.

$1 * 1 + 1 * 3 = 4$ = pass
$1 * 2 + 1 * 4 = 6$ = pass
$1 * 5 + 1 * 5 = 10$ = fail
$1 * 4 + 1 * 5 = 9$ = pass
$1 * 6 + 1 * 4 = 10$ = fail
$1 * 6 + 1 * 6 = 12$ = fail

This helps us determine the threshold of 10. A score $>=10$ leads to the output 'fail'

Grade A is higher than B, and B in higher than C. If a similar ordering is preserved with label encoding, label encoding can be a good choice.

3.4.2 Frequency-based vectorizers

Text can be passed through vectorization techniques which work by breaking down the text into tokens (also called terms) and counting token occurrences in the text. Tokens can be single words, n-grams, or phrases.

Count vectorization

A count vector is formed using the count of occurrences of terms comprising the text. For example, 'I like NLP like ML' -> 'I' : 1, 'like' : 2, 'NLP' : 1, 'ML' : 1

You can use **sklearn's** CountVectorizer to implement this in Python.

```
from sklearn.feature_extraction.text import CountVectorizer

text = ["I like NLP like ML"]
vectorizer = CountVectorizer()
# you can also create count vectors for n-grams
# e.g., CountVectorizer(ngram_range=(2,2)) for bigrams
vectorizer.fit(text)
vector = vectorizer.transform(text)

print(vectorizer.vocabulary_)
# >> {'like': 0, 'nlp': 2, 'ml': 1}
print(vector.toarray())
# >> [[2 1 1]]
```

Hash vectorizer

In general, a hash function is any function that can be used to map data of arbitrary size to fixed-size values. A hash vector in NLP is produced when term frequency counts are passed through a hash function that transforms the collection of documents into a sparse numerical matrix. This sparse matrix holds information regarding the term occurrence counts.

What's a document? A text sample is also called a document in a corpus containing many text samples (called documents).

'processing the language using natural language processing'

processing	the	language	using	natural
2	1	2	1	1
hash application to each term				

Sparse matrix encoding
[0.0, -0.38, -0.76, ..., 0.38, ..., 0.0, 0.38, ...]

One advantage over a count vectorizer is that a count vector can get large if the corpus is large. Hash vectorizer stores the token as numerical values as opposed to a string. The disadvantage of a hash vectorizer is that the features can't be retrieved once the vector is formed.

```
from sklearn.feature_extraction.text import HashingVectorizer

text = ["I like natural language processing"]
vectorizer = HashingVectorizer(n_features=10)
vector = vectorizer.transform(text)

print(vector.shape)
# >> (1, 10)
print(vector.toarray())
# >> [[  0.40824829 0. 0. 0.  -0.40824829 -0.81649658 0. 0. 0. 0.]]
```

Term frequency – inverse document frequency (TF-IDF)

TF-IDF is the count of the frequency of occurrences of tokens (also called terms) comprising the document, downweighed by importance of the terms which is calculated by dividing number of documents by number of documents containing the term (IDF). Breaking it down, document frequency for a term is defined as the number of documents a term is contained in divided by the total no. of documents. IDF is just the inverse of that. The IDF reflects how important each term is in a particular document corpus. So, if a word occurs too frequently, for example, 'the' or 'and' , then their document frequency counts will be high, resulting in a low IDF. It is a common practice to have a threshold for min_df and max_df to ignore very highly occurring terms and very rare terms.

Mathematically,

$$TF - IDF = TF(t, d) * IDF(t)$$

where,

TF (t, d) = no. of times term t occurs in a document

IDF (t) = ln((1+n)/(1+df(d, t))) + 1

n = no. of documents

df(d, t) = document frequency of the term t

The library sklearn can be used to build a TF-IDF vector.

```
from sklearn.feature_extraction.text import TfidfVectorizer

x = ["i like nlp", "nlp is fun", "learn and like nlp"]
vectorizer = TfidfVectorizer()
vectorizer.fit(x)
tfidf_x = vectorizer.transform(x)
```

TF-IDF is a basic approach that is computationally less expensive compared to word embeddings, which we'll learn about shortly. However, the vector length depends on the size of the corpus and hence can be very large. Further operations on large vectors can get computationally expensive and feature reduction processes may be required.

3.4.3 Co-occurrence matrix

A co-occurrence matrix measures the relationship between the terms that occur together in a context. The main use of this representation is the indication of connection between notions. A simple example is as follows.

'Sky is blue. Grass is green.' →'sky blue', 'grass green'

	sky	blue	grass	green
sky	1	1	0	0
blue	1	1	0	0
grass	0	0	1	1
green	0	0	1	1

To implement, we can define a function as follows.

```
! pip install pandas==1.5.2
! pip install numpy==1.23.5
! pip install scipy==1.9.3
! pip install ntlk

import numpy as np
import pandas as pd
import scipy
from nltk.tokenize import word_tokenize

def create_cooccurrence_matrix(sentences, window_size=2):
  vocabulary = {}
  data = []
  row = []
  col = []
  for sentence in sentences:
    tokens = [
      token
      for token in word_tokenize(sentence.strip())
      if token != u""
    ]
    for pos, token in enumerate(tokens):
      i = vocabulary.setdefault(token, len(vocabulary))
      start = max(0, pos-window_size)
      end = min(len(tokens), pos+window_size+1)
      for pos2 in range(start, end):
        j = vocabulary.setdefault(tokens[pos2], len(vocabulary))
        data.append(1.)
        row.append(i)
        col.append(j)
  cooc_matrix_sparse = scipy.sparse.coo_matrix(
    (data, (row, col))
  )
  return vocabulary, cooc_matrix_sparse
```

Passing sample documents through the function to retrieve the co-occurrence matrix can be done as follows.

```
sentences = [
  'grass green',
```

```
    'sky blue',
    'green grass forest',
    'blue sky clouds'
]
vocab, coocc_matrix = create_cooccurrence_matrix(sentences)
df_coocc = pd.DataFrame(
    coocc_matrix.todense(), index=vocab.keys(), columns = vocab.keys()
)
df_coocc = df_coocc.sort_index()[sorted(vocab.keys())]

print(df_coocc)
# >>       blue   clouds   forest   grass   green   sky
# blue     2.0    1.0      0.0      0.0     0.0     2.0
# clouds   1.0    1.0      0.0      0.0     0.0     1.0
# forest   0.0    0.0      1.0      1.0     1.0     0.0
# grass    0.0    0.0      1.0      2.0     2.0     0.0
# green    0.0    0.0      1.0      2.0     2.0     0.0
# sky      2.0    1.0      0.0      0.0     0.0     2.0
```

3.4.4 Word embeddings

Imagine you have a corpus with very long sentences. Numerical representations such as one-hot encoding or TF-IDF become sparse representations, meaning there will be a lot of 0's in the vector.

Another way to represent text is using dense representations. One such way is using word embeddings. Word embeddings are a way to numerically represent every word in a corpus. The resultant is a numerical vector for each term in the corpus. Every vector is the same size that is usually much smaller than a TF-IDF or one-hot encoded vector.

How are we able to represent each word in a small-sized vector? The simplest way to understand this is using the following example.

Let's say our corpus has terms – 'king', 'queen', 'boy', 'girl', 'apple', and 'mango'. We can represent each word by the features that define it. These features can be gender, royal, fruit, etc., and each feature occupies a position in the vector. For instance, some sample vectors for the different words can be seen in Table 3.1. We see the word 'queen' will have a high score for royal feature, and a low score for fruit feature, while the opposite is true for the word 'apple.' Representing the word based on different features or attributes gets us a smaller-sized representation, which equals the number of features in length. In this example, we defined features like gender, royal, etc. In reality, models can learn different features by looking at large datasets and how certain words occur with other words.

The idea behind word embeddings is based on distributional hypothesis and semantics, which means that words with similar meanings will likely be used together in sentences more often. If every word is represented as a vector, words occurring in similar contexts tend to be closer to each other in the vector space, i.e., the distance between such vectors will be small. For instance, 'cat' and 'dog' are words that are more likely to be used more in combination with 'veterinarian' than 'football'.

TABLE 3.1 Word vectors based on features.

	gender	royal	fruit	...
'queen'	1.00	0.98	0.02	...
'king'	-1.00	0.94	0.01	...
'apple'	0.00	0.01	0.92	...

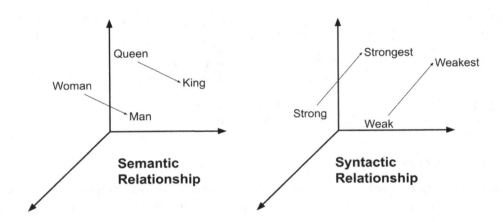

FIGURE 3.4 Relationships between words using distances between word embeddings.

Once you have word embeddings, these can be used in the input to train a machine learning model. They can also be used to determine the relationship between words by calculating the distance between their corresponding vectors. Word embeddings capture the meanings of words, semantic relationships, and the different contexts. Using word embeddings, Apple the company and apple the fruit can be distinguishable. While trying to get word pairs, e.g., 'queen' -> 'king' , 'woman' -> ?, word embeddings can be used to find the difference between vectors for 'king' and 'queen' , and find the corresponding word for 'woman' that exhibits a similar vector difference with the word 'woman' . See Figure 3.4.

Models

Word embedding models can be generated using different methods like neural networks, co-occurrence matrix, probabilistic algorithms, and so on. Several word embedding models in existence include Word2Vec[5], fastText[6], Doc2Vec[7], GloVe embedding[8], ELMo[9], transformers[10], universal sentence encoder [44], InferSent [52], and

---

[5]https://radimrehurek.com/gensim/models/word2vec.html
[6]https://ai.facebook.com/tools/fasttext/
[7]https://radimrehurek.com/gensim/models/doc2vec.html
[8]https://nlp.stanford.edu/projects/glove/
[9]https://paperswithcode.com/method/elmo
[10]https://www.sbert.net/docs/pretrained_models.html

Open-AI GPT.[11] Let's look at the implementation of various of them using Python. We'll also leverage these in Section V for various tasks.

Word2Vec

Word2Vec is a popular word embedding approach. It consists of models for generating word embeddings. These models are shallow two-layer neural networks having one input layer, one hidden layer, and one output layer. Word2Vec utilizes two models within.

A sentence is divided into groups of n words. The model is trained by sliding the window of n words.

- Continuous bag of words (CBOW)

  CBOW predicts the current word based on other words within the same context in a specific n-word window. The input layer of the neural network is the context words and the output layer contains the current word.

- Skip gram

  Skip gram works the other way round. It predicts the surrounding context words for an input word.

The main disadvantage of Word2Vec is that you will not have a vector representing a word that does not exist in the corpus. For instance, if you trained the model on biological articles only, then that model will not be able to return vectors of unseen words, such as 'curtain' or 'cement' .

> Word2Vec is trained on the Google News dataset[a], which contains about 100 billion words.
>
> ---
> [a]`https://research.google/tools/datasets/`

You can produce Word2Vec embeddings using the library `Gensim` or `spaCy`.

`spaCy` offers many built-in pre-trained models which form a convenient way to get word embeddings quickly. `spaCy` offers these models in several languages. The most popularly used models for the English language are `en_core_web_sm`, `en_core_web_md`, `en_core_web_lg`, `en_core_web_trf`.

`spaCy` parses blobs of text and seamlessly assigns word vectors from the loaded models using the tok2vec component. For any custom corpus that varies vastly from web documents, you can train your own word embeddings model using spaCy.

```
! pip install spacy
! python -m spacy download "en_core_web_sm"
```

---
[11]`https://openai.com/api/`

```
import spacy

nlp = spacy.load("en_core_web_sm")
doc = nlp(u'hot chocolate is filling')

doc.vector
```

spaCy offers pre-trained models. Gensim does not provide pre-trained models for word2vec embeddings. There are models available online to download for free that you can use with Gensim, such as the Google news model[12].

```
! pip install gensim

import gensim.downloader as api

model = api.load('word2vec-google-news-300')

print(model['river'])
```

fastText

fastText was developed by Facebook. This architecture considers each character in a word while learning the word's representation.

The advantage of fastText over Word2Vec is that you can get a word representation for words not in the training data/vocabulary with fastText. Since fastText uses character-level details on a word, it is able to compute vectors for unseen words containing the characters it has seen before. One disadvantage of this method is that unrelated words containing similar characters/alphabets may result in being close in the vector space without semantic closeness. Example, words like 'love' , 'solve', and 'glove' contain many similar alphabets 'l' , 'o' , 'v' , 'e' , and may all be close together in vector space.

> fastText is trained on web-based data, including Common Crawl[a] and Wikipedia[b].
>
> ---
> [a]https://commoncrawl.org/
> [b]https://www.tensorflow.org/datasets/catalog/wikipedia

```
! pip install gensim

from gensim.models import FastText

tokens_doc = [
  ['I', 'like', 'nlp'],
  ['nlp', 'and', 'machine', 'learning']
]
fast = FastText(
  tokens_doc,
  size=20,
```

---
[12]https://code.google.com/archive/p/word2vec/

```
   window =1 ,
   min_count =1 ,
   workers =5 ,
   min_n =1 ,
   max_n =2
)

# vector for word 'nlp'
fast.wv['nlp']
```

Doc2Vec

Doc2Vec is based on WordVec except it is suitable for larger documents. Word2Vec computes a feature vector for every word in the corpus, whereas Doc2Vec computes a feature vector for every document in the corpus.[13] is an example of training Doc2Vec.

GloVe

GloVe stands for global vectors. GloVe model trains on co-occurrence counts of words and produces a vector by minimizing the least square error.

Each word in the corpus is assigned a random vector. If two words are used together more often, i.e., they have a high co-occurrence, then the vectors of those words are moved closer in the vector space. After various rounds of this process, the vector space representation approximates the information within the co-occurrence matrix. In mathematical terms, the dot product of two words becomes approximately equal to the log of the probability of co-occurrence of the words. This is the principle behind GloVe.

Glove vectors treat each word as one, without considering the same word can have multiple meanings. The word 'bark' in 'a tree bark' will have the same representation as 'a dog bark' .

Since it is based on co-occurrence, which needs every word in the corpus, glove vectors can be memory intensive based on corpus size.

Word2Vec, skip-gram, and CBOW are predictive and don't account for scenarios where some context words occur more often than others. They capture local context rather than global context, whereas GloVe vectors capture the global context.

> GloVe is trained on Wikipedia, Common Crawl, and Twitter data[a].
>
> ---
> [a]https://nlp.stanford.edu/projects/glove/

```
! pip install wget
! python -m wget http://nlp.stanford.edu/data/glove.6B.zip
! unzip glove*.zip

emmbed_dict = {}
with open('/content/glove.6B.200d.txt','r') as f:
```

---
[13]https://github.com/RaRe-Technologies/gensim/blob/develop/docs/notebooks/doc2vec-wikipedia.ipynb

```
  for line in f:
    values = line.split()
    word = values[0]
    vector = np.asarray(values[1:], 'float32')
    emmbed_dict[word] = vector

print(emmbed_dict['river'])
```

ELMo

ELMo is a deep contextualized word representation model. It considers the complex characteristics of words and how they vary across different contexts. Each term is assigned a representation that is dependent on the entire input sentence. These embeddings are derived from a Bi-LSTM model. We'll go over Bi-LSTM later in Chapter 4 (Section 4.2.2.4).

ELMo can handle words with different contexts used in different sentences, which GloVe is unable to. Thus the same word with multiple meanings can have different embeddings.

> ELMo is trained on a large text corpus comprising 5.5 billion words.

```
! pip install tensorflow==2.11.0
! pip install tensorflow-hub==0.12.0

import tensorflow_hub as hub
import tensorflow.compat.v1 as tf

tf.disable_eager_execution()

# Load pre trained ELMo model
elmo = hub.Module(
  "https://tfhub.dev/google/elmo/3",
  trainable=True
)

# create an instance of ELMo
embeddings = elmo(
  [
  "I love to watch TV",
  "I am wearing a wrist watch"
  ],
  signature="default",
  as_dict=True
)["elmo"]
init = tf.initialize_all_variables()
sess = tf.Session()
sess.run(init)

print('Word embeddings for the word "watch" in the 1st sentence')
print(sess.run(embeddings[0][3]))
print('Word embeddings for the word "watch" in the 2nd sentence')
print(sess.run(embeddings[1][5]))
```

Different vectors are returned as follows.

Word embeddings for the word 'watch' in the 1st sentence

[0.14079624 -0.15788543 -0.00950474 ... 0.43005997 -0.52887076 0.0632787]

Word embeddings for the word 'watch' in the 2nd sentence

[-0.08213369 0.01050352 -0.01454161 ... 0.48705414 -0.5445795 0.52623963]

Universal Sentence Encoder

The Universal Sentence Encoder model is based on transfer learning and is a sentence-level encoder [44]. It encodes text into high dimensional vectors and finds applications in text classification, semantic similarity, clustering, and more.

> It is trained on Wikipedia, web news, web question-answer pages, and discussion forums.

The pre-trained Universal Sentence Encoder is available in TensorFlow Hub[14].

```
! pip install tensorflow
! pip install tensorflow_hub

import tensorflow_hub as hub
import tensorflow.compat.v1 as tf

embed = hub.load(
  "https://tfhub.dev/google/universal-sentence-encoder/4"
)
sentences = [
  "I love to watch TV",
  "I am wearing a wrist watch"
]
embeddings = embed(sentences)
```

Transformers

Since the past few years, there has been heavy research on transformer-based (neural network architecture) models that are suitable for many tasks, one being generating word embeddings. We'll dig into transformers in Chapter 4 (Section 4.2.3). We will also learn more about the BERT (Bidirectional Encoder Representations from Transformers) model.

> BERT models are pre-trained on BooksCorpus [210] and Wikipedia.

Sentence-BERT (SBERT) is a smaller version and modification of the pre-trained BERT model [141].

```
! pip install transformers==4.17.0
! pip install sentence-transformers==2.2.2
```

---

[14]https://tfhub.dev/

```
from sentence_transformers import SentenceTransformer

docs = ["NLP method for feature extraction."]
sbert = SentenceTransformer('bert-base-nli-mean-tokens')
sentence_embeddings_BERT = sbert.encode(docs)

print(sentence_embeddings_BERT)
```

There are many models offered with **sentence-transformers**[15] that can be used to generate embeddings. Different models are suitable for different applications.

You can also use the library **transformers** to get numerical features from text as follows.

```
from transformers import pipeline

feat_extractor = pipeline("feature-extraction")
feature = feat_extractor("NLP method for feature extraction.")

print(feature)
```

All the code for numerical feature generation demonstrated above can be found in the notebook section3/features.ipynb.

As we have seen, there are several options for extracting word embeddings using a pre-trained model. It is also possible to train a custom model on your own data.

---

[15]https://www.sbert.net/docs/pretrained_models.html

TIP

With so many options for extracting numerical features, which one to choose and when?

The models you try should depend on your data and application. For instance, if you have strings representing finite categories, then using one-hot encoding will make sense. If you have sentences, then using a count vectorizer, hash vectorizer, TF-IDF, or word embeddings could be good solutions. Different models are trained on different datasets and have some advantages and drawbacks as we discussed above. A model trained on data similar to your data can work well. It also depends on your end goal. If you want to get words similar to input words, using word embeddings will make the job simpler.

Often, there is no one right answer. It is a common practice to try a few different transformations and see which one works better. For instance, trying TF-IDF, and a couple of word embedding models followed by comparing the results of each can help with the process of selecting the feature generation method while creating a text classification model. The comparison can comprise evaluating which model yields better results when used with a fixed classifier model and/or how much computation time and resources are required. For instance, word embeddings are more complex than TF-IDF as they use a model to generate numerical representation.

## CHAPTER 4

Data Modeling

4.1 DISTANCE METRICS

Many applications in NLP comprise tasks such as computing similarity between two pieces of text. This can be at different levels - word level, phrase level, sentence level, and document level. The interest may be to find syntactic similarity or semantic similarity. We will discuss some popular distance metrics that can be used to create a model for solving text data challenges, especially when it is related to finding the difference or similarity between two words or sentences.

Moreover, the similarity measure can be in different contexts. Are the words related in the way they are spelled or sound? Are the words similar in their meaning? Let's look at some similarity metrics below.

4.1.1 Character-based similarity

Character level similarity looks at how different two strings are from one another based on characters within.

A popular approach to measure this difference is called **Longest Common Substring**, which finds the maximum length of a contiguous chain of characters from both strings being compared. Applications include data deduplication and plagiarism detection.

Another popular measure is called the **Levenshtein edit distance**. This distance is calculated between two strings by counting the minimum number of operations needed to transform one string into the other. The operations include insertion, deletion, replacement, or substitution of a character. A common application is spelling correction, which we have covered earlier in Chapter 3 (Section 3.1.2).

Hamming distance refers to the number of positions with the same character in both strings. This only works on strings with the same length.

Several other distance metrics find use in different applications, such as Longest Common Subsequence, Jaro Wrinkler distance, etc. [45] is a good resource to learn further about other distance metrics. Implementing these distances for applications is less common as there exist many open-source tools that contain implementations

DOI: 10.1201/9781003264774-4

that can be used out of the box. One such library containing implementations of multiple distance metrics is pyStringMatching[1].

```
from pyStringMatching import matcher

# Longest Common Subsequence (LCS)
lcs, lcs_len = matcher.LCS("string", "strings")

# Longest Common Sub-string (LCSubStr)
lcsubstr = matcher.LCSubStr("string", "strings")

# Levenshtein distance between 2 strings
lev = matcher.levenshtein("string", "strings")

# Jaro similarity between 2 strings
j_similarity = matcher.jaro_similarity("string", "strings")

# Jaro-Winkler similarity between 2 strings
jw_similarity = matcher.jaro_winkler_similarity(
   "string", "strings"
)
```

4.1.2 Phonetic matching

Phonetic matching is finding similarities between two words on how they may sound rather than their precise spelling. The process includes creating an alphanumeric code for an input word and comparing the code for two words. Applications include spelling corrections and searching large text corpora. Soundex and Metaphone are two popular phonetic algorithms [199]. In Python, you can implement it as follows.

```
# Dictionary which maps letters to soundex codes.
# Vowels and 'H', 'W' and 'Y' will be represented by '.'
codes = {
   "BFPV": "1", "CGJKQSXZ": "2",
   "DT": "3",
   "L": "4", "MN": "5", "R": "6",
   "AEIOUHWY": "."
}
def soundex_generator(token):
   token = token.upper()
   soundex = ""
   soundex += token[0]

   # Enode as per the codes
   for char in token[1:]:
      for key in codes.keys():
         if char in key:
            code = codes[key]
            if code != '.':
               if code != soundex[-1]:
                  soundex += code
```

---

[1]https://github.com/jsingh811/pyStringMatching

```
# Trim or Pad to make a 4-character code
soundex = soundex[:7].ljust(7, "0")

return soundex
print(soundex_generator('natural'))
# >> N364000
print(soundex_generator('natuaral'))
# >> N364000
```

You can also use the library `fuzzy`. Some users have reports errors using this tool off late, hence we wanted to share the above implementation as well.

```
! pip install fuzzy

import fuzzy
soundex = fuzzy.Soundex(4)
soundex('fuzzy')
# >> F200
```

4.1.3 Semantic similarity metrics

Below are some popular distance metrics used to find semantic similarity. Semantic similarity is calculated using the numerical representation of text. Hence, we share examples of calculating these on vectors rather than text. In practice, the numerical representation of text can be calculated using techniques discussed in the previous chapter.

Euclidean distance

The Euclidean distance between two points is the length of the path connecting them. This distance is useful when the length of text plays a role in determining similarity. Note that if the length of the sentence is doubled by repeating the same sentence twice, the euclidean distance will increase even though the sentences may have the same meaning. A popular open-source library containing this implementation is `sklearn`.

```
from sklearn.metrics.pairwise import euclidean_distances

print(euclidean_distances([[1.0, 2.0, 3.0]], [[1.0, 2.0, 3.0]]))
print(euclidean_distances([[1.0, 2.0, 3.0]], [[2.0, 4.0, 6.0]]))
```

[[0.]]

[[3.74165739]]

Cosine distance

Cosine distance is the most popularly used metric for measuring distance when the differences in document lengths (magnitude of the vectors) do not matter. Many libraries in Python contain the implementation of cosine distance. The cosine distance between 'I love ice cream' and 'I love ice cream I love ice cream I love ice cream' will be 0 because occurrences of terms within each sample follow to the same distribution. `sklearn` can be used to compute cosine similarity.

$$\text{Consine similarity} = 1 - \text{Cosine distance}$$

```
from sklearn.metrics.pairwise import cosine_similarity

print(cosine_similarity([[1.0, 2.0, 3.0]], [[1.0, 2.0, 3.0]]))
print(cosine_similarity([[1.0, 2.0, 3.0]], [[2.0, 4.0, 6.0]]))
```

[[1.]]

[[1.]]

Jaccard index

The Jaccard index is another metric that can be computed by calculating the number of words common between two sentences divided by the number of words in both sentences combined. This metric is also helpful while assuming the relationship between semantic similarity and word usage.

When to use which metric?

Let's say we build a numerical vector for each document that is computed based on the counts of words present. The magnitude of the vector may vary if the counts of words in two sentences differ, even though the two sentences are similar otherwise. This will give rise to a higher Euclidean distance. The main advantage of cosine similarity is that it does not depend on the length differences. If the two similar documents are far apart by the Euclidean distance because of the length, (for example 50 occurrences of the word 'basketball' in one document versus 10 occurrences of the same word in another) they could still have a smaller angle between them. Smaller the angle, the higher the similarity.

The code used in this section can be found in the notebook section3/distance.ipynb.

4.2 MODELING

In a general sense, a model is a representation of a system. In data science, a model can be software that consists of logical operations being performed on the input data resulting in an output. A simple example is checking whether the input is present in the look-up list and returning its corresponding value as illustrated in Figure 4.1. A model could also be based on machine-learning algorithms that follow a different set of steps for processing input data. Below, we'll describe some common types of machine learning models for text data.

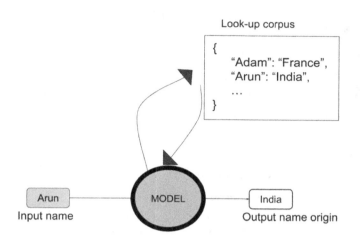

FIGURE 4.1 An example of a look-up based model.

Machine learning models can be of different types, including supervised learning and unsupervised learning. In supervised learning, labeled data is required to train the model to learn the input-output relationships. Supervised learning include classification (where output is categorical) and regression (where output is continuous). An example of classification model is a sentiment classification model (the output can be among a fixed set of categories). An example of regression model is a model that predicts stock price (price is not categorical and is fluid). In text data, the most common types of machine learning models built are classification and clustering. Regression models are also built depending on the problem at hand (such as predicting price for stocks based on social media text data) but are less common in comparison.

Once we have the numerical features built from text data, we can pass them into any clustering or classification/regression model. We'll primarily keep our focus on classification compared to regression, but the basic concept for most models discussed for classification also applies to same model's regressor. Figure 4.2 shows a summary of popularly used models for language tasks. This does not imply the models not listed don't perform well. Different models can work differently depending on the data and goal.

We will go over some popular classic machine learning models as well as deep learning models. Classic machine learning models include models that are lightweight and simpler than the latest deep learning architectures. Classic ML models are very

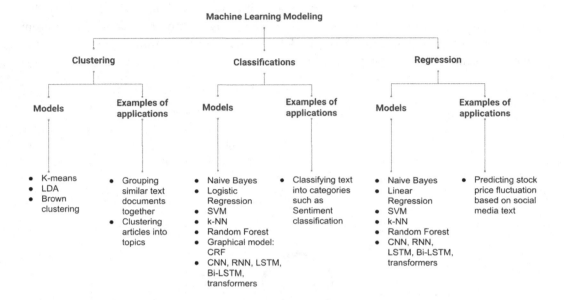

FIGURE 4.2 Popular ML models for text-based applications.

popularly used in the industry today and serve great solutions for a wide range of problems.

Did you know that classic ML models are used very popularly in the industrial domain, while deep learning models find heavier use in research domains?

This is because the resources needed to train a model along with the speed of getting predictions out are important considerations in the industry and are usually constrained. On the contrary, research teams are funded for getting access to extra resources for their projects. For example, if 2% loss in accuracy means the model size can be reduced to half, it may be a preferable solution. If you are an early data science professional in the industry or currently interviewing, you may observe that the focus in many data science interview assignments is not about the higher accuracy, but your overall approach, considerations, and thought process. Investment in compute resources to get a small % increase in accuracy is more common in research-front domains, such as the education sector and large organizations with dedicated research teams.

Did you know that large language models (LLMs) that have been developed in the recent years, such as GPT-3 [143] (not open-sourced, runs on OpenAI's API) and PaLM [151] (developed by Google), have taken weeks and months to train with the training cost of millions of dollars? The recent model - BLOOM [33] took more than three months to complete training on a supercomputer and consists of 176 billion parameters. It was trained using $7 million in public funding. However, that is the state-of-the-art for language models and is not what industries adopt for common use cases.

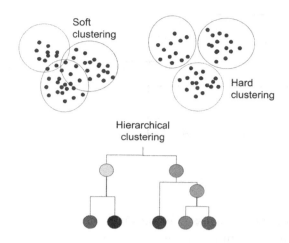

FIGURE 4.3 Different types of clustering.

4.2.1 Classic ML models

We will dig into some of the popular classic ML models below.

4.2.1.1 Clustering

Clustering refers to organizing data into groups (also called clusters or cohorts). In machine learning, clustering is an unsupervised algorithm, which means that what data sample belongs to which cluster is not known and the algorithm tries to establish clusters on its own. The number of clusters an algorithm will divide the data into is on the user. Often, there is some experimentation involved by trying few different number of clusters. The library `sklearn` can be used to train clustering models.

At a high-level, clustering can be of a few different types. As illustrated in Figure 4.3, hard clustering separates the data samples into clusters without any overlap between the clusters. This means that every data sample can only belong to one cluster. Soft clustering, on the contrary, assumes that a data sample can be a part of multiple clusters and there is no perfect separation between the clusters. Hierarchical clustering forms clusters in a hierarchical manner where the clusters can end up in one root. Any clustering that is not hierarchical is called flat or partitional clustering.

Any clustering algorithm can be applied to text data's numerical representations (also called numerical features). Let's look at some popular ones below.

- K-means[2]

  K-means is a hard, flat clustering method. It works by assigning k random points in the vector space and the initial 'means' (mathematic mean) of the k clusters. Then, it assigns each data point to the nearest cluster 'mean'. Then the 'mean' is recalculated based on the assignments, followed by reassignment of

---

[2]`https://scikit-learn.org/stable/modules/generated/sklearn.cluster.KMeans.html`

	word1	word2	...
Document 1			
Document 2			
...			

	Topic 1	Topic 2	...
Document 1			
Document 2			
...			

	word1	word2
Topic 1		
Topic 2		
...		

FIGURE 4.4 Matrix factorization in LDA.

the data points. This process goes on until the cluster 'means' stop changing.[3]
is a good resource for more details on k-means.

Other vector space-based methods for clustering include DBSCAN [65] which
favors densely populated clusters. Another method is called expectation maxi-
mization (EM) [138] which assumes an underlying probabilistic distribution for
each cluster.

Here's how an implementation in Python looks like.

```
from sklearn.cluster import KMeans

kmeans = KMeans(n_clusters=2).fit(X)
```

- Latent Dirichlet Allocation (LDA)[4]

LDA is the most popular topic modeling algorithm. Topic modeling is an unsupervised learning method to discover latent topics in large text corpora. The
idea behind topic modeling is different from other clustering approaches as it
assumes that a document can contain multiple topics. This approach is similar
to soft clustering where a data sample can belong to multiple clusters. The
output of a topic modeling algorithm is a list of topics with associated word
clusters.

In this algorithm, topics are realized as a mixture of words where each word has
some probability score for being associated with a topic. Every text sample (or
document) can be made up of a combination of topics with some probability.
Each document is seen as a composition of words. The order of the words is
not considered in this model. Mathematically, LDA works by decomposing the
corpus document-word matrix into two matrices: the document-topic matrix
and the topic-word matrix. This technique is also called matrix factorization
[39]. To learn further about the workings of LDA, more details can be found in
this article [35]. Figure 4.4 represents this idea behind LDA.

---

[3]https://www.youtube.com/watch?v=_aWzGGNrcic
[4]https://scikit-learn.org/stable/modules/generated/sklearn.decomposition.
LatentDirichletAllocation.html

An implementation of the LDA model can be seen in Chapter 8 (Section 8.2). Here's some sample code using Python.

```
from sklearn.decomposition import LatentDirichletAllocation

lda = LatentDirichletAllocation(n_components=5)

lda.fit(X)
```

Some other topic modeling algorithms include latent semantic analysis (LSA) [87] and probabilistic latent semantic analysis (PLSA) [94].

- Brown clustering

  Brown clustering is a hierarchical clustering method. The underlying method revolves around the distributional hypothesis. A quality function is used to describe how well the surrounding context words predict the occurrence of the words in the current cluster. This is also called mutual information.

  More on brown clustering can be found here [81].

  Other approaches include graph-based clustering (also known as spectral clustering). Examples include Markov chain clustering [89], Chinese whispers [32], and minimal spanning tree-based clustering [135].

[101] is an informative article for further details on clustering.

4.2.1.2 Classification

Classification is a supervised learning technique. Classification models require labeled input training data containing data samples and the corresponding label/class. The model then tries to learn from the known input-output relationships and can be used to classify new/unseen data samples.

There exist many classification models. The list below contains some of the popular ones used in NLP. The library `sklearn` can be used for training a model using these algorithms.

- Naive Bayes[5]

  A Naive Bayes model is a probabilistic model that is based on Bayes theorem [78]. Naive Bayes model is scalable, requiring the same number of parameters as the features. In classification, this model learns a probability for each text document to belong to a class and then chooses the class with the maximum probability as the classification. Such models are also called generative models.

  There are three types of Naive Bayes models that are commonly used - Gaussian Naive Bayes, Multinomial Naive Bayes, and Bernoulli Naive Bayes. For text classification, Multinomial Naive Bayes is commonly used and is a popular choice for establishing a baseline.

---

[5]https://scikit-learn.org/stable/modules/generated/sklearn.naive_bayes.MultinomialNB.html

> What does establishing a baseline mean?
>
> When starting a classification problem (or any modeling problem), the first step is to judge the viability of creating a model that can do the job. Practitioners either look for existing models that can be used for the classification or create a simple model to access viability. The latter includes taking a simple feature extraction technique along with a simple model and running evaluation. If the results show promise, i.e., they are better than randomly guessing classifications of each sample, then practitioners spend further time cleaning the data, experimenting with different features and feature parameters, tuning the model, and trying different models.
>
> For example, let's say you are building a model to classify text into two categories. You have an equal amount of labeled samples for each category. You take your raw data, perform some basic preprocessing, extract TF-IDF, and train a Multinomial Naive Bayes classification model. You observe a per class accuracy of > 60%. This model is already better than randomly guessing classes, which will get you a 50% accuracy at best. Thus it would be worth putting more work into this model to make it better.

For more on this model, [47] contains a step-by-step breakdown.

Here's how to build this model in Python.

```
from sklearn.naive_bayes import MultinomialNB

clf = MultinomialNB()

clf.fit(X, y)
```

- Logistic regression[6]

  Logistic Regression is a discriminative classifier that learns weights for individual features that can be linearly combined to get the classification. In other words, this model aims to learn a linear separator between different classes. The model assigns different weights to each feature value such that the sum of the product of each feature value and weight decides which class the sample belongs to. Despite the term 'regression' in its name, it is a classification model. This is also a popular model for establishing baselines.

  Further explanation can be found here [181].

  Here's how to build this model in Python.

  ```
  from sklearn.svm import LogisticRegression
  ```

---

[6]https://scikit-learn.org/stable/modules/generated/sklearn.linear_model.LogisticRegression.html

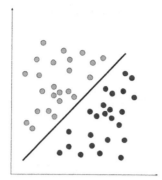

FIGURE 4.5 SVM hyperplane separating data samples.

```
clf = LogisticRegression()

clf.fit(X, y)
```

- Support vector machine (SVM)[7]

  The best way to understand SVM is using the illustration in Figure 4.5. SVM algorithm computes a hyperplane that best separates the data samples. This hyperplane is just a simple line in two dimensions. This line is also called the decision boundary. All samples falling to one side of this boundary belong to class 1, and the samples falling to the other side of the boundary belong to class 2. SVM also works with non-linearly separable data using suitable kernels [59] (kernels transform linearly inseparable data to linearly separable data).

  These models are small and work well with a limited number of samples. Hence, it is a popular choice in the industry.

  For further details, [163] is a good resource.

  Here's how to build this model in Python.

```
from sklearn.svm import SVC

clf = SVC()

clf.fit(X, y)
```

- Random forest[8]

  Random forest algorithm constructs a multitude of decision trees [85]. In a decision tree structure, leaves of the tree represent class labels and branches represent features that result in those labels. An example can be seen in

---

[7]https://scikit-learn.org/stable/modules/generated/sklearn.svm.SVC.html
[8]https://scikit-learn.org/stable/modules/generated/sklearn.ensemble.
RandomForestClassifier.html

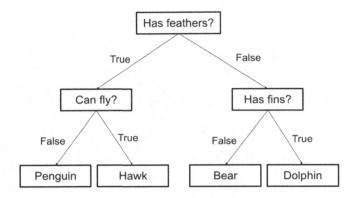

FIGURE 4.6 An example of a decision tree.

Figure 4.6. The output of the model is the class that is selected by most trees for the sample. [134] contains step-by-step details on this algorithm.

Here's how to build this model in Python.

```
from sklearn.ensemble import RandomForestClassifier

clf = RandomForestClassifier()

clf.fit(X, y)
```

- K-nearest neighbors (KNN)[9]

  This algorithm classifies a data sample by finding known classes of samples that are nearest to it. The number of nearest neighbors looked at is defined by 'k', which is chosen by the user. More details can be found in this guide [29].

  Here's how to build this model in Python. Here, 'k' = n_neighbors.

```
from sklearn.neighbors import KNeighborsClassifier

clf = KNeighborsClassifier(n_neighbors=3)

clf.fit(X, y)
```

- Conditional random fields (CRFs)[10]

  CRF is a type of classifier where the predictions for a sample considers context into account by looking at neighboring samples. The predictions are modeled as a graph representing dependencies between predictions. The type of graph used varies for different applications. In NLP, linear chain CRFs are commonly used where each prediction relies only on its immediate neighbors. Reference [102] is the original paper containing further details about CRFs.

---

[9]https://scikit-learn.org/stable/modules/generated/sklearn.neighbors.KNeighborsClassifier.html

[10]https://sklearn-crfsuite.readthedocs.io/en/latest/

```
import sklearn_crfsuite

crf = sklearn_crfsuite.CRF(
    algorithm='lbfgs',
    c1=0.1,
    c2=0.1,
    max_iterations=100,
    all_possible_transitions=True
)
crf.fit(X_train, y_train)
```

4.2.2 Deep learning

The human brain is composed of a network of neurons. These neurons help transmit signals. For instance, you smell pizza and think about how much you like pizza. Then, you decide on getting some pizza for yourself. Then you remember that you had decided to cut down on pizza and cook your meals instead. But then, you think one more pizza can't hurt. You decide to eat the pizza. See how an event as such involves multiple layers of information processing? The information flows from one layer to the other. Artificial neural networks (ANN) are inspired by the working of the human brain to have a machine understand available information and make decisions. The simplest ANN consists of an input layer (the information/data), an output layer (where the system decides the action), and a hidden layer (where the information is processed). ANNs can have multiple hidden layers. An ANN made up of more than three layers is called a deep neural network (DNN). DNNs form the basis of deep learning. Deep learning allows the program to train itself to learn from the data.

The `Keras` [48] library in Python can be used to build these deep learning models.

There are different types of deep learning models. Some popular ones include the following.

4.2.2.1 Convolutional neural network (CNN)

CNNs are multi-layered artificial neural networks. They are popularly used for image-processing tasks such as satellite image processing, medical image processing, object detection, and time series forecasting. CNN is a feed-forward network (information is processed in one direction only and connections between the nodes do not form a cycle) and treats data as spatial. For example, an eye in an image of a person's face is a part of the image and not the entire image by itself. The CNN retains spatial context to make that distinction.

For text, CNNs are used to create text classification models, such as category classification.

A CNN consists of the following layers. Each layer's task is to extract features to find patterns in data.

Convolution layer: It works by placing a filter over parts of the data sample and creates a convolved feature map.

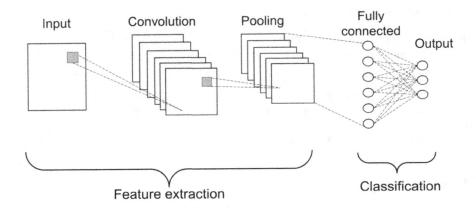

FIGURE 4.7 CNN architecture.

Pooling layer: This layer reduces the sample size of a feature map, as a result, it reduces the number of parameters the network needs to process. The output is a pooled feature map. Two methods of doing this are max pooling and average pooling.

Fully connected layer: This layer flattens the data and allows you to perform classification.

An activation function is a mathematical function used in neural networks to enable the modeling of complex, non-linear relationships between inputs and outputs. The absence of an activation function would limit the network to a linear combination of its inputs. Common activation functions include sigmoid, hyperbolic tangent, ReLU, and its variants, with each having its own set of properties that can be used in different types of neural networks depending on the problem being solved. Often CNNs will have a Rectified Linear Unit or ReLU after the convolution layer that acts as an activation function to ensure non-linearity as data moves through the layers in the network. ReLU does not activate all the neurons at the same time. Using ReLU helps prevent exponential growth in the computation required to operate the neural network.

Figure 4.7 shows a diagram of a basic CNN. There can also be multiple convolutional+ReLU and pooling layers in models.

More details on CNN can be found in this article [178].

Sequential is the easiest way to build a model in `Keras`. It allows you to build a model layer by layer. You can then use the `add()` function to add layers to the model.

```
# Imports
from keras.layers import (
  Dense,
  Embedding,
  Conv1D,
  MaxPooling1D,
  Flatten
)
from keras.models import Sequential
```

We define some parameters we will use to create an embedding layer. The embedding layer helps convert each word into a fixed length vector of defined size. The embedding layer will also be used for other types deep neural network models such as recurrent neural networks (RNNs) that we will build later in this section.

```
MAX_WORDS_IN_VOCAB = 20000 # Size of the vocabulary
EMBEDDING_DIM = 100 # Dimension of the dense embedding
MAX_SEQUENCE_LENGTH = 300 # Length of input sequences

model = Sequential()

# An embedding layer maps a sequence of word indices to embedding
#   vectors and learns the word embedding during training
model.add(
  Embedding(
    MAX_WORDS_IN_VOCAB,
    EMBEDDING_DIM,
    input_length=MAX_SEQUENCE_LENGTH
  )
)
```

Now, we can build our CNN. First we add a convolutional and pooling layer. We can add multiple pairs of convolutional and pooling layers.

```
# Convolution layer
model.add(Conv1D(128, 5, activation="relu"))

# Pooling layer
model.add(MaxPooling1D(5))
```

Next, we add a Flatten layer to flatten the data to a single dimension for input into the fully connected layer (dense layer).

```
# flattens the multi-dimension input tensors into a single dimension
#   for input to the fully connected layer
model.add(Flatten())

## Fully connected layer
#Hidden dense layer
model.add(Dense(128, activation="relu"))

# Output layer
# The softmax function turns a vector of N-real-values
#   into a vector of N-real-values that sum to 1
model.add(Dense(2, activation="softmax"))
```

To compile the model, we run `model.compile`. `model.summary` prints a summary of the model, which includes the names and types of layers in the model, output shape for each layer, number of weight parameters of each layer, and more.

```
# Model compilation
model.compile(
  loss="categorical_crossentropy",
  optimizer="rmsprop",
  metrics=["acc"]
)
print(model.summary())
```

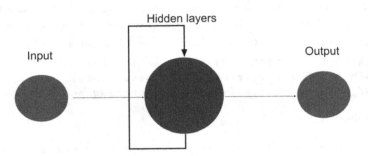

FIGURE 4.8 RNN architecture.

Finally, to fit the model on your data, the following command can be used.

```
# Training
model.fit(xs, ys, epochs=20, verbose=1)
```

> What is an epoch?
>
> Epochs is the number of passes of the entire training dataset that have gone through the training or learning process of the algorithm. Datasets are usually grouped into batches (especially when the amount of data is very large).

We'll build a CNN model on a sample dataset for demonstration of a text classification example in Chapter 8 (Section 8.3.2.2).

4.2.2.2 Recurrent neural network (RNN)

RNNs are a type of artificial neural networks where connection between the nodes can create a cycle, i.e., the output from some nodes impact subsequent input to the same node. This means that RNNs are fundamentally based on feedback, i.e., output of the current layer is dependent on the previous layer as well. Hence, these are not feedforward neural networks.

RNNs work well with sequential tasks where the order matters. RNNs can use their internal state or internal memory to process variable-length sequences of inputs. Popular applications include time-series forecasting, speech recognition, music composition, and natural language processing. An example includes the prediction of the next word in a sequence. 'The clouds are in the __' -> sky.

RNN's architecture has an input layer, hidden layers, and an output layer. The hidden layer does the looping and has memory to store feedback from previous layers. Figure 4.8 shows the diagram for a RNN.

More details on RNNs can be found here [153].

LSTMs and BiLSTMs are two types of RNNs that find popular use in text applications.

4.2.2.3 Long short term memory (LSTM)

'I grew up in France. I speak fluent __.' Nearby words suggest that the next word is likely a language, but the name of the language needs to know about the context from further away, i.e., 'France'. When the gap between the relevant information and the point where it is needed becomes very large, RNNs no longer perform well. LSTMs are a type of RNN that can memorize long-term dependencies. LSTMs include a memory cell that allows it to maintain information for longer periods of time that standard RNNs lack.

In LSTM neural networks, gates are special structures that control the flow of information through the network. LSTM has three main gates - *forget gate* (decides how much of the previous data will be forgotten versus used), *input gate* (quantifies the importance of new information carried by the input), and *output gate* (determines the value of next hidden state). These gates are neural networks themselves and are thought of as filters. Each gate consists of a sigmoid activation function and a pointwise multiplication operation. The sigmoid is a mathematical function that maps input values to a value between 0 and 1. This allows for control over amount of information that is allowed to pass through the gates. Values close to 0 indicate that the information should be discarded, while values close to 1 indicate that the information should be retained. Let's consider a simple example.

'Bob loves to swim. Jim likes coffee.' Once the first sentence is over, the second one is no longer about Bob. The new subject is Jim. The *forget gate* allows forgetting about Bob and retaining Jim as the subject.

'Jim likes coffee. He told me over the phone that he owns a limited edition brewing machine.' Here, we can see three pieces of information. Jim likes coffee, he used the phone, and he owns a limited edition brewing machine. In the context of the first sentence, the critical information from the second sentence is the ownership of the limited edition brewing machine, and not that he was on the phone. This is the task of the *input gate*.

'I grew up in France. I speak fluent __.' Based on the context of the first sentence, the blank word is likely to be 'French'. This is the function of the *output gate*.

Using gates, LSTM networks can selectively store, alter, or retrieve information for an extended duration, making them ideal for sequential data or time-series analysis. More about LSTMs can be found here [153].

Using **Keras**, the following is an example of creating a LSTM model.

As we are dealing with text, we first create an embedding layer.

```
from tensorflow.keras.layers import Embedding, LSTM, Dense

MAX_WORDS_IN_VOCAB = 20000 # Size of the vocabulary
EMBEDDING_DIM = 100 # Dimension of the dense embedding
MAX_SEQUENCE_LENGTH = 300 # Length of input sequences

model=Sequential()

# An embedding layer maps a sequence of word indices to
#  embedding vectors and learns the word embedding during training
model.add(
```

```
Embedding(
  MAX_WORDS_IN_VOCAB,
  EMBEDDING_DIM,
  input_length=MAX_SEQUENCE_LENGTH
  )
)
```

Then, we can add multiple LSTM layers.

```
# LSTM layer
model.add(LSTM(128, activation='relu', return_sequences=True))
# When return_sequences  set to true,
#  it returns a sequence of output to the next layer
# Set to True if the next layer is also a Recurrent Network layer

# Adding a second LSTM layer
model.add(LSTM(128, activation='relu'))
```

Next, we add a fully connected layer. In this layer, each neuron is connected to the neurons of the preceding layer.

```
# Dense hidden layer
model.add(Dense(32, activation='relu'))
```

Finally, we add an output layer, compile the model and fit it on the data.

```
# Output layer
# The softmax function turns a vector of N-real-values
#  into a vector of N-real-values that sum to 1
model.add(Dense(4, activation='softmax'))

# Model compilation
model.compile(
  loss='sparse_categorical_crossentropy',
  optimizer='adam', metrics=['accuracy']
)
print(model.summary())

# Training
model.fit(xs, ys, epochs=20, verbose=1)
```

4.2.2.4 Bi-directional LSTMs (BiLSTMs)

Bi-directional LSTMs consider the past as well as future contexts. Outputs from two LSTMs are concatenated, where one processes the sequence from left to right, the other one processes the sequence from right to left. More about BiLSTMs can be found here [50].

An implementation of a simple BiLSTM model is as follows.

```
from tensorflow.keras.layers import (
  Embedding, Bidirectional, LSTM, Dense
)

MAX_WORDS_IN_VOCAB = 20000 # Size of the vocabulary
EMBEDDING_DIM = 100 # Dimension of the dense embedding
MAX_SEQUENCE_LENGTH = 300 # Length of input sequences
```

```
model = Sequential()
# embedding layer to map word indices to vectors
model.add(
  Embedding(
    MAX_WORDS_IN_VOCAB,
    EMBEDDING_DIM,
    input_length=MAX_SEQUENCE_LENGTH
  )
)
# Bidirectional LSTM
model.add(Bidirectional(LSTM(64)))

# Dense layer to get the output
model.add(Dense(MAX_WORDS_IN_VOCAB, activation="softmax"))

# Model compilation
model.compile(
  loss="categorical_crossentropy",
  optimizer='adam', metrics=["accuracy"]
)
# Training
model.fit(xs, ys, epochs=20, verbose=1)
```

We'll build a BiLSTM model for next word prediction classification in Chapter 11 (Section 11.2).

> *TIP*
>
> CNNs can be used to build text classification models where the sequence of words is not relevant. In other text applications such as sentiment analysis and next-word prediction, the order of the words matters to create a meaningful sentence. CNNs do not do well in solving sequence models. For sequential text data, RNNs (especially LSTMs and BiLSTMs) are the most popular.

4.2.3 Transformers

You might have heard all the buzz around transformers in NLP. Transformer models have achieved state-of-the-art status for many major NLP tasks in the past few years.

Transformer is a type of neural network architecture. But so is RNN, right? How is a transformer different?

In NLP, before transformers, RNNs were used more profoundly for developing state-of-the-art models. As we saw in the previous section, an RNN takes in the input data sequentially. If we consider a language translation task, an RNN will take the input sentence to be translated one word at a time, and translate one word at a time. Thus, the order of words matters. However, word-by-word translations don't always yield an accurate sentence in a different language. So while it can work well for next-word prediction models, it will not work well for language translation. Since it takes in data sequentially, processing large text documents is hard. It is also difficult to parallelize to speed up training on large datasets. Extra GPU (GPU, or graphics processing unit, is a specialized processing unit with enhanced mathematical computation capability) doesn't offer much help in this case. These are the drawbacks of RNNs.

On the contrary, transformers can be parallelized to train very large models. Transformers are a form of semi-supervised learning. They are trained on unlabeled data, and then fine-tuned using supervised learning for better performance. They were initially designed for language translation.

4.2.3.1 *Main innovations behind transformers*

There are three main innovations behind the original transformers.

1. Positional encoding

   Let's use language translation as an example. Each word in a sentence sequence is assigned an ID. The order of the words in the sentence is stored in the data rather than the structure of the network. Then, when you train a model on large amounts of data, the network learns how to interpret the positional encodings. In this way, the network learns the importance of word order from data.

   This makes it easier to train a transformer than an RNN.

2. Attention

   Attention is a useful concept. The first transformer model's paper was titled 'Attention is all you need' [187].

   As we learned before, transformers were originally built for language translation. Hence, we will use language translation examples to understand this concept better as well.

   The attention mechanism is a neural network structure that allows the text model to look at every word in the original sentence while making decisions on how to translate it.

   'The agreement on the European Economic Area was signed in August 1992'. This sentence's word-by-word translation to French does not yield a correctly formed French sentence. 'the European Economic Area' translates to 'la européenne économique zone' using a word-by-word translation, which is not a correct way of writing that in French. One of the correct French translation for that phrase is 'la zone économique européenne'. In French, the equivalent word for 'economic' comes before the equivalent word for 'european' and there is a gendered agreement between words. 'la zona' needs the word translation on 'European' to be in the feminine form.

   So for successful translation using the attention concept, 'european' and 'economic' are looked at together. The model learns which words to attend to in this fashion on its own from the data. Looking at the data, the model can learn about word order rules, grammar, word genders, plurality, etc.

3. Self attention

   Self attention is the concept of running attention on the input sentence itself.

   Learning from data, models build internal representation or understanding of language automatically. The better the representation the neural network learns, the better it will be at any language task.

   For instance, 'Ask the server to bring me my check' and 'I think I just crashed the server', both contain the word server, but the meaning is vastly different in each sentence. This can be known by looking at the context in each sentence. 'server' and 'check' point to one meaning of 'server'. 'serve' and 'crash' point to another meaning of 'server'.

   Self attention allows the network to understand a word in the context of other words around it. It can help disambiguate words and many other language tasks.

Architecture

Transformers have two parts - encoder and decoder. The encoder works on input sequences to extract features. The decoder operates on the target output sequence using the features. The encoder has multiple blocks. The features that are the output of the last encoder block become the input to the decoder. The decoder consists of multiple blocks as well.

For instance, in a language translation task, the encoder generates encodings that determine which parts of the input sequence are relevant to each other and passes this encoding to the next encoder layer. The decoder takes encodings and uses derived context to generate the output sequence. Transformers run multiple encoder-decoder sequences in parallel. Further information can be found at [225].

4.2.3.2 Types of transformer models

Transformer models can be of different types. The types include autoregressive models, autoencoding models, and seq-to-seq models.

Below are some notes on some of the most popular transformer models. Going into further details on each one's architecture is out of the scope of this book. Additional resources are linked for curious readers.

1. Autoencoding models

   Autoencoding models are pre-trained by corrupting the input tokens and then trying to reconstruct the original sentence as the output. They correspond to the encoder of the original transformer model and have access to the complete input without any mask. Those models usually build a bidirectional representation of the whole sentence. Common applications include **sentence classification, named entity recognition (NER)**, and **extractive question answering**.

(a) BERT

BERT [62] stands for Bidirectional Encoder Representations from Transformers. One of the most popular models, BERT is used for many NLP tasks such as text summarization, question and answering system, text classification, and more. It is also used in Google search, and many ML tools offered by Google Cloud. It is a transformer-based machine learning technique for NLP pre-training and was developed by Google. BERT overcomes the limitations of RNN and other neural networks around handling long sequences and capturing dependencies among different combinations of words in long sentences. BERT is pre-trained on two different, but related, NLP tasks - Masked Language Modeling and Next Sentence Prediction. Masked Language Modeling training aims to hide a word in a sentence and has the algorithm predict the masked/hidden word based on context. Next Sentence Prediction training aims to predict the relationship between two sentences. BERT was trained using 3.3 billion words total with 2.5 billion from Wikipedia and 0.8 billion from BooksCorpus [97].

(b) DistilBERT

DistilBERT is a distilled version of BERT, smaller, faster, cheaper, and lighter than BERT. It was built using knowledge distillation during the pre-training phase that reduced the size of a BERT model by 40% while retaining 97% of its language understanding capabilities and being 60% faster [147].

(c) RoBERTa

RoBERTa [112] is a robustly optimized method for pre-training natural language processing systems that improve on BERT. RoBERTa is different from BERT in the masking approach. BERT uses static masking, which means that the same part of the sentence is masked in each epoch. On the contrary, RoBERTa uses dynamic masking where different parts of the sentences are masked for different epochs. RoBERTa is trained on over 160GB of uncompressed text instead of the 16GB dataset originally used to train BERT [152].

2. Autoregressive models

A statistical model is autoregressive if it predicts future values based on past values. In language, autoregressive models are pre-trained on the classic language modeling task of guessing the next token having read all the previous ones. They correspond to the decoder of the original transformer model, and a mask is used on top of the full sentence so that the attention heads can only see what was before in the text, and not what's after[11]. **Text generation** is the most common application.

---

[11]https://huggingface.co/docs/transformers/model_summary

(a) XLNet

XLNet [203] is an extension of the Transformer-XL model (a transformer architecture that introduces the notion of recurrence to the deep self-attention network [56]) pre-trained using an autoregressive method where the next token is dependent on all previous tokens. XLNet has an architecture similar to BERT. The primary difference is the pre-training approach. BERT is an autoencoding-based model, whereas XLNet is an autoregressive-based model. XLNet is known to exhibit higher performance than BERT. XLNet is also known for overcoming weakness of BERT on tasks such as question answering, sentiment analysis, document ranking, and natural language inference.

(b) GPT-2

GPT-2 [136] (generative pre-trained transformer model - 2nd generation) was created by OpenAI in February 2019 which is pre-trained on a very large corpus of English data in a self-supervised fashion. It is autoregressive model where each token in the sentence has the context of the previous words. GPT-2 was to be followed by the 175-billion-parameter GPT-3, revealed to the public in 2020. GPT-2 has been well known for tasks such as translating text between languages, summarizing long articles, and answering trivia questions. GPT-2 was trained on a dataset of 8 million web pages. GPT-2 is open-sourced.

(c) GPT-3

GPT-3 (generative pre-trained transformer model - 3rd generation) [38] is an autoregressive language model that produces text that looks like it was written by a human. It can write poetry, draft emails, write jokes, and perform several other tasks. The GPT-3 model was trained on 45TB of text data, including Common Crawl, webtexts, books, and Wikipedia. GPT-3 is not open-source. It is available via OpenAI's API, which is reported to be expensive as of 2022. The chat-based tool, ChatGPT, is based on GPT-3.

The only difference between autoregressive models and autoencoding models is in the pre-training. Therefore, the same architecture can be used for both autoregressive and autoencoding models.

3. Seq-to-seq models

These models use both the encoder and the decoder of the original transformer. Popular applications include **translation**, **summarization**, **generative question answering**, and **classification**.

(a) T5

T5 [226] is a text-to-text transfer transformer model which is trained on unlabeled and labeled data, and further fine-tuned to individual tasks for language modeling. T5 comes in multiple versions of different sizes; t5-base, t5-small (smaller version of t5-base), t5-large (larger version of t5-base), t5-3b, and t5-11b. T5 uses a text-to-text approach. Tasks including translation, question answering, and classification are cast as feeding text to the model as input and training the model to generate some target text. T5 trained on the c4 Common Crawl web corpus.

(b) BART

BART [108] was developed by Facebook AI in 2019. BART is a transformer encoder-encoder (seq2seq) model with a bidirectional (BERT-like) encoder and an autoregressive (GPT-like) decoder. BART is pre-trained by corrupting text with an arbitrary noising function and learning a model to reconstruct the original text. BART has proven to be highly effective when fine-tuned for text summarization and translation type tasks but also works well for tasks such as text classification and question answering. The BART model provided by Hugging Face is trained on the CNN/Daily Mail News Dataset.

(c) PEGASUS

PEGASUS (Pre-training with Extracted Gap-Sentences for Abstractive Summarization) was developed by Google AI in 2020 [209][12]. They propose pre-training large transformer-based encoder-decoder models on massive text corpora with a new self-supervised objective. This is currently the state-of-the-art for abstractive summarization [193] on many benchmark datasets.

We'll be using several of these models in Section V for different popular applications.

For each of the different types of models above, one may perform better than the other based on the dataset and task. Table 4.1 contains a summary of applications of these models.

4.2.3.3 *Using transformer models*

The general strategy behind training transformer models is to increase the model's size as well as the size of the data used for pre-training. **Pre-training** here is the act of training a model from the raw data available. Transformer models learn patterns from language input and hence are trained on very large datasets. The training process requires massive compute resources and time of up to several weeks. It has been reported to have a significant amount of carbon emissions. For reducing environmental impact, time, and compute resources, model sharing has become paramount.

Fine-tuning is a process that comes after pre-training. Fine-tuning helps train a pre-trained model with data specific to a task. Since pre-training is done on large datasets, fine-tuning requires much lesser data. The time and resources required are also lower for fine-tuning models. For instance, a model pre-trained on a general English dataset can be fine-tuned for scientific/research applications using arvix data[13]. Since what the model learns is based on the knowledge that has been transferred to it, the term transfer learning is commonly used in transformers.

---

[12]https://huggingface.co/docs/transformers/model_doc/pegasus
[13]https://huggingface.co/datasets/arxiv_dataset

TABLE 4.1 Transformer models and applications.

Type	Models	Popular Applications
Autoencoding	BERT RoBERTa DistilBERT	Sentiment classification Sentence classification Word sense disambiguation
Autoregressive	XLNET GPT-2 GPT-3	Text generation Question answering Document ranking Natural language inference Writing emails / poetry / jokes
Seq-to-seq	T5 BART PEGASUS	Language translation Text summarization Question answering Classification

An example of the pre-training and fine-tuning flow can be seen in Figure 4.9.

The Hugging Face `transformers`[14] library in Python provides thousands of pre-trained and fine-tuned models to perform different tasks such as classification, information extraction, question answering, summarization, translation, and text generation, in over 100 languages. Thousands of organizations pre-train and fine-tune models and open-source many models for the community. Some of these organizations include the Allen Institute of AI, Facebook AI, Microsoft, Google AI, Grammarly, and Typeform.

You can use `transformers` library - `pipeline()` function to use transformers. Here's an example.

```
from transformers import pipeline

sa_model = pipeline("sentiment-analysis")
sa_model("Do you really think I love headaches?")
```

[‘label’: ‘NEGATIVE’, ‘score’: 0.9915459752082825]

By default, the sentiment-analysis pipeline selects a BERT-based pre-trained model that has been fine-tuned for sentiment analysis in the English language, called `distilbert-base-uncased-finetuned-sst-2-english`. Some other available pipelines include `feature-extraction`, `fill-mask`, `ner` (for NER), `question-answering`, `summarization`, `text-generation`, `translation`, `zero-shot-classification` (for classification on the fly as shown below). Code samples for many of these are present in the notebook section3/transformers.ipynb.

```
from transformers import pipeline
```

---

[14]https://huggingface.co/docs/transformers/index

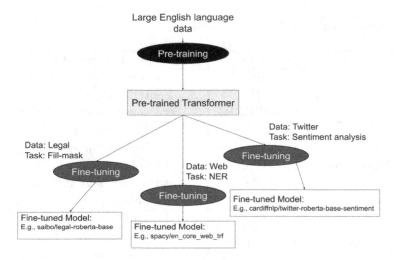

FIGURE 4.9 Examples of the pre-training and fine-tuning flow in transformer models.

```
osc_model = pipeline("zero-shot-classification")
osc_model(
  "This is a book about NLP.",
  candidate_labels=["education", "politics", "business"]
)
```

'sequence': 'This is a book about NLP.',

'labels': ['education', 'business', 'politics'],

'scores': [0.5546694397926331, 0.26519840955734253, 0.1801321655511856]

To select a specific model for these tasks, the `pipeline()` takes a keyword argument `model`. Depending on your application, you can search for domain-specific models. For example, `nlpaueb/legal-bert-base-uncased` is a BERT-based legal domain model fine-tuned for `fill-mask` tasks. You can find all available models to use at[15]. Use the tag of the model you want to use as the value of the keyword argument `model`.

There are several popular transformer models apt for different applications. We will demonstrate these for different applications in Section V. You can also fine-tune models on a custom dataset for several tasks using a pre-trained model[16]. We will demonstrate an implementation for fine-tuning using a custom dataset in Chapter 7 (Section 7.1.1.4) for NER.

Hugging Face transformers require either `PyTorch` or `Tensorflow` to be installed since it relies on either one of them as the backend, thus make sure to have a working version before installing `transformers`.

---

[15]https://huggingface.co/models

[16]https://huggingface.co/docs/transformers/training

TABLE 4.2 ML models and applications.

Type of ML Model	Applications
Classic ML models	Well suited for training models for simple tasks in text classification, regression, and clustering.
CNNs	Well suited for training models on large datasets for text classification tasks where word order is not relevant.
LSTMs and BiLSTMs	Well suited for training models on large datasets tasks where order of words matter, such as next-word prediction and sentiment analysis.
Transformers	Well suited for simple classification tasks as well as complex tasks such as text generation, language translation, text summarization, and question answering. For practical use in the industry, many pre-trained and fine-tuned models can be leveraged.

[17]This short course by Hugging Face is a great resource to learn further about transformers.

Limitations

The biggest limitation of the transformer models is that it is trained on large datasets scraped from the web and unfortunately include the good and the bad from the Internet. There have been reports of gender and racial biases in the results of these models. Fine-tuning the pre-trained models to your dataset won't make the intrinsic bias disappear. Hence, be sure to test your models thoroughly before deploying them in your organization.

In this section, we covered classic machine learning models, CNNs, RNNs, and transformers. Table 4.2 contains popular applications these models are used for in NLP.

4.2.4 Model hyperparameters

There are many parameters in a model, some of which are learned by the algorithm's training process itself, and some of them are user-defined and taken in as the input before training the model.

A hyperparameter is a parameter whose value is explicitly set by the user and can be used to control the learning process. Generally, any machine learning model you use will have some hyperparameters that you can experiment with until you get the best performance. The hyperparameters are set before the learning algorithm begins training the model.

What are these hyperparameters depends on the model you choose and the algo-

---

[17]https://huggingface.co/course/chapter1/1?fw=pt

TABLE 4.3 Common hyperparameters of classic ML classification models. Attached URLs contain further details for each hyperparameter.

Model	Commonly tweaked hyperparameters
Multinomial NaiveBayes[18]	alpha
Logistic Regression[19]	C, penalty, solver
SVM[20]	C, gamma, kernel
kNN[21]	n_neighbors
RandomForest[22]	n_estimators, max_features, max_depth, min_samples_split, min_samples_leaf, bootstrap
CRF[23]	algorithm, c1, c2 max_iterations, all_possible_transitions

rithm behind it. For example, the k in kNN, the number of clusters in a clustering algorithm, and the number of hidden units, epochs, and number of nodes in a neural network model are some examples of hyperparameters. The tool you use to implement the different models in Python specifies what these hyperparameters are. Tables 4.3 and 4.4 contain a list of common hyperparameters for some popular classic ML classification models and deep learning models in language tasks and links to resources with further details.

Hyperparameter tuning is a popular practice and refers to the task of fine-tuning your model with parameters that yield the best results. The evaluation of results is discussed in the next section. We'll discuss more on hyperparameter tuning in the next section as well and share an example using kNN classifier.

4.3 MODEL EVALUATION

Often, there are multiple models known to be well suited for a particular type of task. It is a common practice to build multiple models and compare certain metrics to pick the best model. Once you pick a model, it is a good practice to perform hyperparameter tuning to pick a good set of parameters to return the best results. These results are nothing but metrics that make the best sense for your application,

---

[18]https://scikit-learn.org/stable/modules/generated/sklearn.naive_bayes.MultinomialNB.html

[19]https://scikit-learn.org/stable/modules/generated/sklearn.linear_model.LogisticRegression.html

[20]https://scikit-learn.org/stable/modules/generated/sklearn.svm.SVC.html

[21]https://scikit-learn.org/stable/modules/generated/sklearn.neighbors.KNeighborsClassifier.html

[22]https://scikit-learn.org/stable/modules/generated/sklearn.ensemble.RandomForestClassifier.html

[23]https://sklearn-crfsuite.readthedocs.io/en/latest/

TABLE 4.4 Common hyperparameters of deep learning-based classification models. Attached URLs contain further details for each hyperparameter.

Model/Layer	Commonly tweaked hyperparameters

Deep Neural Networks[1]: Embedding layer	Embedding layer :
	   input_dim (Size of the vocabulary)
	   output_dim (Dimension of the dense embedding)
	   input_length (Length of input sequences)
	   Usage: `Embedding(input_dim, output_dim, input_length=10)`

Specific to CNN	Convolutional layer :
	   Number of convolutional layers
	   filters (Number of kernels of each convolutional layer)
	   kernel_size (Kernel size in each convolutional layer)
	   activation (Activation function in each convolutional layer) [2]
	   Usage: `Conv1D(filters, kernel_size, activation=None)`
	 Pooling layer :
	   pool_size (Pooling size after each convolutional layer)
	   Usage: `MaxPool1D(pool_size=2)`

Specific to LSTM & BiLSTM	LSTM layer :
	   Number of LSTM layers
	   units (Number of units)
	   activation (Activation function)
	   Usage: `LSTM(units, activation="tanh")`

Common	Dense layer :
	   Number of dense layers
	   units (Number of units in each dense layer)
	   Usage: `Dense(units, activation=x)`
	 model.compile : loss, metrics, optimizer (learning_rate)
	   Usage: `model.compile(optimizer="adam", metrics=["acc"],`
	   `loss="categorical_crossentropy")`
	 model.fit : epochs, batch_size, validation_split
	   Usage: `model.fit(x, y, batch_size=10, epochs=1,`
	   `validation_split=0.0)`

[1]https://keras.io/api/layers/
[2]https://deepai.org/machine-learning-glossary-and-terms/activation-function

such as accuracy. In this section, we'll discuss model evaluation practices, what these metrics are, and how to know which metrics make the best sense for your model.

While evaluating the model, learning about how it predicts on the very same data it was trained on is not sufficient. The training data is what the model has already seen, thus it may be better at predicting the training data as opposed to unseen samples. A common practice is to break your data into training and testing samples. The training samples go into training your model, and the testing samples are saved for evaluating your model later. That way, you can verify the results of your model on samples unseen during the training process. Some practitioners split the data into three groups instead - training, testing, and validation samples. In that case, the validation sample set is commonly used for hyperparameter tuning of the model.

> *TIP*
>
> Ensure you separate your data well enough so no common link remains in your testing and training samples. Let's consider an example where your data comprises YouTube video descriptions (from videos created by many different content creators). Since multiple videos can be posted by the same user, video descriptions can have common text that content creators put in every description, such as where else to follow them, their taglines, etc. If your training and testing samples have videos from the same source, then the test can produce biased results.

The code used in this section below can be found in the notebook section3/evaluation-metrics.ipynb.

Cross-validation

Another recommended practice is performing cross-validation. In this technique, your data is split between training and testing samples x times (x can be user-defined -> x-fold cross-validation). A fold refers to a run. 5 folds means that the training and testing will be done five times on different splits of data. Each fold, the testing samples can be different from all other folds, or you can also decide to turn that off and pick a random sample each time. Evaluating the x models and their results help understand if you have enough data and whether your model has any bias or high-variance issues. Here's how to implement it using `sklearn`.

```
from sklearn.datasets import load_iris
from sklearn.linear_model import LogisticRegression
from sklearn.model_selection import cross_val_score

# sample data for demo
X, y = load_iris(return_X_y=True)
clf = LogisticRegression()

# 5-fold cross validation
```

BINARY CLASSIFICATION

	Actual = YES	Actual = NO
Prediction = YES	63 (TP)	6 (FP)
Prediction = NO	7 (FN)	62 (TN)

MULTI-CLASS CLASSIFICATION

	Actual = class 1	Actual = class 2	Actual = class 3	Actual = class 4
Prediction = class 1	28	5	3	7
Prediction = class 2	3	34	5	5
Prediction = class 3	4	4	32	1
Prediction = class 4	3	2	6	29

FIGURE 4.10 An example of a confusion matrix for a binary classification case and a multi-class classification case. TP stands for true positives. TN stands for true negatives. FP stands for false positives. FN stands for false negatives.

```
cross_val_score(clf, X, y, cv=5)
```

Confusion matrix

A confusion matrix can be useful in understanding model performance by each class in a classification problem. Figure 4.10 shows how a confusion matrix looks like. Adding up the actual columns will give you the number of samples for the respective classes in the dataset.

```
from sklearn.metrics import confusion_matrix

y_true = [2, 0, 2, 2, 0, 1]
y_pred = [0, 0, 2, 2, 0, 2]

confusion_matrix(y_true, y_pred)
# >> array([[2, 0, 0],
# [0, 0, 1],
# [1, 0, 2]])
```

4.3.1 Metrics

Important evaluation metrics include the following. The below metrics can be calculated per class or at an overall aggregate level.

- Accuracy/Recall
  Accuracy is the measure of how correct your predictions are compared to the truth/actual labels. The formula is as follows for a class. The term recall refers to the accuracy of a particular label/class.

$$\text{recall} = \frac{\text{correct classifications for a class}}{\text{count of samples actually belonging to the class}}$$

Looking at the confusion matrix from Figure 4.10 for the multi-class classification, for class 1, the recall will be

$$\frac{28}{28+3+4+3}$$

For binary classification, the recall can also be defined as

$$\frac{\text{true positives}}{\text{true positives + false negatives}}$$

- Precision
  Precision is a measure of how correct your predictions are compared to other predictions. The formula is as follows for a class.

$$\text{precision} = \frac{\text{correct classifications for a class}}{\text{count of all samples classified with the class}}$$

Looking at the confusion matrix from Figure 4.10 for the multi-class classification, for class 1, the precision will be

$$\frac{28}{28+5+3+7}$$

For binary classification, the precision can also be defined as

$$\frac{\text{true positives}}{\text{true positives + false positives}}$$

Let's look at an example where precision is more important than recall. Let's say there are 100 culprits of a crime in a crowd of 200 people. It is important that no innocent person is punished. Recognizing culprits correctly is more important than missing a few culprits rather than potentially punishing an innocent individual. If you found 45 culprits correctly, your precision becomes 100%, whereas your overall accuracy is 72.5%, and your recall for the class culprit is 45%. In such a case, getting a high precision is a more important metric.

- F1

  The F1 score is the harmonic mean of precision and recall. It is computed using the following formula

$$\frac{2 * \text{precision} * \text{recall}}{\text{precision} + \text{recall}}$$

The maximum possible value is 1.0 indicating a perfect recall and precision. The F1 score takes into account how the data samples might be distributed among the classes. For example, if the data is imbalanced (e.g., 80% of all players do not get drafted and 10% do), the F1 score provides a better overall assessment compared to accuracy.

Let's consider an example to understand the precision and recall and why looking at these metrics per class can be beneficial in understanding your model. Your model has two classes with the same number of samples each (let's call the number of samples as sample1 and sample2 for class 1 and class 2, respectively). Let's say your model predicts class 1 for all samples.

Overall :

$$\text{Recall} = \frac{\text{prediction(class 1) in samples1} + \text{prediction(class2) in samples2}}{\text{samples1} + \text{samples2}} = \frac{x+0}{x+x} = 50\%$$

$$\text{Precision} = \frac{\text{prediction(class 1) in samples1} + \text{prediction(class2) in samples2}}{\text{prediction(class 1)} + \text{prediction(class2}} = \frac{x+0}{2x+0} = 50\%$$

Per class :

$$\text{Recall class 1} = \frac{\text{predicted(class 1) in samples1}}{samples1} = \frac{x}{x} = 100\%$$

$$\text{Precision class 1} = \frac{\text{predicted(class 1) in samples1}}{\text{predicted(class 1)}} = \frac{x}{2x} = 50\%$$

$$\text{Recall class 2} = \frac{\text{predicted(class 2) in samples2}}{samples2} = 0\%$$

$$\text{Precision class 2} = \frac{\text{predicted(class 2) in samples2}}{\text{predicted(class 2)}} = 0\%$$

These indicators help understand model results for the different classes and bring forward any bias that might exist.

> **TIP**
>
> It is important to understand which metric is most important for your use case before you start trying to make the model 'better'. For example, if it is important to have the least amount of false classifications, then precision is an important metric to monitor. Accuracy is important when the correct classifications are more important. F1-score is a good metric when there is class imbalance. F1 score is also popularly used when practitioners care about both precision and recall.

These scores can be calculated using the `sklearn` library as follows.

```
from sklearn.metrics import precision_recall_fscore_support

y_true = ['lion', 'dog', 'tiger', 'lion', 'dog', 'tiger']
y_pred = ['lion', 'dog', 'lion', 'dog', 'dog', 'tiger']

precision, recall, fscore, _ = precision_recall_fscore_support(
    y_true, y_pred, average='macro'
)
# macro: Calculates metrics for each label, and finds their mean.
# micro: Calculates metrics globally by counting the
#  total true positives, false negatives, and false positives.
# weighted: Calculates metrics for each label, and finds their
    average
# weighted by the number of true instances for each label.
```

precision=0.7222222222222222

recall=0.6666666666666666

fscore=0.6555555555555556

Table 4.5 contain a summary of these evaluation metrics.

TABLE 4.5 ML model evaluation metrics.

Metric	Formula
Recall	$\dfrac{\text{correct classifications for a class}}{\text{count of samples actually belonging to the class}}$
Precision	$\dfrac{\text{correct classifications for a class}}{\text{count of all samples classified with the class}}$
F1	$\dfrac{2 * \text{precision} * \text{recall}}{\text{precision} + \text{recall}}$

4.3.2 Hyperparameter tuning

Hyperparameters make a difference in the goodness of model results. The goodness can be determined based on the evaluation metric that makes sense for your model. Let's look at an example below using accuracy as our evaluation metric.

```
from sklearn.neighbors import KNeighborsClassifier
from sklearn.metrics import accuracy_score

clf1 = KNeighborsClassifier(n_neighbors=3)
clf1.fit(X_train, y_train)
y_pred1 = clf.predict(X_test)
acck3 = accuracy_score(y_test, y_pred1)
# >> 0.67


clf2 = KNeighborsClassifier(n_neighbors=50)
clf2.fit(X_train, y_train)
y_pred2 = clf2.predict(X_test)
acck50 = accuracy_score(y_test, y_pred2)
# >> 0.82
```

```
"""
Improvement in accuracy
"""

clf3 = KNeighborsClassifier(n_neighbors=70)
clf3.fit(X_train, y_train)
y_pred3 = clf3.predict(X_test)
acck70 = accuracy_score(y_test, y_pred3)
# >> 0.80
"""
No additional improvement in accuracy
"""
```

You can see the how the accuracy changes with different values of `n_neighbors`. Practitioners also plot the change in accuracy with the hyperparameter value for visually understanding the impact.

As we saw in Table 4.3 and Table 4.4, there are can be many hyperparameters to tune per model. Fortunately, there are many methods that can be leveraged to hyperparameter-tune models. These include the following.

- Grid search : Exhaustive search through manually defined hyperparameter value options.

- Random search: Rather than an exhaustive search, this method randomly selects combinations of parameters. It is known to do better than grid search for deep learning models.

- Other methods include bayesian optimization [182], gradient-based optimization [28], evolutionary algorithms [60], population-based optimization [206], and paramILS [72].

In the below example, we use `sklearn` to perform grid search to find the good hyperparameters for a kNN classifier.

```
from sklearn.model_selection import GridSearchCV
from sklearn.neighbors import KNeighborsClassifier

grid_params = {
  "n_neighbors": [3, 5, 7, 10, 15, 20, 25, 35],
  "weights": ["uniform", "distance"],
  "metric": ["euclidean", "manhattan"]
}

gs = GridSearchCV(
  KNeighborsClassifier(),
  grid_params,
  cv=10,
  verbose=1
)

gs_results = gs.fit(X, y)

# best param and scores for your model can be obtained as follows
```

```
print(
  "Best k: ",
  gs_results.best_estimator_.get_params()["n_neighbors"]
)
print(gs_results.best_score_, gs_results.best_params_)
```

In the above grid search, there are 8 possibilities for n_neighbors, 2 possibilities for weights, 2 possibilities for metric, and 10 cross-validations. The model in run 8 * 2 * 2 * 10 = 320 times to find the best hyperparameters.

The following code can be used to random search instead.

```
from sklearn.model_selection import RandomizedSearchCV
from sklearn.neighbors import KNeighborsClassifier

grid_params = {
  "n_neighbors": [3, 5, 7, 10, 15, 20, 25, 35],
  "weights": ["uniform", "distance"],
  "metric": ["euclidean", "manhattan"]
}

rs = RandomizedSearchCV(
  KNeighborsClassifier(),
  param_distributions=grid_params,
  n_iter=10
)

rs_results = rs.fit(X, y)

# best param and scores for your model can be obtained as follows
print(
  "Best k: ",
  rs_results.best_estimator_.get_params()["n_neighbors"]
)
print(rs_results.best_score_, rs_results.best_params_)
```

Another option is to use the KerasTuner[24] library. This library allows for optimal hyperparameter searching for machine learning and deep learning models. The library helps find kernel sizes, learning rate for optimization, and other different hyper-parameters. Here is an example.

```
! pip install keras-tuner==1.1.3

import keras_tuner
from tensorflow import keras

def build_model(hp):
  model = keras.Sequential()
  model.add(
    keras.layers.Dense(
      hp.Choice('units', [8, 16, 32]), # choice of param values
      activation='relu'
    )
  )
```

---

[24]https://keras.io/keras_tuner/

```
model.add(keras.layers.Dense(1, activation='relu'))
model.compile(loss='mse')
return model

# Random searching for best hyperparameter
tuner = keras_tuner.RandomSearch(
    build_model,
    objective='val_loss',
    max_trials=5
)
tuner.search(
    x_train, y_train,
    epochs=5,
    validation_data=(x_val, y_val)
)
best_model = tuner.get_best_models()[0]
```

[3] walks through an example of optimizing a CNN model using KerasTuner.

All the code used for hyperparameter tuning in this section can be found in the notebook section3/hyperparameter-tuning.ipynb.

Windup

In this section, we covered several concepts necessary to start building NLP applications. We discussed practical implementations of cleaning and standardizing text. For most applications based on text data, cleaning the data is the biggest and most time-consuming step. We looked at various libraries that can be used in Python to achieve text preprocessing. Most preprocessing tasks can be solved using regex or libraries such as `NLTK` and `spaCy`. Different text-based datasets can have different noise elements within. It is a good practice to manually look at some data samples to gauge the data quality and what cleaning steps it might require. If the task is just to understand what's in the text, you can directly resort to data visualization or printing words with the most occurrence. This is often the demand for many data analytics-based tasks. We also discussed that simple yet effective data augmentation techniques can come in handy when you are lacking data samples.

For building any predictive models, you need to further transform your text to create numerical features. We discussed the various ways to get these features, including logical operations on text, word frequency-based counts, and more advanced word embedding techniques. Once generated, the features can then be used to find similar words or for building machine learning models. For applications like finding similar words, distance metrics can be used to compute similarities and differences between words in a corpus. We went through the commonly used distance metrics in NLP. The most popular one for finding context/semantic similarity is cosine distance. For applications requiring modeling, we discussed classic machine learning models, deep neural networks such as CNN, LSTM, and BiLSTM, and neural network-based transformer models. As a practitioner working in the industry, classic machine learning models are very popular, especially when building the first solution for a problem. CNN is used when larger datasets are available to create better text classification models. LSTM and BiLSTM models can be built for tasks where word orders are important, such as next-word prediction models. Transformer models are trained on very large datasets, which is not typically done for solving NLP tasks in industry domains other than large research organizations. Many transformers-based pre-trained and fine-tuned models are accessible with Hugging Face that are pre-trained on large language datasets and can be used out-of-the-box for several NLP tasks, such as document summarization or for extracting word embeddings to use with other models for custom tasks.

TIP

The more complex the model, the better the results? No.
Transformer-based models are not always going to give better results. It depends on your application and it is very much possible that a simple TF-IDF with a logistic regression model meets your needs. It is recommended to start with the easiest and quickest solutions first.

We then looked at several model evaluation metrics and hyperparameter tuning examples to help identify the best model for your application.

We covered a lot of ground in this section. Now, we are ready to use all this NLP understanding and build actual stand-alone NLP applications. It is important to understand the need for NLP across industries to know what we are trying to solve. In Section IV, we will discuss NLP applications by industry vertical, and in Section V, we will implement NLP applications using Python. Tying the knot between using NLP in the enterprise and implementing applications in Python, we will build some industrial projects using real-world scenarios in Section VI.

IV

NLP Applications across Industry Verticals

Natural language processing (NLP) finds application in a wide range of industry verticals. With the rise of the Internet, high volumes of text data are getting produced across the globe, including 300 billion emails [165] and 18.7 billion text messages [150] each day. With the availability of large volumes of text, many industry verticals have started leveraging natural language processing techniques to understand and analyze their data. This usage is increasing as we speak and spreading into more and more domains and applications. In this section, we will go through 15 industry verticals and discuss how they are using and researching NLP today. There are interesting examples in history of how a process from one domain formed the basis for an invention in a completely different domain. James Dyson created the Dyson vacuum design as an inspiration from how sawmills use cyclone force to eject sawdust [64]. In the mid-'90s, a Children's hospital in the UK improved its ICU hand-off process by consulting with the Ferrari F1 pit crew team. Their error rate reportedly reduced from 30% to 10% with the adoption of the F1 recommended protocol [189]. In the late 1800s, French doctor Etienne Tarnier was looking for a solution to save the lives of babies that were born prematurely. On a visit to a Paris zoo, he saw poultry incubators and borrowed the inspiration to make a baby incubator [128].

Below, we will discuss the following industries and how they leverage NLP today. Even if you don't envision working in a particular industry vertical, read through it as we progress through this section. You never know what inspires you for solving a different problem.

- Social media

- E-commerce

- Travel and hospitality

- Marketing

- Insurance

- Finance

- Healthcare

- Law

- Real estate

- Oil and gas

- Supply chain

- Telecommunication

- Automotive

- Serious gaming

- Education and research

- Other popular applications: writing and email, home assistants, and recruiting

## CHAPTER 5

NLP Applications – Active Usage

5.1 SOCIAL MEDIA

5.1.1 What is social media?

People from across the globe use social media platforms daily. Some of the popular global social media platforms include Twitter, Facebook, Instagram, TikTok, YouTube, Twitch, LinkedIn, Reddit, Pinterest, and others. Source [125] suggests that there were 3.78 billion social media users worldwide in 2021, which marks a five percent increase from 2020. As seen in Figure 5.1, the number of users on social media increased from 2.86 billion in 2017 to 3.78 billion in 2021. This marks a whopping 32.17% increase in four years. The average annual growth in social media consumers has been 230 million between 2017 and 2021. A common pattern between the dynamics of these platforms revolves around two themes – content creation and content consumption. Let's consider YouTube as an example. Content creators (individuals or brands) create videos and upload them on YouTube. Consumers of these videos search for content and watch the videos of interest. The viewer can also leave a comment and other signals such as a like, dislike, share, add to a playlist, and so on.

5.1.2 Language data generated

The major sources of language data on social media include user comments and social media posts. Data attached to social media posts include post titles, descriptions, post audios, and closed captions.

5.1.3 NLP in social media

Amid a regular video-watching experience, have you ever noticed an advertisement popping up right before your video starts, or sometimes in the middle of it? How about when you watch one video, the sidebar floods with videos around the same and alike topics as seen in Figure 5.2? Every such experience involves NLP in the

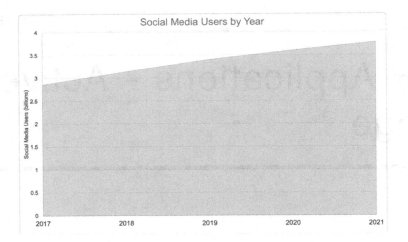

FIGURE 5.1 Global count of social media users by year.

background. Every text signal you leave as comments is also analyzed using NLP to help content creators understand audience sentiment and demand.

Recommendations

Recommendation systems are not only common in the social media space, but also in many other industries like retail and real estate that recommend items based on your previous selections. Notice how often the suggestions on social media are much alike what you previously watched or searched for? What about when you have

FIGURE 5.2 Social media content recommendations on the right based on the currently viewed content.

a typo in your search term as in Figure 5.3? It still shows you the most relevant and usually the item you meant to search for.

Showing results for **natural language processing**   Search instead for **natu lange processing**

FIGURE 5.3   Search typo correction on social media.

There's a lot that goes in the background of a recommendation engine as such. A part of it uses NLP on the text fields of these videos/posts and matches them with other items' text fields to measure content similarity.

Comment analysis

A lot of companies perform sentiment analysis on public tweets, posts, and comments from several different social media platforms. This helps them analyze the audience's response to something which in turn helps inform business decisions on content creation and marketing. Other applications that go beyond just sentiment analysis include emotion analysis and topic classification to categorize the text from social media for different business needs. An example would include an analysis of tweets to help predict stock market changes. Several open-sourced and proprietary company-owned algorithms have floated around to solve the use case. Another example includes analysis of a brand's social media channels, which helps them gauge consumer sentiment, and further assess their complaints in negative sentiment comments algorithmically. This saves hours of manual effort in going through each comment.

Chatbots

Have you noticed that you can reach out to businesses now using social media? Facebook messenger and Instagram messenger are some examples. Several companies have deployed chatbots on their different social media pages. The bot helps answer straightforward questions automatically and connects to an agent if it is unable to handle the query. Examples include the chatbots of brands such as Kayak, T-Mobile, Expedia on Facebook messenger, KLM Airlines on WhatsApp, and many others helping you with hotels, rental cars, flights, and accommodation-related queries. Figure 5.4 shows an example of a conversation with a chatbot using social media messengers.

Fake news detection

Several news items are shared on social media platforms. With this free-flowing information, it has been important to separate the untrue from the truth due to incidents involving fake news spread. Many data points are used for creation of such models, including NLP to use text inputs for classifying information as fake and detection of inappropriate content using text descriptions.

Post comments using AI

You would have noticed people leaving comments on products and ads on Facebook and Instagram. Let's take MAC (the beauty brand) as an example. On MAC's

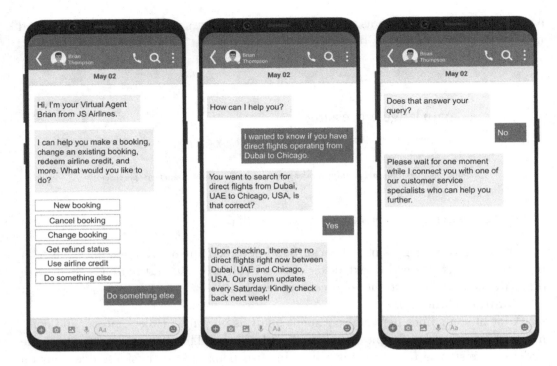

FIGURE 5.4 Brand chatbots on social media messengers.

posts on Facebook, people leave thousands of comments. Their AI-based solution saves human effort and leaves a personalized-looking response to user comments. These responses help answer user questions and market MAC products. The bot uses NLP, specifically natural language understanding (NLU), to decipher the context and intent of the customer and construct human-like-looking responses automatically.

Such bots also analyze customer sentiment and respond accordingly. Just like any algorithm, sentiment analysis has its drawbacks in detecting sarcasm. As an example, a user on social media once posted about an airline's service as seen in Figure 5.5 where the bot detected the sentiment as positive and left a 'thank you' comment accordingly. Such occurrences are typically much fewer than successful detections.

Language translation

Social media platforms offer automatic language translations for enabling global information sharing.

Speech-to-text

Converting social media audio or video post to text is done to create subtitles and transcribe posts. NLP plays an important role in the underlying algorithms.

Ads

What you search, browse, and consume on social media reflects your interests. Based on the audience segment a brand may be targeting, ads show up on your screen when you are browsing the platform. NLP is a part of the solution and helps categorize social media data to aid the overall advertising field.

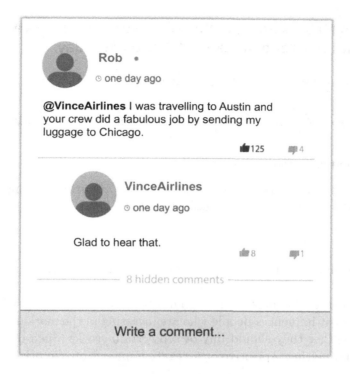

FIGURE 5.5 Sentiment analysis gone wrong.

Image-to-text

Conversion of text within images to text of string-form using optical character recognition (OCR) is of use to analyze and understand content within social media posts such as memes.

Research

Social media data is used for several research efforts studying employability measurement [20], suicidal risks [55], travel trend analysis [155][1], audience analytics and interest indexing [157], marketing optimization [158], and many more applications.

5.2 FINANCE

5.2.1 What is finance?

The finance industry is a broad range of businesses that surround everything to do with managing money. Examples include banks, credit unions, credit card companies, companies managing investment funds, stock brokerages, and so on.

---

[1]https://github.com/jsingh811/pyYouTubeAnalysis/blob/master/samples/report/travel_vlogs_report.pdf

Elon Musk said "use Signal" and confused investors sent the wrong stock up 438% on Monday.

Published Monday, Jan 11 2021 - 6.39PM EST

FIGURE 5.6 Impact of a social media post on an unrelated stock price.

5.2.2 Language data generated

The finance sector consists of text data sources primarily coming from financial records, legal documents, user interactions, and receipts.

5.2.3 NLP in finance

When we are thinking of finance, one particular use case comes to mind - stock price predictions.

News in general influences people around the world. Especially when the news is related to stocks, it influences people who are investing in the market and makes them think about whether they should buy or sell certain stocks. Such decisions taken by the investors have either a positive or a negative impact on the price of stock trading on exchanges. In 2021, Elon Musk tweeted about 'signal', encouraging his followers to use it. This led to a surge in an unrelated stock with a very similar name as seen in Figure 5.6 [124].

The applications of NLP in finance range broadly.

Text categorization

Finding financially relevant content from social media posts and news is required because people are posting about many different topics. Finding what the relevant topics are about certain businesses, politics, global news, or stocks forms a baseline for analyzing content for stock price impact.

Sentiment analysis

Sentiment analysis on news text and social media posts helps identify cunsumer reactions and affinities. Sentiment analysis combined with social media post classification and topic identification helps build stock price prediction algorithms.

Language translation

Language translation offerings break language and geographical barriers between consumers and businesses. Real-time translation of content, especially agreements, from one language to another finds application in this industry.

Legal documents review

There are usually large amounts of legal documents that exist in the domain. It can be time-consuming to go through documents to find anything that could raise flags. NLP reduces the time and effort involved by extracting required information from documents, finding relevant documents, and summarizing documents. Companies like Deloitte, Ernst & Young, and PwC provide actionable yearly audits of a company's performance. For example, Deloitte's Audit Command Language uses

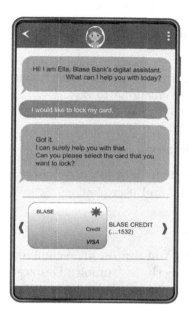

FIGURE 5.7 A bank's chatbot.

NLP-based approaches to examine contract documents and long-term procurement agreements, particularly with government data for accounting and auditing [218].

Chatbots

Chatbots are to help people with any concerns, and any basic questions before actually connecting to a human customer service representative. Customer record analysis helps serve consumers better by analyzing interactions to identify traits and trends surrounding customer needs and expectations. Conversational history further helps with the identification of audiences that may be suitable for certain credit card offers and other financial products and/or services. Other basic actions can be taken by chatbots in this domain as well. An example of a chatbot is shown in Figure 5.7. Such chatbots exist for many banks. For example, Bank of America's chat assistant, Erica, uses NLP to chat with customers.

Image-to-text

Many receipts and documents in this sector need to be converted to data that can be processed by a machine, such as bank checks. OCR is applied to automatically extract the different fields within a check that allows depositing checks from any location into an account within a matter of minutes.

5.3   E-COMMERCE

5.3.1   What is e-commerce?

E-commerce is the buying of goods and services on the Internet. There are different types of e-commerce businesses, generally classified into three categories.

1. Business-to-business, such as Shopify where businesses sell to other businesses.

2. Businesses-to-consumer, where businesses sell to consumers such as amazon and target.

3. Consumer-to-consumer, such as eBay where consumers post products and other consumers are directly engaging to buy.

5.3.2   Language data generated

The primary source of language data in an e-commerce setting comes from product descriptions, user comments, and user chat.

5.3.3   NLP in e-commerce

Let's consider an example. You are on an e-commerce website and you search for 'tumbler' but spell it incorrectly as 'tumblr.' Despite the error, the search engine is able to understand what you meant and returns tumbler products as in Figure 5.8.

1971 results for "tumbler"

Stainless Steel Tumbler	Glass Tumbler with lid 20oz	Carnival cup with lid and straw
Strong Systems	Eigen	Heaven Gifts
$9.99	$12.99	$19.99
In Stock	In Stock	In Stock
Free Shipping	Free Shipping	Free Shipping
Buy Now	Buy Now	Buy Now

FIGURE 5.8   Results on an e-commerce website from search with a spelling error.

Now, when a tumbler with a straw is clicked on (Figure 5.9), you see in the 'more to consider' section, a lot of other tumblers, most with a straw as in Figure 5.10, show up because that's what the kind of tumbler image you first clicked on.

Carnival cup with lid and straw
Heaven Gifts

$19.99
★★★★★ 1876

In Stock
Free Shipping

Quantity
1

Add to
cart

FIGURE 5.9 Tumbler with a straw - product page.

More to consider

Glass Tumbler 3 pk
$32.99

Glass Tumbler 20oz
$12.99

Coffee tumbler
$19.99

Simple sipper
$9.99

FIGURE 5.10 Tumbler with a straw – more to consider section.

Overall, popular applications of NLP in e-commerce include the following.

Product recommendations

From detecting typos to surfacing results most relevant to the search presented by different users, NLP powers intelligent search functionality and recommendations. Using NLP on product descriptions and past search data, similar items that may be of interest to consumers are recommended and this is a widely popular application in this industry. An example can be seen in Figure 5.10.

Comment classification

Analyzing comments at an individual level or an aggregated level helps e-commerce businesses understand their product attractions and shortcomings. NLP is used for the classification of customer comments into topics based on the content contained within the comment and product information. These classifications can also be made available to the end user for sifting through relevant review comments.

Let's say you're searching for formal pants on an e-commerce website, and then you click on a product. There are a lot of reviews, and a platform for customers to rate and categorize their reviews, such as their product size, how they rate the 'true to size' metric, etc. But then some categories are not filled in by the customer but are embedded in their comment - such as size, fit, and color. The comment could contain information about the size, fit, and/or color of the product, but there may not be a straightforward way to find that out without reading through all the comments. With NLP, these comments are categorized algorithmically so that the consumer is able to get the right view of the attributes that they might be interested in, that they would not have the insights to otherwise. This can be seen in Figure 5.11.

Sentiment analysis

Sentiment analysis helps businesses understand their product shortcomings by analyzing reviews of customers who have purchased a product.

Chatbots

Amazon, Zara, and many such businesses offer their customers the option of using chat to interact with customer service. When you start the chat, typically there are a few questions that the chatbot asks you and tries to give you automated answers before it transfers you to a customer service representative. Something really basic like order status or return status can be easily communicated without actually connecting you to a human representative. The chatbot can also guide you to answers to frequently asked questions (FAQs) as seen in Figure 5.12. It is a popular use case for creating quicker solutions where some of the answers can be presented to the user without the need for human-to-human interactions, along with the round-the-clock availability of such services.

Customer interaction analytics

Calls or chats happening between customers and customer service representatives are analyzed to better solve consumer complaints and questions and make their experience better in the future. NLP helps analyze when a user may be frustrated or happy to optimize the interaction. Furthermore, data generated from the chat is used to train models that recommend responses that the customer service representatives can use for chatting with customers.

Another area of analytics is the search queries used by users. This helps identify trends and popular product types which can help inform stocking decisions.

Marketing

NLP helps inform marketing efforts by analyzing searches and identifying the keywords that should be on different types of products for increased discoverability.

Language translation

Language translation enhances the quality of a business's global reach. Language translation services are built using NLP to translate text on websites in different geographical regions.

Reviews related to

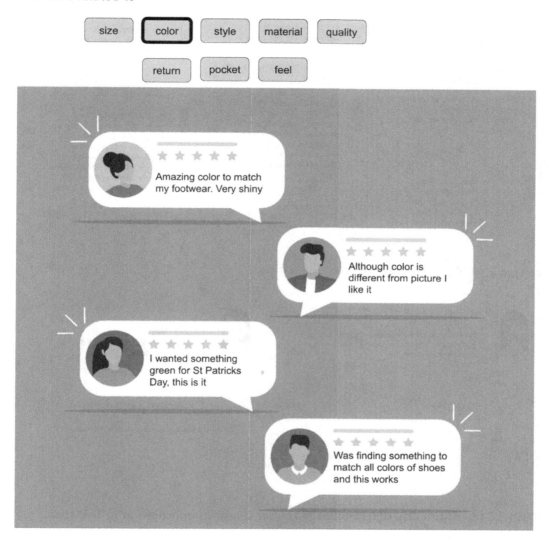

FIGURE 5.11 Customer review section showcasing comment classification into types.

Sensitive information removal

Any sensitive information that a user may enter in comments or chat can be identified and removed using NLP. To protect the company from privacy invasion claims, Figure 5.13 shows an example where a potential credit-card number is censored and edited in a live chat before the message is sent to the agent.

Ads

Just like the social media space, text data on e-commerce websites are categorized using NLP to aid the advertising field.

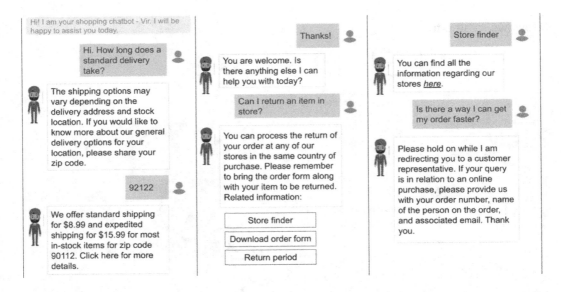

FIGURE 5.12 E-commerce chatbot.

FIGURE 5.13 Automatic detection of potential sensitive information in live chat.

5.4 TRAVEL AND HOSPITALITY

5.4.1 What is travel and hospitality?

The travel and hospitality industry includes a broad range of businesses including airlines, hotels, tour operators, travel consolidators, tourist boards, cruise lines, railroads, private transportation providers, car rental services, resorts, and lodging. The global tourism and travel industry contributed USD 5.8 billion to the global GDP in 2021 [91, 160].

5.4.2 Language data generated

The main sources of text data in this domain comes from user comments and interactions with customer service, followed by hotel, rooms, bookings, and airline descriptions.

5.4.3 NLP in travel and hospitality

Machine Learning and deep learning have helped the industry resort to data-driven smart decisions around pricing, customer service, and marketing areas. NLP improves the efficiencies of some major processes in this domain. A large number of businesses leverage NLP in this domain. For example, Placemakr, a technology-enabled hospitality company in the USA, explores NLP, statistical modeling, and machine learning for understanding customer engagement, optimizing operations, and maximizing revenue for hotels and multi-family properties across the country.

Some of the applications of NLP in travel and hospitality include the following.

Chatbots

Chatbots provide an easy and resource-efficient solution to common customer requirements such as retrieving bookings, making new bookings, inquiring about upcoming travel, finding information for a booking, and sorting out common complaints. Chatbots are capable of answering questions such as; does the hotel have free Wi-Fi? What is my seat number?

Chatbots are also useful in providing 24x7 service to customers without the involvement of actual human agents. An example of such a chatbot can be seen in Figure 5.14. Furthermore, only special requests that the chatbot can't resolve are forwarded to human agents as default, which helps make the operations efficient.

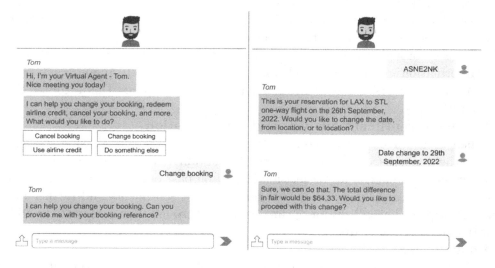

FIGURE 5.14 Hospitality bookings chatbot.

Chatbots are also built across the social media pages of businesses. For instance, the Kayak chatbot is simple to engage with and easy to interact with. You type a message to @Kayak within Facebook Messenger and the bot immediately responds with an option to help you find a flight, hotel, rental car, and more. An example of such a chatbot can be seen in Figure 5.4.

Personalized tour recommendation

User search preferences regarding their holidays can form an analytical data piece for personalized recommendations. In the past decade, big data technologies have allowed businesses to collect such information at scale and build personalized recommendation systems. NLP tools aid in creating custom tour packages that rightly fit the individual's pocket while providing them the desired experience [91].

Marketing

An important aspect of travel and hospitality includes marketing efforts. Understanding the consumer segments and their response to select offers and services aids in structuring efficient marketing strategies. Any interaction with consumers in terms of surveys and comments helps establish trends and create customer groups (also called segments). Each customer segment can then be targeted in ways that are most likely to appeal to the segment. For example, it was reported that after deploying IBM Watson Ads conversational system, Best Western Hotels and Resorts achieved a 48% incremental lift in visits [221]. This system delivered unique responses to each customer.

Document analysis

NLP-based tools find use in document classification and helping technicians find relevant information from complex databases of manuals. For instance, airline and aircraft maintenance procedures can be significantly helped by NLP document analysis and search functionalities [92].

Furthermore, in the age of digitization, any handwritten notes can be converted to text using NLP techniques.

Mosaic ATM[2] is a Virginia, US-based company that provides AI-powered aviation solutions. They use NLP to gather insights from text, voice, audio, image, and speech to inform operational and strategic decision-making across any aerospace business unit. Services provided include document anomaly detection, aircraft maintenance using information extraction and classification, aviation safety report analysis, and more. Their customers include United Airlines, Hawaiin Airlines, Delta, United States Navy, and NASA.

Comment sentiment analysis and categorization

When users leave negative comments about a hotel or flight, businesses need to address the concerns of the individuals to maintain trust in their service quality. Today, consumers make a lot of decisions based on past online reviews of a business. NLP algorithms can classify comments into different sentiments and further bucket them into topics. This allows for optimally sifting through user comments to address concerns and analyze feedback.

Image-to-text

OCR is used in hospitality to convert receipts and invoices into digital records that can be extracted for accounting and analytical purposes.

---

[2]https://mosaicatm.com/aviation-natural-language-processing/

5.5 MARKETING

5.5.1 What is marketing?

Marketing is a broad industry associated with promoting or selling products and services. It includes market research and advertising.

The four P's of marketing; product, price, place, and promotion; make up the essential mix a company needs to market a product or service. The term marketing mix was coined by Neil Borden who was a professor of advertising at the Harvard Graduate School of Business Administration [195].

Marketing is a need that applies to most industry verticals. One of the main objectives is to identify ideal customers and draw their attention to a product or service.

5.5.2 Language data generated

Text data for this domain largely comes from product descriptions, customer interactions, comments, and website descriptions.

5.5.3 NLP in marketing

I was searching for king bed frames using Google Search, and later on, while browsing a social media platform I came across ads for king mattresses. See Figures 5.15 and 5.16. Has something like this happened to you? This is an example of advertising.

Advertisers want their ads to get in front of the desired audience and attain this with the help of ad publishers for hosting the ads. Entities from New York Times to part-time bloggers are considered digital publishers. Advertisers want to reach their desired audience, and publishers publish the ads and use them to monetize their content and fund their overheads.

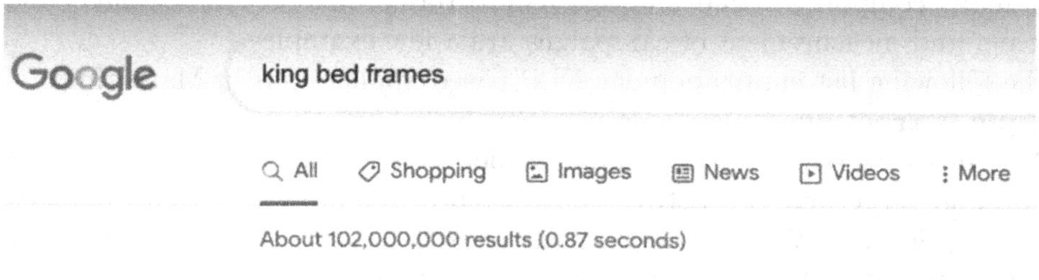

FIGURE 5.15 Searching the web for king bed frames.

The target audience is identified using cookies and IP addresses. These are essentially text files in your browser that track the information you search for. An IP address is like a house address for your computer that shows where you are located. Both cookies and IP addresses together help advertisers reach you. This is how searching for content in one place leads to related ads in another.

Many companies such as IBM (IBM Watson Advertising) and Salesforce [222] leverage NLP for marketing-related offerings. They serve several clients in their mar-

FIGURE 5.16 Advertisement on social media for king mattress.

keting efforts. For example, Salesforce Einstein's predictions are leveraged by Marriott hotels, furniture seller Room & Board, and others [223]. The Marketing domain includes many components that leverage NLP. Product and service verbiage, audience targeting, and measurement of campaigns are a few examples.

The following list entails popular NLP-based applications in Marketing.

Topic extraction

Content categorization is a popular implementation of NLP for effective content creation and targeting. Extracting topics from a free-form text that your audience is interested in, including the kind of keywords that they may be drawn towards, is bucketed into topics for categorical filtering. This not only informs about audience interests but also aids in analysis reports and recommendations of what brands can create that will resonate with their audience.

Sentiment analysis

Sentiment analysis on free-form text enables the understanding of consumer interaction and reaction to a product or a service. Using this analysis, marketers are able to structure their own product or service in a way to best serve the customers.

Audience identification

Audience identification is helpful for target messaging so that delivered content resonates with consumers and is presented to them in the way that is most likely to receive engagement. Since the audience interacts with a lot of text on the web, text data forms a large part of identifying audiences and their affinities.

Creating buyer personas in marketing campaigns is based on the product or services defined by common traits of the people they want to reach. This definition depends on the social, demographic, economical, and topical interests of the target audience, for instance-males, 55+, living in North Carolina, and interested in baseball. The interest in baseball is determined by related content searched for and browsed. Not just the term 'baseball', but also other terms like 'Aaron Judge' convey interest in the topic. NLP helps with establishing such relationships and classifications.

Chatbots

Chatbots are used in many companies to support marketing efforts. Answering basic questions, improving customer service, and analyzing user intent assists in round-the-clock service, understanding consumers, and selling relevant products. Customers are also targeted using chats. As we mentioned in the section on travel and hospitality, Best Western Hotels and Resorts achieved a 48% incremental lift in visits after deploying IBM Watson Ads [221]. This conversation system delivered unique responses to each customer based on their questions.

Another use case is analyzing chat data and presenting advertisements based on the identified topics and interest relevance.

Trend identification

Identification of trends that vary by consumer segment or time is important in this domain. Trends using search history, product descriptions, articles, and social media data inform marketing strategies.

AI-based slogan writing

AI technologies are popularly used for the automated identification of trends and for coming up with slogan recommendations. Catchy slogans are known to help in marketing content. The online tool - Frase [175] is a slogan generator powered by NLP. Figure 5.17 shows a slogan recommendation for a ring size adjustment product.

Image-to-text

Understanding purchase history, location, image posts, and comments help with brand strategy and analytics. OCR is used for such record digitization.

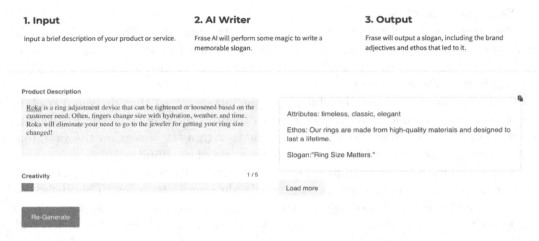

1. Input

Input a brief description of your product or service.

2. AI Writer

Frase AI will perform some magic to write a memorable slogan.

3. Output

Frase will output a slogan, including the brand adjectives and ethos that led to it.

Product Description

Roka is a ring adjustment device that can be tightened or loosened based on the customer need. Often, fingers change size with hydration, weather, and time. Roka will eliminate your need to go to the jeweler for getting your ring size changed!

Attributes: timeless, classic, elegant

Ethos: Our rings are made from high-quality materials and designed to last a lifetime.

Slogan:"Ring Size Matters."

Creativity   1 / 5

Load more

Re-Generate

FIGURE 5.17   AI-based slogan recommendation. Source [175].

5.6   INSURANCE

5.6.1   What is insurance?

Insurance is a type of risk management commonly used to protect against the risk of uncertain financial loss. Some popular types of insurance include home or property insurance, medical insurance, life insurance, disability insurance, automobile insurance, travel insurance, fire insurance, and marine insurance.

Insurance typically consists of a legal agreement between you and the insurer containing terms of the policy and coverages. To request your insurance to cover a loss, a formal request needs to be filed, also called a claim. A claim is a request for payment for loss or damage to something your insurance covers. Claim errors cause insurance companies to lose money if the risk is not estimated correctly. For example, there have already been 2,950 pandemic-related employment claims in the United States including disputes that range from remote work to workplace safety and discrimination [213]. Underwriters (members of financial organizations that evaluate risks) benefit from risk mitigation by adding restrictions to new or renewed policies.

Fraud has a large financial impact on this industry. Property-casualty fraud leads to loss of more than USD 30 billion from businesses each year, while auto insurance 'premium leakage' is a USD 29 billion problem [213]. Identification of fraud is key.

5.6.2   Language data generated

A lot of text data is generated in insurance companies, including claim forms, applications, emails, chat-based conversations with customers, marketing documents, and contracts [212]. Other types of data containing text include bills and receipts.

5.6.3   NLP in insurance

NLP saves the insurance industry both time and money. For instance, Lemonade [176] is an insurance company that provides personalized insurance policies and quotes to customers through the use of its chatbot, Maya. Maya has reportedly processed a theft claim in the past for a USD 979 lost coat within 3 seconds. This process included reviewing the claim, cross-referencing it with the customer's policy, running 18 anti-fraud algorithms, approving the claim, wiring instructions to the bank, updating the customer, and closing the claim [115].

Sprout.AI [177] is another example of a company offering end-to-end claim automation for insurers. They use image recognition and OCR, audio analysis, and automatic document analysis using NLP techniques to analyze text data from insurance claims. They also pair text with external real-time data like weather and geolocation to enrich their analysis. The startup's technology reportedly settles claims within minutes, while also checking for fraud [115].

A few key areas that have benefitted from NLP in Insurance include customer service and satisfaction, underwriting automation, fraud detection, risk assessment, and claims management.

The following examples showcase applications of NLP in Insurance.

Chatbots

A survey indicated more than 80% of insurance customers want personalized offers and recommendations from their auto, home, and life insurance providers [115]. Virtual assistants such as chatbots can help with this problem. With chatbots, services as such can be available 24x7. Moreover, virtual agents can be trained to deliver a more personalized experience to customers, as if the user is talking to one of the human agents.

Allstate partnered with Earley Information Science to develop a virtual assistant called ABIe [171] to help human agents know better about their products. This was especially helpful when Allstate launched its business insurance division. ABIe can process 25k inquiries per month, leveraging NLP and helping make corporate agents more self-sufficient to better sell products to their customers [115].

Amelia is a technology company that was formerly known as IPsoft. They developed a conversational AI technology [172] for processing claims. Amelia's conversational agent can pull up a user's policy information, verify their identity, collect information relevant to the claim the user wants to file, and walk them through the process step-by-step.

An example of an insurance chatbot can be seen in Figure 5.18.

Customer service analysis

Analysis of customer interactions helps identify customers who might be at risk of cancellation of services, or on the other hand interested in further products. Customer conversation or comment analysis helps improve customer support.

Information classification

Information classification helps agents look up information faster without having to manually sift through documents. Much of the labor goes into the correct classification of information so that the text can be routed appropriately or acted upon based on the business need. NLP-based solutions have proven helpful for this use case. For example, Accenture developed its own NLP-based solution for document classification named MALTA [170]. Its job is to automate the analysis and classification of text to help with fast and easy information access. Accenture claimed the solution provided 30% more accurate classification than when the process was done manually [115].

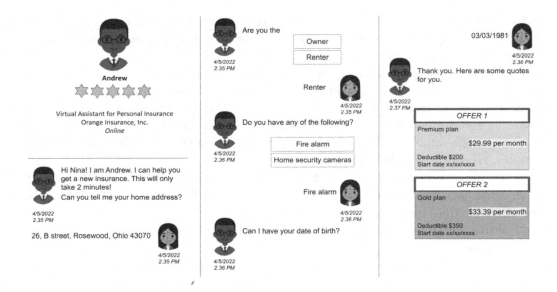

FIGURE 5.18 Insurance chatbot example.

Fraud detection

Insurance frauds are estimated to be more than USD 40 billion per year in cost by the FBI [5]. Insurance frauds cause high premiums and impact insurers as well as customers. NLP-based solutions are able to better analyze fraudulent claims and increase their correct detection.

The company, Shift Technology, developed an NLP-based technology to help insurers detect fraudulent claims before they pay them out. Their service is called FORCE and it applies a variety of AI technologies, including NLP, to score each claim according to the likelihood of fraud. The performance of their service is gaining appreciation resulting in the company signing a partnership with Central Insurance Companies to detect fraudulent claims in the auto and property sectors [16].

Risk assessment

Natural disasters are unavoidable and in the US alone, the cost of billion-dollar disasters has been on the rise. The average over the past five years is 16 events per year, costing just over USD 121 billion per year [103]. NLP-based tools have been a popular component in risk assessment. As per a survey examining the adoption of AI by risk and compliance professionals, 37% of respondents claimed that NLP was a core component or extensively used in their organization [46].

The consulting company - Cognizant, uses NLP to predict flood risks in the United States to better underwrite policies for their insurance clients [103]. They claimed that NLP helped with a more accurate definition of risks, provided useful insights to help with policy refinement, and resulted in a 25% improved policy acceptance rate.

Information extraction

The process of underwriting requires the availability of analysis of policies and documents in bulk quantities. This part of the insurance process is highly error-prone as it depends on how well the analysis was performed. With NLP, relevant information extraction can help underwriters access risk levels better. Entity extraction such as dates, names, locations, etc., help underwriters find information that would've taken a much longer time to look up manually.

For example, DigitalOwl [174] and Zelros [208] are two companies that have developed solutions to analyze, understand and extract relevant information from documents to help underwriters make their decisions faster, and with more accuracy [115].

This also finds application in claim management. Processing claims can be time-consuming. With NLP, agents are able to auto-fill details of a claim by using communication from customers in natural language.

Image-to-text

Several invoices are available on paper rather than a digital format. It is important to place automation to process such documents to increase processing speed. Thus conversion of such records to text is an important application that allows the usage of NLP on the text extracted for processing, analytics, classification, or a combination thereof. This is done using OCR. An example can be seen in Figure 5.19.

Date	Description		Charges	Credits
07-12-22	Guest Room		179.00	
07-12-22	State Tax		10.74	
07-12-22	City/Local Tax		19.69	
07-12-22	State-Cost Recovery Fee		1.10	
07-13-22	Guest Room		179.00	
07-13-22	State Tax		10.74	
07-13-22	City/Local Tax		19.69	
07-13-22	State-Cost Recovery Fee		1.10	
07-14-22	Guest Room		179.00	
07-14-22	State Tax		10.74	
07-14-22	City/Local Tax		19.69	
07-14-22	State-Cost Recovery Fee		1.10	
07-15-22	Visa	XXXXXXXXXXXX0395 XX/XX		631.59

FIGURE 5.19 Conversion of invoices to text using OCR.

5.7 OTHER COMMON USE CASES

We have observed that chatbots happen to be an application spread across most industry verticals. Sentiment analysis appears to be another common application that is used for a multitude of reasons across industries. Text similarities, topic modeling, and classification are some others that find use in applications across domains. Other than the ones we have looked at, there are some applications that are spread across in terms of usage by individuals and/or industries. These include products that people interact with often. Let's look at them below.

5.7.1 Writing and email

Several individuals leverage writing improvement tools for different communications, such as emails, work documents, etc. Services such as Grammarly[3] help restructure a sentence using NLP. Auto-complete on your phones and emails (see Figure 5.20) helps with common sentence completion. Microsoft Word, Google Docs, and many text editors also help identify potential spelling mistakes, excessive word repetitions, and grammatical errors.

Many organizations also use domain-specific autocomplete / next-word prediction models to speed up the documentation process for their employees.

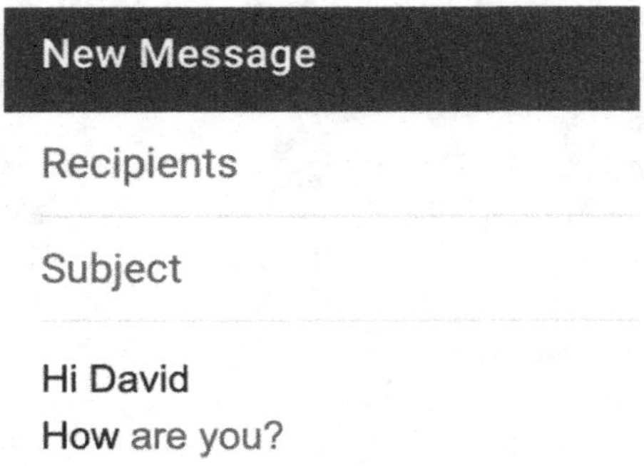

New Message

Recipients

Subject

Hi David
How are you?

FIGURE 5.20 Auto sentence completion suggestions in Gmail.

Writing emails has become a part of all work cultures today. Other than that, NLP has aided technologies to help in spam detection (Figure 5.21). We still may get some spam emails into our regular inbox, but technology plays a major role in separating out true spam, thus saving users time and preventing clicks on unsolicited URLs.

Other applications include bucketing email into different categories, such as primary, social, promotions, and more, as seen in Figure 5.22.

5.7.2 Home assistants

Ever owned or heard of Amazon Echo and Google Home? These are little devices you can plug into any socket in your home and ask questions, make them play your music, ask for the news, set alarms, and turn on your lights, oven, or TV when paired with

---

[3]https://app.grammarly.com/

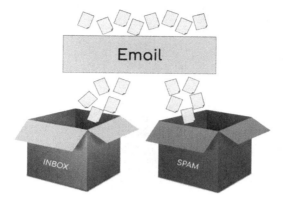

FIGURE 5.21 Email filtering leading to division of incoming mail between inbox and spam.

Categories

Social   1,922

Updates   4,190

Forums

Promotions   11

FIGURE 5.22 Email classification in Gmail.

other smart devices. Several devices get launched each year that integrate with your existing smart home set-up to make your home a smart home. With home assistants like Echo and Google Home, a lot is happening at the backend with models in the cloud, but the start of it remains the voice commands. It needs the ability to listen to you, understand what you are asking for, and then provide you with the best answer. How does that work? Your voice is translated into text and further processing happens thereafter on the text data for understanding intent. That's right, NLP powers the technology providing critical abilities without which we wouldn't know these virtual home assistants.

5.7.3 Recruiting

Recruiting is a common process across industry verticals. When an open job position gets bulk of applications, NLP techniques can sift through various PDF resumes to filter down to ones that match the closest to the open position requirements.

## CHAPTER 6

NLP Applications - Developing Usage

6.1 HEALTHCARE

6.1.1 What is healthcare?

The healthcare industry (also called the medical industry or health economy) is a collection of sectors that provide goods and services to treat people with medical needs. Drugs, medical equipment, healthcare facilities like hospitals and clinics, and managed healthcare including medical insurance policy providers belong to this domain. Insurance is a large field on its own, which we have looked into as a separate industry vertical in the previous chapter. Here, we will look into the other aspects of the healthcare industry and how NLP makes a difference.

6.1.2 Language data generated

The healthcare industry consists of many sources of text data. This includes patient records, drug-based information, doctor notes, policies, research documents and studies, and legal documents.

6.1.3 NLP in healthcare

NLP is gaining popularity in healthcare due to its potential of analyzing large volumes of patient data. Physicians spend a lot of time inputting the 'how' and the 'why' of what's happening with their patients into chart notes. When the doctor sits down with you, and documents your visit in a case note (a summary and analysis of a single case), those narratives go into the electronic health record systems (EHRs) and get stored as free text [71]. Any data embedded in the unstructured format is harder to make use of. Big data analytics in healthcare shows that up to 80% of healthcare documentation is unstructured, and therefore goes largely unutilized, since mining and extraction of this data are challenging and resource intensive [71].

According to a recent report, global NLP in the healthcare and life sciences market is expected to reach USD 3.7 billion by 2025, at a Compound Annual Growth Rate of 20.5% [106].

DOI: 10.1201/9781003264774-6

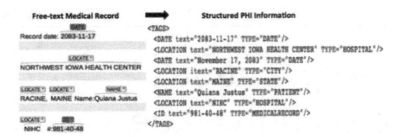

FIGURE 6.1 Classification of text into protected health information (PHI) categories. Source [202].

```
 1 Record date: 2067-11-24
      (LOCATE *)
 3 HUNTINGTON EMERGENCY DEPT VISIT

      (NAME *)              (ID *)                            (DATE)
 7 THOMAS-YOSEF,JULIA    840-91-51-9         VISIT DATE: 11/24/67
                  (NAME *)
 9 This patient was seen with Dr. Earley.
10 The patient was interviewed

12 and examined by me.
13 Resident's note reviewed and confirmed.
14 The

16 plan of care was discussed with the patient.
17 Please see chart for

19 details.
                                                    (AGE)
21 HISTORY OF PRESENTING COMPLAINT: Briefly, this is a 47-year-old

23 woman with a history of asthma and non-insulin-dependent diabetes

25 mellitus who has had three weeks of progressive substernal chest

27 pain radiating to the back with associated nausea, vomiting,

29 shortness of breath, and diaphoresis.
```

FIGURE 6.2 Example of clinical record with annotated PHI categories. Source [202].

Let's look at some applications of NLP.

Protected health information (PHI) detection

Health insurance portability and accountability act (HIPAA) requires healthcare providers, health plans, and other covered entities to protect sensitive patient health information from being disclosed without the patient's consent or knowledge. NLP finds use in automatically identifying pieces of content containing PHI using entity recognition and text classification. Figures 6.1 and 6.2 show sample classification of text to PHI from a 2014 paper [202] titled *Automatic Detection of Protected Health Information from Clinic Narratives.*

Clinical trials

Using NLP, healthcare providers can automatically review massive quantities of unstructured clinical and patient data and identify eligible candidates for clinical trials [106]. Furthermore, for doctors finding relevant clinical trials or patient data surrounding a set of symptoms can require sifting through thousands of records. With NLP, finding records similar to another record or related to a complex search query can be made easier.

Clinical support

Analyzing patient documents to cross-link symptoms embedded in unstructured text and finding case studies surrounding similar symptoms can be aided by NLP using text classification, similarity measurement, and analysis.

Research

NLP techniques help summarize large chunks of text into key points or summaries. This helps consolidate large records and documents into a readable summarized form allowing doctors and researchers to get context without having to dig through every document where applicable. Figure 6.3 depicts the algorithmic process and target.

Other research applications include algorithmically studying drug side effects, people's sentiment for pain medication, and studying a variety of symptoms and relationships using NLP.

Texts-to-text

BACKGROUND: ... Cobalamin (vitamin B12) deficiency is particularly common in the elderly ... The objective of this review is to evaluate the efficacy of oral cobalamin treatment in elderly patients.

TARGET: The efficacy was particularly highlighted when looking at the marked improvement in serum vitamin B12 levels and hematological parameters... Our experience and the present analysis support the use of oral cobalamin therapy in clinical practice

Inputs: study abstracts, BACKGROUND statement

Output: TARGET statement

FIGURE 6.3 Document summarization in medical records. Source [63].

Speech-to-text

Many doctors today use audio recording devices to capture notes from patient visits. These are then translated into the text to fill up patient chart notes and visit summaries. This saves doctors typing time. Abridge[1] and Medrecorder[2] are examples of audio recording products and transcribing services.

Language interpretation and translation

Translators and interpreters both work to provide meaningful communication between different languages. Translators work with written words, while interpreters work with spoken words. Helping patients with communication barriers to get medical help is greatly advanced by the help of NLP in language translation technologies. Many businesses offering these services exist today and leverage NLP. Healthcare facilities like UCSD Health are able to partly adopt such services, but still keep an on-site human language translator [73]. With time and increased efficiencies with NLP, there is a large opportunity for growth in such services.

Imparied speech-to-text applications

Speech impairment in different individuals may not follow a standard pattern. It is custom to each individual. Hence, it has been a technological challenge to develop

---

[1] https://www.abridge.com/
[2] https://www.medcorder.com/

intelligent applications that can help individuals with speech impairment communicate. Google has been researching techniques to make this possible. Translation of impaired speech-to-text finds applications in engaging in complete communication with other individuals where the technology is able to fill in the gaps to make the language understandable. The challenge of needing custom models per user remains an issue. Research is being conducted on building models that are custom trained on an individual's voice samples [40].

Drug interactions

Detecting drug-to-drug interactions (DDI) is important because information on DDIs can help prevent adverse effects from drug combinations. This field is especially of use to the Pharma industry. There is always an increasing amount of new drug interaction research getting published in the biomedical domain. Manually extracting drug interactions from literature has been a laborious task. Drug interaction discovery using NLP by sifting through millions of records has been a subject of research recently and has proved to show good accuracy improvements in DDI [110, 149].

Image-to-text

Medical notes, prescriptions, and receipts are passed through digitization techniques for information extraction and record-keeping using OCR.

6.2 LAW

6.2.1 What is law?

Law is a system of rules that are enforceable by governmental institutions. The legal industry is all about sectors that provide legal goods and services. A lawyer is a person who practices law. People need lawyers in many stages of life, including work, marriage, and beyond. The size of the legal services market worldwide in 2020 was reported at USD 713 million and is expected to reach USD 900 million + by 2025 [61].

6.2.2 Language data generated

This industry vertical is all about documents and paperwork. Thus, the most common sources of text data comprise legal documents.

There is a large pool of associated data for this industry, especially around text documents. LexisNexis and Westlaw (acquired by Thomson Reuters), Wolters Kluwer, and Bloomberg Law are the big players in the legal database world and most law firms have subscriptions to most or all of these.

6.2.3 NLP in law

Just like the rest of the industry domains, AI is beginning to find use in legal sector operations. While AI adoption in law is still new, lawyers today have a wide variety of intelligent tools at their disposal [70]. NLP happens to be an important sub-division of AI in the field of law. Legal document automation is arguably among the earliest commercial natural language generation systems [57].

Legal systems became a popular topic starting in the 1970s and 1980s. Richard Susskind's Expert Systems in Law, Oxford University Press, 1987 is a popular example exploring artificial intelligence and legal reasoning [167]. In recent years, the field has become increasingly popular with the rise of many start-ups that make use of deep learning techniques in the context of legal applications.

CaseText [86] and CaseMine [42] were both founded in 2013 and provide interfaces to help find relevant material by uploading a passage or even an entire brief that provides context for the search. Another example is Ross Intelligence which was founded in 2014 and offers the ability to make a query (ask a question) as you would naturally talk to a lawyer.

Some of the ways NLP is getting used in law are as follows.

Legal research

Legal research is one of the most popular applications of NLP in law. The crux of any legal process involves good research, creating documents, and sifting through other relevant documents. It is popularly known that the legal processes take time and this is one of the reasons why. NLP can help shorten this time by streamlining the process. NLP-powered applications are able to convert a natural language query into legal terms. It becomes easier to find documents relevant to the search query, thus enabling a faster research process. NLP can also help find similar case documents to help lawyers with references.

In a patent dispute case between Apple and Samsung (the years 2011–2016), Samsung reportedly collected and processed around 3.6TB or 11,108,653 documents with a processing cost of USD 13 million over 20 months. Today, a heavy focus is on creating optimized techniques for categorizing the relevancy of documents as quickly and efficiently as possible [57].

Language translation

Contract review programs can process documents in 20 different languages, helping lawyers to understand and draft documents across geographies. OpenText has introduced an e-discovery platform called Axcelerate; and SDL, known for its translation products and services, provides a Multilingual eDiscovery Solution, enabling access to foreign language case-related content via translation [57].

Chatbots

A survey taken in 2018 highlighted that 59% of clients expect their lawyers to be available after hours [49]. Chatbots are of great help to answer straightforward questions of clients. It gives customers access to communication beyond regular working hours without the involvement of actual humans working off hours. Such services also field people's initial questions to direct them to the services they need faster [70]. An example includes a chatbot based on IBM Watson created by Norton Rose Fulbright, an Australian law firm, to answer standard questions about data breaches and was active until 2022 [21]. Figure 6.4 shows an example of such a chatbot.

Document drafting, review, and analysis

Word choice is prime in legal documents. Any errors in a contract can open it up to unintended consequences. With the help of NLP tools, lawyers can get documents cross-checked without spending additional manual hours. ContractProbe [53] and PrivacyPolicyCheck are some examples that let you upload documents for review.

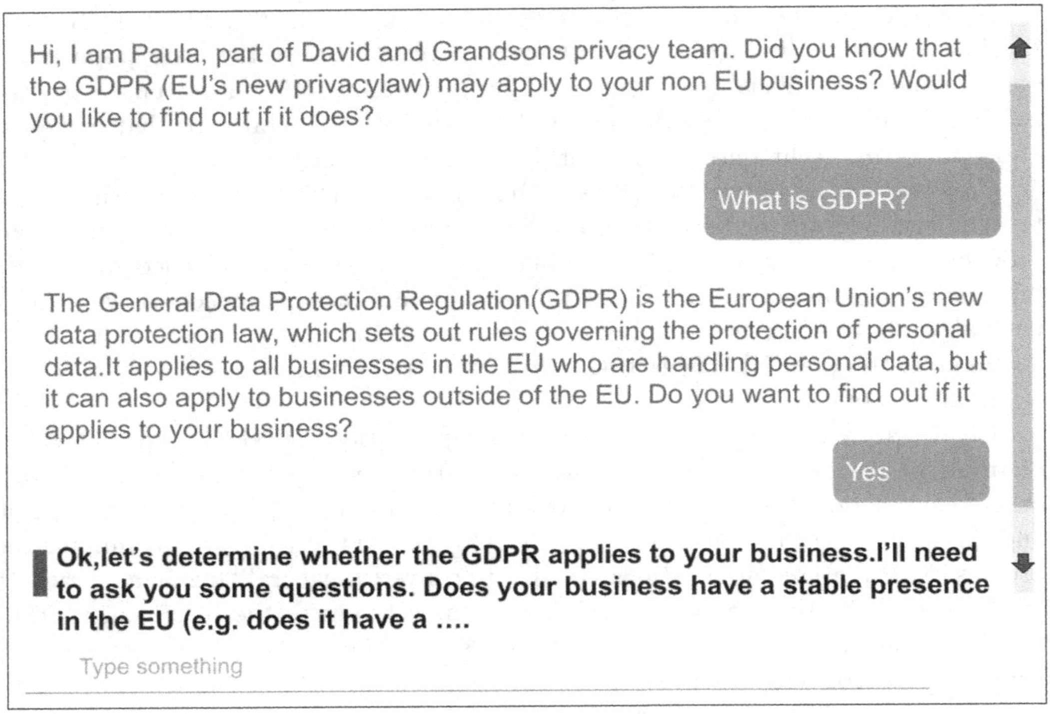

Hi, I am Paula, part of David and Grandsons privacy team. Did you know that the GDPR (EU's new privacylaw) may apply to your non EU business? Would you like to find out if it does?

What is GDPR?

The General Data Protection Regulation(GDPR) is the European Union's new data protection law, which sets out rules governing the protection of personal data.It applies to all businesses in the EU who are handling personal data, but it can also apply to businesses outside of the EU. Do you want to find out if it applies to your business?

Yes

Ok,let's determine whether the GDPR applies to your business.I'll need to ask you some questions. Does your business have a stable presence in the EU (e.g. does it have a ....

Type something

FIGURE 6.4 A GDPR compliance guidance chatbot.

Furthermore, services are available that create templates for contracts based on a law or a policy using NLP. This helps create basic versions of contracts. Kira Systems [98], founded in 2015, and Seal Software, founded in 2010 and acquired by DocuSign in 2020 for USD 188 million, offer pre-built models for hundreds of common provisions covering a range of contract types.

Other services also help organize and file documents automatically based on contained language. NLP aids in the automation of such processes, thereby saving lawyers time and enabling them to assist more clients.

6.3 REAL ESTATE

6.3.1 What is real estate?

Real estate is a broad categorization that refers to property consisting of land and improvements or development made on top of the land. There are different types of real estate.

1. Land: Vacant land or undeveloped property.

2. Residential: Types of properties where humans reside, such as single-family homes, condominiums, apartments, and townhomes.

3. Commercial: Office buildings, shopping malls, stores, parking lots, medical centers, and hotels are examples of this type of real estate.

4. Industrial: Factories, mechanical productions, research and development, construction, transportation, logistics, and warehouses are examples of this type of real estate.

The real estate industry includes many branches, including developers, brokerages, sales and marketing, property lending, property management, and professional services.

6.3.2 Language data generated

The main forms of language data generated in real estate include property listing descriptions, legal documents, and customer interactions.

6.3.3 NLP in real estate

Let's talk about a full-service real estate brokerage such as Redfin (`https://www.redfin.com/`). On this platform, people can post about properties they want to sell, and interested buyers can look at available properties and their details. Sellers can describe their property on Redfin using an address, price, available date, home tour schedule, and details such as square footage, number of bedrooms, number of bathrooms, and other features. This is further broken down into sqft. area of the bedrooms, appliances, homeowner's association (HOA) fees, etc. Furthermore, they can also add a text-based description of their property to highlight the listing and its attractive features.

For listings missing key pieces of information, the information can be extracted from text descriptions so it is easier to find and filter for buyers [15]. This helps improve the searchability of properties and checks mismatches between descriptions and explicitly filled-out columns.

Many companies leverage AI for real estate [224]. A study [66] reported that NLP analyzes hidden values in text descriptions, increasing the property value between 1% and 6% on average.

Popular uses of NLP in real estate are as follows.

Information extraction

The ability to extract relevant entities such as the number of bedrooms, solar panels, square footage area, etc., from text is advantageous for the industry. It finds use in auto-filling fields from property descriptions as seen in Figure 6.5.

Chatbots

Chatbots reduce manual effort and improve customer experience. They also help in handling large amounts of customer volume thereby only routing the needed requests to human agents. Furthermore, feedback from recorded customer interactions further helps with analytics and improvements in the service.

Chatbots in real estate usually assist users in searching for inventory. Figure 6.6 shows an example of such a chatbot. Another example is AIRE Software

Beautiful 3 bedroom 3 bathroom single family home. The gated community offers (2) swimming pools and a children's playground. Enjoy newer dual paned, energy efficient windows throughout the home. You will easily notice the charming, newer mantle above the inviting fireplace, that you can nestle in front of on chilly winter evenings. There is also a newer screen door at front entry, and an energy efficient, leased solar system which was installed approximately (4) years ago for big energy savings.

3 bedroom
3 bathroom
Swimming pool
Children's playground
Dual paned windows
Fireplace
Leased solar system

FIGURE 6.5 Real estate listing description with information extraction results on the right to identify key pieces of information.

(getaire.com.au/meet-rita/), an Australian startup that offers an AI-powered virtual assistant for real estate companies called *Rita*. *Rita assists* real estate agents in lead generation by integrating customer relationship manager (CRM) data and property data.

Legal document review

Brokerages have millions of documents stored in their digital archives. NLP systems can go through large amounts of these documents and help with document summarization to present shorter summaries. NLP also helps find relevant docu-

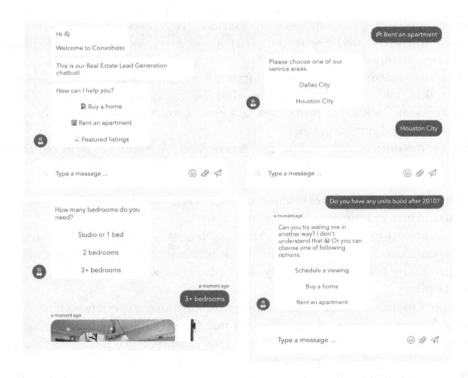

FIGURE 6.6 Convoboss: Real estate chatbot for 24/7 lead generation. Source [54].

ments and filter down large corpora for a given use case. For example, a Brazilian startup, Beaver (beaver.com.br/), leverages NLP to improve the working efficiency of real estate agents by speeding up document analysis [224]. They extract information from documents surrounding property registrations and purchase contracts to create summarized reports.

For instance, underwriting is the process through which an individual or institution takes on financial risk (e.g., loans, insurance, or investment) for a certain fee. The process of underwriting requires the availability of an analysis of policies and documents in large quantities.

Compliance assurance

General data protection regulation (GDPR) and California consumer privacy act (CCPA) compliances are in place to protect consumer privacy. GDPR helps ensure a user's information is not stored by a business outside of geographical bounds. CCPA-compliant businesses must ensure a user's information is erased from their systems if a California user issues such a request. NLP techniques help identify and remove consumer information.

Personal identifiable information (PII) identification and removal

PII refers to information that can reveal the identity of an individual, such as email ID, phone number, government ID number, etc. At times certain personal information may make its way into property listings or documents unintentionally. NLP algorithms help with automatically identifying such information from free-form text with the help of named entity recognition (NER).

6.4   OIL AND GAS

6.4.1   What is oil and gas?

Oil and natural gas are high-impact industries in the energy market and play an influential role in the global economy as the world's primary fuel source. Production and distribution of oil and gas are complex and capital-intensive tasks, often requiring state-of-the-art technologies.

This sector can widely be divided into three operational areas; upstream for exploration and production of oil and natural gas, midstream for transportation and storage, and downstream for refining and selling.

6.4.2   Language data generated

In general, data generated in this field commonly includes well and reservoir reports, measurements, risk logs, and injury records, often combined with other data modalities.

Finding appropriate quality and quantity of data is often the biggest hindrance in AI. This has been a large concern in oil and gas. The terminology of the text is also highly technical involving a lot of codes and jargon. Furthermore, reasons for data limitation can stem from a variety of factors, including privacy terms, regulatory terms, copyright, IP protection, or simply lack of proper collection and storage. As part of digital transformation in oil and gas, the DELFI cognitive E&P environment and industry-wide collaboration at the Open Subsurface Data Universe (OSDU) Forum have undertaken to make data availability easier with the digitization of decades-old reports and documents [26]. Such availability makes NLP applications a large and increasing possibility in the industry.

6.4.3 NLP in oil and gas

Usage of NLP in the oil and gas industry may seem odd at first, but several publications and articles have exposed various applications and advantages of NLP including a reduction in procurement costs, data-driven well and reservoir planning, maximizing efficiency, improving safety analysis, and minimizing risks.

Alejandro Betancourt, who leads the analytics team at Columbian oil and gas company Ecopetrol, suggests that oil and gas companies can potentially improve their enhanced oil recovery (EOR) rates by using NLP, computer vision, and machine learning for drilling and exploration data [30].

Below are the primary NLP applications.

Risk identification

NLP finds use in the oil and gas industry for risk identification and assessment. For experienced drilling engineers, their past experiences have historically been the driving factor for risk assessments. With NLP, bulk logs going outside the scope of one engineer's experience can assist in the process. Chevron [173] maintains datasets on prior risk assessments and prior issues encountered in disparate systems. The risk assessment database contains descriptions of risks from historical risk assessments, and the well operations database contains descriptions of unexpected events and associated unexpected-event codes, which categorize the unexpected events [200]. A system was created for allowing a project drilling engineer to query for risk in natural language and get back drilling codes related to the risk. Additionally, the system returned statistics showing how often related events happened in the past and the likelihood of the issue occurring in certain fields.

Injury classification

Classifying injury logs to help identify potential risky operations and environments is yet another application of NLP. For instance, let's say a user wants to query a database of safety logs for foot injuries. Querying by searching for foot injuries using hard-set keywords such as 'foot' or 'foot injury' are likely to return a combination of relevant and irrelevant records, thus narrowing the insights. False matches for keywords like 'foot' might be common given that it is also a word used for the measurement unit 'foot'.

Per [200], a keyword search of the safety logs of a large utility company for 'lower body injuries' resulted in 534 entries. A semantic search, which included related terms such as 'leg', 'foot', or 'toe', returned 1027 results, many of which had nothing to do with actual injuries. A cognitive search using natural language processing techniques resulted in more accurate output with 347 incidents, with correct identification of dual-meaning words like 'foot' thereby pinpointing results to injury-related context.

A sentence like *'Was hit by a piece of plastic that had come loose while working solo on a rig.'* can be correctly classified into solo working injuries with NLP. Finding such injuries is further made easier with NLP by mapping the employee's question in natural language like 'Find incidents involving debris falling on lone employees' to the right type of classifications and results [200].

Chatbots

A virtual agent that technicians and engineers can interact with aids in making operations more time efficient. It is often critical that problems are resolved given the delicate and volatile nature of the job. With NLP employment, engineers and technicians can engage in a full dialog to get their questions answered. This enables safer and faster troubleshooting by reducing resource downtime because of unexpected issues [144].

Other than employees, chatbots are also built for businesses. For example, Shell launched an AI-based Chatbot for B2B (business-to-business) lubricant customers and distributors. Chatbots as such help find lubricants, alternatives, the right oil for a machine, and more. An example of such a virtual agent can be seen in Figure 6.7.

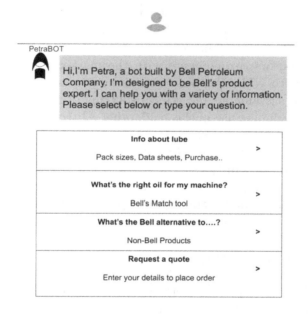

FIGURE 6.7 Petroleum company chatbot example.

Analysis of logs from employees as well as clients helps analyze feedback that in turn informs process improvements.

Crude oil price forecasting

A paper in 2019 published by Li, Shang, and Wang [109] explored a text-based crude oil price forecasting approach using deep learning, where they leveraged data from the crude oil news column from Investing.com. Topic modeling followed by the analysis of each word within the topics helped them develop the approach.

6.5 SUPPLY CHAIN

6.5.1 What is supply chain?

A supply chain is a network between a business and its suppliers to produce and distribute a specific product to the end buyer. Key functional areas of the supply chain include purchasing, manufacturing, inventory management, demand planning, warehousing, transportation, and customer service.

6.5.2 Language data generated

Primary sources of language data come from supply chain process documents, order forms and logs, and communication logs.

6.5.3 NLP in supply chain

There have been several articles and publications exploring the possibilities of using NLP for supply chain operations [216, 217]. Retailers can state requirements and place orders using natural language. The request can be analyzed with NLP techniques. Suppliers and distributors can compete with the market trends based on relevant data identification with NLP. Furthermore, manufacturers can perform automated analyses for ensuring sustainable and ethical sourcing of raw materials by suppliers. While NLP is still developing use in this field, other AI techniques are being explored for supply chain applications as well [220].

Breaking it down, some popular NLP applications include the following.

Shipment document analysis

Analyzing large volumes of shipment documents can be done faster using NLP. Techniques such as information extraction have been explored in this domain. Document analysis further has the potential of providing supply chain insights to identify areas of lag.

Relevant data identification

NLP can help identify and scan online resources for information about industry benchmark rates for transportation costs, fuel prices, and labor costs. This data also helps compare costs to market standards and identify cost optimization opportunities [105]. Since the same location or process name can be written in different ways, NLP aids in mapping data to standardized labels. Dynamically identifying relevant market data and extracting relevant information can be automated with NLP. With correct data identification and analysis, suppliers and distributors can monitor competitor data to quickly adapt to changing market trends.

Language translation

To communicate across locations for global businesses, language translation techniques with NLP help in breaking communication barriers. Stakeholders throughout the supply chain use language translation to communicate with other individuals in their native language.

Chatbots

Just like other industry domains, chatbots help reduce human time involvement by automatically answering questions across the supply chain domain. Chatbots touch several different use cases in this industry as can be seen in Figure 6.8. Tradeshift [13] is an example of a company using a procurement assistant, and there are several other advancements and potentials being explored in this domain [114]. Figure 6.9 shows a conversation with a chatbot for procurement after reported damage. Other examples include fetching natural disaster information via news sources and identifying overlap between routes and timelines to inform users of the situation, loss, and/or alternatives.

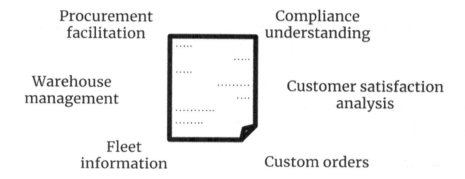

FIGURE 6.8 Uses of chatbots in different supply chain operations.

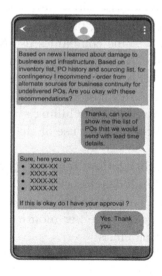

FIGURE 6.9 An example of a supply chain procurement chatbot.

Supply risk management

Comments by planners can be analyzed to identify risks and automate the risk management process in the supply chain [169]. For instance, 'Units in Chandigarh awaiting local release. Local release delay due to artwork issue.' In this comment, the cause of the interruption is an artwork issue that can be automatically extracted and classified with NLP. Companies like Coupa and Oracle leverage natural language processing for supplier risk assessment [219].

6.6 TELECOMMUNICATION

6.6.1 What is telecom?

Telecommunications (also called telecom) is defined as communicating over a distance [11]. The telecommunications industry is made up of cable companies, internet service providers, satellite companies, and telephone companies. The global telecom services market size was estimated at USD 1,657.7 billion in 2020 [75].

6.6.2 Language data generated

The primary types of language data include call audio, text messages, emails, customer interactions, and support/assistance requests.

6.6.3 NLP in telecom

The usage of NLP in telecom is gaining prominence with time. A great number of telecom operators have started deploying AI-powered solutions in both business-to-business and companies' internal processes [2].

Applications such as an automated system that can debug complaints of a consumer from an SMS using NLP techniques are prime use cases in the telecom industry. The applications do not comprise NLP alone, but the interaction and conglomeration of several NLP algorithms, engineering pipelines, and interactive services. Let's dig through some examples of how some companies use NLP for different applications.

A popular 2004 example of NLP in telecommunications is the natural-language customer service application for a telephone banking call center developed as part of the AMITIÉS dialogue project (Automated Multilingual Interaction with Information and Services) [77]. It facilitates an easier billing system that the telecom customers can directly interact with. Ever since the use of chatbot services in telecom has been on the rise.

Telia Company AB is the fifth largest telecom operator in Europe with more than 20,000 employees and over 23 million subscribers [2]. It is present in Sweden, Finland, Norway, Denmark, Lithuania, Latvia, and Estonia. Reports claim that the company saved 2,835 hours of human agent time per month [12] with a reported savings of 1 million Euros [2] by automating chats.

China Mobile is the world's largest mobile provider with more than 450 thousand employees and reported revenue of 768.1 billion CNY in 2020 [7]. It has over 942 million subscribers [161]. The company leverages NLP techniques for fraud detection. Their big data-based anti-fraud system, Tiandun, is able to detect spam and fraudulent activity in calls and texts.

Vodafone Group is a British multinational telecommunications company with more than 265 million subscribers [27]. Vodafone uses a chatbot named TOBi [100]. The group has a presence across 46 spoken languages and 26 countries, where only 10% of their consumer base speaks English as their native language [100]. They implemented NLP-based techniques into their virtual assistant TOBi. TOBi is a text bot that is able to directly answer most customer questions and recommend products or solutions to their queries.

See Figure 6.10 for an example of a Telecom company's chatbot.

FIGURE 6.10 Telecom company's chatbot.

Telenor is a large Danish Telecommunication company. They built an NLP algorithm to streamline customer center function by analyzing emails and suggesting appropriate answers in response. Their NLP-based algorithm attained an 80% accuracy rate and significantly improved time-to-respond rate [211].

Breaking it down, the following NLP applications are seen popularly in telecom.

Language translation

Given the number of global telecommunication companies, dealing with multiple languages remains a challenge. Language translation techniques are used to parse and process text for further analysis.

Chatbots

Intelligent virtual agents have gained traction in the telecommunication sector. Customer service and satisfaction hold a supreme spot in the success of businesses, which virtual assistants help improve. The main attraction of virtual assistants for telecom providers is to optimize the processing of bulk volumes of support requests for troubleshooting, debugging, billing inquiries, assistance, and maintenance. Service-type questions can be handled by AI-powered assistants allowing faster turnaround times and efficient request volume management.

Support request assistance

Telecom companies receive inquiries for a large volume of support issues each day. Text classification helps route the inquiry to the right category. This method also helps prioritize support requests.

Spam and fraud detection from calls and text

NLP techniques are used to parse text and audio from calls and extract features useful in building a fraud detection model. A smart AI-based solution for fraud detection is gaining prominence with many companies following the trend with time.

Customer segmentation

Customer behavior segmentation helps companies understand their audience better and it is partly dependent on text data generated by the customers, amongst interaction transcripts, subscription patterns, lifecycle, and migration data.

Recommendation system Attributes from customer profiles, interactions, and the items the customer expresses interest in are used to recommend products and services with the help of NLP.

Review and Sentiment analysis

Understanding customer sentiment towards a product or service to get feedback and further improve upon offerings is a popular use case. Sentiment analysis further helps in improving customer experience. Segmenting negative comments to automatically classify problem areas saves the manual effort of sifting through comments or custom interaction logs.

Invoicing automation

Auto-detecting relevant information from bills, automatically performing checks for the correctness of the information, or helping answer customer questions on a billing statement are popular NLP examples. Further image-to-text techniques (OCR) help parse pictures of bills into digitized and organized text for easier processing.

6.7 AUTOMOTIVE

6.7.1 What is automotive?

Automotive is one of the world's largest industries by revenue. The automotive industry comprises a wide range of companies involved in different components of building and selling vehicles including design, development, manufacturing, marketing, and sales.

6.7.2 Language data generated

Primary sources of language data are user interactions in the form of text and voice commands. Other sources include manuals and reports.

6.7.3 NLP in automotive

AI in Automotive primarily revolves around the interactions between the passenger and the vehicle. The autonomous vehicle (AV) industry is the main one leveraging computing power, AI, and NLP. There is an opportunity to enhance the interactive experience for passengers who will be the only occupants of the vehicles with L5 full autonomous 'no driver' vehicles [168]. However, there is a need for the ecosystem that joins NLP and AV to bring NLP-powered technologies to every car. NLP comes under the top two technologies in the Lux Research Foresight 2021 report for autonomous vehicles with a 44% annual growth rate of patents published over the past five years in NLP [168].

While we wait for the industry of autonomous vehicles to become more mainstream, many companies have started integrating AI into existing vehicles for supporting drivers and passengers. For instance, Mercedes launched its AI-powered OS in A-Class cars in 2018. Dubbed Mercedes-Benz User Experience (MBUX) responds to the conversational commands of drivers using NLP-powered technology. Other information such as the status of bad roads, vehicle location, weather information, and more can be delivered to the driver using voice commands. The CEO of Daimler, Ola Källenius, calls this AI-powered digital assistant a 'very good butler' since it learns and adapts to the driver's preferences over time [180].

It was reported in [116] that several companies have started providing AI services for the automotive industry. Intellias is a European company founded in 2002 with KIA as one of its key clients. Berlin-based company Kopernikus Automotive was founded in 2016 and has built AI and ML components for autonomous systems deployed in passenger vehicles. Their key client is Porche. Ukraine-based Diceus is a development company that delivers end-to-end, enterprise-grade solutions and custom software to large corporations in more than 20 countries. They use machine learning and artificial intelligence for automotive applications and help their clients to analyze, optimize, and migrate existing automotive software.

Let's look at some NLP applications below.

Dialog with the vehicle in natural language

In new developing technologies, NLP is envisioned to play a vital role. In self-driving cars, from requesting destinations to changes in the route taken, stopping at a restaurant on the way, communicating in natural language makes the entire experience seem natural and effortless as it would with a human-driven car. How do I open the hood? What is the current oil level? NLP can make getting answers to simple questions easy and automated.

Similar dialog-based systems can also be used to engage with the entertainment systems inside the vehicle. Figure 6.11 shows an example of a smart car assistant.

FIGURE 6.11   Infotainment systems in vehicles.

Language translation

While this technology is not yet a part of widely used vehicles, it has started finding use in the automotive industry. For vehicles meant for tourists, language translation devices are attached to the car to help facilitate communication between the driver and passengers.

Chatbots

Like any other industry, automotive finds use in chatbots as well which help answer customers' common queries in an automated fashion, thereby making customer service available round the clock and engaging human agents only for the needed queries [8]. Chatbots find use in car dealerships to aid in finding suitable vehicles for customers. For instance, DealerAI [215] is a car dealership chatbot platform. Figure 6.12 shows an example of a dealership chatbot.

Topic modeling, text classification, and analytics

There are large documents in an unstructured format that gather around incident reports. To discover trends at a high level, NLP is leveraged to organize text, extract topical information, classify as needed, and provide analytics on key causes of incident reports within a time frame [31].

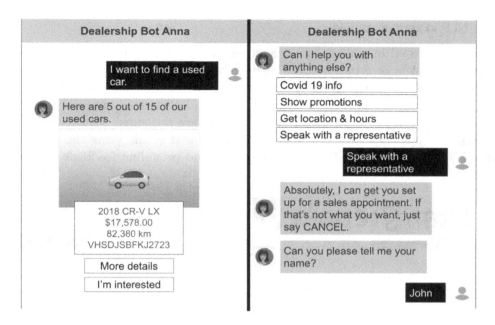

FIGURE 6.12 Chatbot for car dealerships.

6.8 SERIOUS GAMES

6.8.1 What is a serious game?

Video games are electronic games that are played on a computing device such as laptops, cell phones, tablets, etc. The gaming industry is centered around video games, including their development and marketing. The video game industry has grown from focused markets to the mainstream in recent years.

Serious game is a category of games that are designed for purposes other than pure entertainment. Examples include educational games and city planning.

Over the years, there have been several advancements in the gaming experience. Examples include virtual reality, feature enhancements, and the building of virtual conference halls. The latter opened up the possibilities for usage by a larger audience segment, especially with the increased demand during the COVID-19 pandemic when remote working and events gained high traction.

6.8.2 Language data generated

The primary sources of language data in serious games include user-entered text and audio. The text can be conversational, longer sentences, or paragraphs for educational applications.

6.8.3 NLP in serious games

NLP has been used in serious games and communication, translation, and interpretation from spoken or typed natural language for a more real-world feel.

Let's look at a few examples of serious games below that leverage NLP [131].

iSTART [6] is an intelligent tutoring system designed to improve a student's reading comprehension. In iSTART-ME, students are presented with scientific texts and asked to type their own explanations. NLP is used in analyzing the descriptions that are written by the students for assessment and providing feedback. See Figure 6.13.

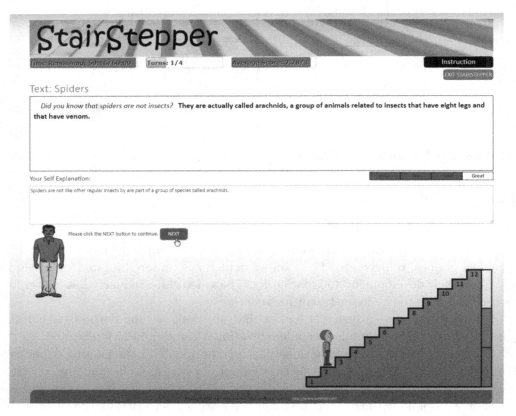

FIGURE 6.13 iSTART self-explanation assessment. Source [6].

Eveil-3D [133] is a language-learning game where NLP is used for the development of speaking and reading skills. In this game, a verbal automatic speech recognizer is trained and used to accept input from students.

I-fleg (interactive French language learning game) [18, 19] aims to present aspects of French as a second language. NLP plays a role in the test exercises that are produced in a non-deterministic manner based on the learner's goal and profile.

Façade [121] is one of the early games allowing a user to type in natural language to control the flow and direction of the game. The game is designed to train students to find arguments in difficult situations. In this game, the user is invited to a dinner during which a marital conflict occurs. The student's goal is to reconcile the couple. With communications from the student, the couple (game) comes back with a predefined context-appropriate response, depending on the utterance category of the student such as praise, criticism, provocation, etc. NLP is used to improve dialogue efficiency between the player and the game (couple). NLP enables pragmatic dialogues between the player and the game, with no emphasis on the syntax or the semantics of the input sentences [131]. Figure 6.14 shows a still from this game.

FIGURE 6.14 Facade game. Source [121].

FearNot! (Fun with Empathic Agents Reaching Novel Outcomes in Teaching) [185] is a story-telling game to teach children strategies to prevent bullying and social exclusion. NLP is used to classify speech and semantic information. Children provide advice to the victimized entity in this application with written free-form text input, which is then elaborated by a language processor.

Mission Rehearsal Exercise [122] presents scenarios of high emotional tension, where the learner decides how to cope with these situations. NLP is used to enable the game to create a virtual experience that matches closely with real human beings.

PlayMancer [9,166] was a live project between 2007 and 2011. It included mini-games meant for cognitive-behavioral therapy sessions. This finds use for patients with behavioral and addictive disorders such as pathological gambling, eating disorders, etc. The objective is to teach patients different ways to overcome their illness. NLP is used to assess a combination of speech, body posture, and emotional state of the patient for defining their behavioral status to adjust the game's interaction.

AutoMentor [191] and Land Science [69] are designed to simulate a human mentor for scientific skills development. NLP is used in this game for human mentor simulation [14].

Operation ARIES! (Acquiring Research, Investigation, and Evaluative Skills) [95] trains students to detect inconsistent and incoherent scientific reasoning and to argue to restore the truth. It is based on the following premise. 'The aliens have invaded the Earth! The Fuaths of the planet Thoth in the Aries constellation are among us and try to destabilize the humans to steal their values by publishing flawed articles. The student has been hired by the Federal Bureau of Science (FBS) to detect the Fuaths as physically they look like humans'. NLP is used for natural language conversations with the learner.

Bucketing some of the common NLP applications below.

Chatbots or virtual communication agents

In most games above, NLP has been explored for simulating conversations between the user and the game. Chatbots are also used in video games in general for assistance. The same technology is also used for automating responses by dummy players in video games.

Text assessment

NLP is used to assess sentences and paragraphs written by players in educational games. Sentiment, intent, and other information embedded in player messages are an integral part of various serious games.

Language translation

Language translation is of great assistance in games for allowing fast and easy switching between languages.

Speech-to-text and vice-versa

A lot of gaming applications work based on a speech or text input that ultimately guides the direction of the game. Using text-to-speech and speech-to-text services helps facilitate the process. Models are popularly built on the translated text rather than audio to update the state and action taken by the game.

6.9   EDUCATION AND RESEARCH

6.9.1   What is education and research?

The education industry comprises establishments whose primary objective is to provide education. These establishments can be public, non-profit, or for-profit institutions and include elementary schools, secondary schools, community colleges, universities, and ministries or departments of education [17]. Research forms a large part of education today, especially in colleges and universities, forming a large part of an individual's education through advanced degrees.

6.9.2   Language data generated

Main sources of text data include research documents, papers, patents, essays, and stories.

6.9.3   NLP in education and research

It is no surprise that the major bulk of communications in an educational context happens through speech and text. Any thesis, publications, or reading materials are all composed of text. With so much text data, NLP finds use in a variety of applications. It is already delivering benefits in an academic setting, and new use cases are being developed and proposed rapidly.

Text summarization

While dealing with documentation, dissertations, and papers, text summarization helps reveal summaries of content captured in long documents, helping sift through information faster and more concisely.

Language translation

Language translation is immensely helpful in the education sector. It not only helps students learn different languages better but also helps break language barriers for making educational material available globally. How many of you use Google Translate whenever you need to find quick translations for a word or sentence? (Figure 6.15)

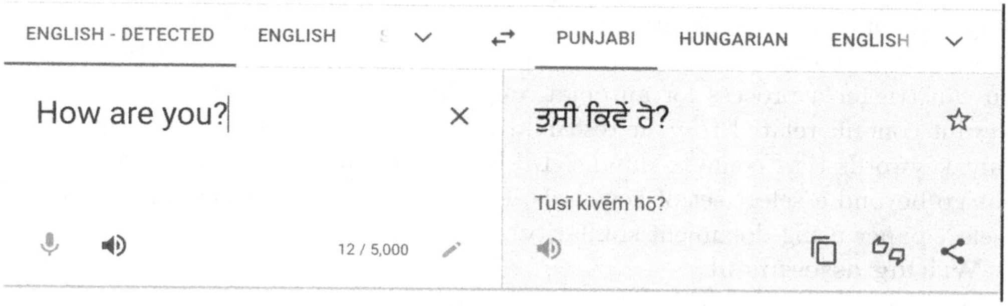

FIGURE 6.15 Google Translate for quick language translation between English and Punjabi.

Academic writing assistance

Historically, NLP has had considerable success in the educational sphere, identifying student grammar and word mechanics problems, and providing holistic scores for five-paragraph essays [74].

Automatic writing evaluation systems assist the writing journeys of authors. A simple example includes spelling error identification and grammar suggestions seen on Microsoft Word, Google Docs, and advanced tools like Grammarly[3]. Furthermore, NLP-powered techniques help with tips on structure, vocabulary, key-topics presence, and plagiarism checks. Another example is the tool jenni.ai that leverages NLP for academic writing assistance.

Semantic and sentiment analysis

Semantic analysis in NLP is to establish the meaning of language. Sentiment analysis helps understand student and teacher feedback in an automated fashion and at a larger data scale.

Administrators and staff at educational institutions can use NLP semantic and sentiment analysis to study students' behavior in response to the instruction they're currently receiving, and the impact of changes in their academic and social environments [74]. This can help analyze the impact of curriculum and teaching approaches.

---

[3]https://app.grammarly.com/

Researchers have begun to apply social network analysis approaches to language data to reveal patterns of collaboration between students in online discussion forums and within Massive Open Online Courses (MOOCs) [74].

Text simplification

Based on ongoing research, different students learn better if the material language was simplified. Using NLP, sentences can be restructured to be more simple to understand for students [74].

Finding relevant material

In a research setting, a literature survey to find out existing material, studies, and development on a topic is a complex process. No matter how much time you spend searching for relevant material, there is always the possibility of having missed something. The number of publications is only increasing with time, thus finding relevant material can at times be challenging and time-consuming. Using NLP techniques, you can trigger a process for automatically sifting through research papers to find relevant content related to your research. Rather than searching using different relevant keywords that come to mind, NLP helps find similarity between blobs of text that go beyond a select set of keywords. Examples include finding papers similar to a select paper using document similarity.

Writing assessment

We discussed many serious games focused on education in the serious games section where students' writing is analyzed and assessed using NLP.

Windup

In this section, we looked at many industry verticals and how NLP is being used today or envisioned being used in research efforts. We shared NLP instances from different industry verticals along with technologies that individuals encounter regularly. Figure 6.16 contains a summary of NLP applications and projects for different industries. Chatbots and text analysis are the most popular applications across domains. Furthermore, language translation (also called machine translation when done by a machine) is a common application for global businesses. NLP techniques including text similarity, text classification, and information extraction power several other common industry applications seen in this section.

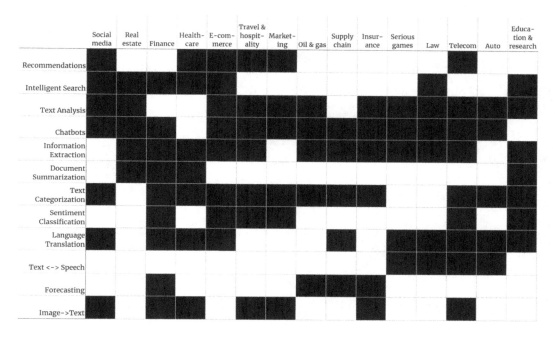

FIGURE 6.16 NLP applications and projects by industry.

How would you take an application and implement it for your use case? Section V is all about implementing different applications. We make use of existing tools and libraries where possible to demonstrate how quickly some of these applications can be brought to life. We take it a notch further in Section VI and build NLP projects and discuss them in an enterprise setting. For example, why would you want to build a chatbot for your company? What are the driving factors for building NLP solutions? And how can you implement that? Section VI contains four industry projects comprising NLP applications that not only contain step-by-step implementations but also aim to give the readers a sense of an actual work setting and how AI fits into broad company goals.

V

Implementing Advanced NLP Applications

We discussed several data sources, data extraction from different formats, and storage solutions in Section II. Once text data is accessible and available, several NLP tools, processes, and models come in handy for different applications, as discussed in Section III. In Section IV, we looked at how several industries are researching and leveraging NLP for different applications.

This section is a guide for implementing advanced NLP applications using concepts learned in the previous chapters, which will prepare you for solving real-world use cases. Each application that we will build in this section can be used stand-alone or in conjunction with other applications to solve real-world problems around text data. These stand-alone applications are like building blocks, that you can combine together to build full-fledged NLP projects, which we will focus on in Section VI along with what it means to build NLP projects in the real-world (in the industry vertical/in an enterprise setting).

In Section IV, we visited popular NLP applications across industry domains. Here, we will pick the most popular applications and implement them using Python tools. The code used in this section can be found at https://github.com/jsingh811/NLP-in-the-real-world under section5. In this section, we will build the following applications.

- Information extraction (IE)

- Text summarization

- Language detection and translation

- Topic modeling

- Text similarity

- Text classification

- Sentiment analysis

## CHAPTER 7

Information Extraction and Text Transforming Models

7.1   INFORMATION EXTRACTION

Information extraction (IE) refers to the task of extracting structured information from semi-structured or unstructured data. Examples include automatic text annotations and image content extraction. In the context of text data, it typically refers to extracting information embedded within a piece of text. Consider the following sentence as an example.

'What is the stock price of Apple?'

Here, 'stock price' is a phrase that conveys meaning. Extraction of phrases from text is the task of **Keyphrase Extraction, or KPE**.

Recognizing 'Apple' as an organization in the above sentence is an example of the task of **Named Entity Recognition, or NER**.

Apple is an organization, but it can also refer to a fruit. In the above sentence, the implied reference is the organization given the context. Disambiguation of 'Apple' here referring to the organization and not the fruit is an example of **Named Entity Disambiguation and Linking**.

All of the above are examples of IE tasks. Let's dive into some popularly applied IE tasks and how you could implement and use them in Python. We'll dive further into Named Entity Recognition and Keyphrase Extraction, as these are the most popular implementations in the industry. Most other IE tasks we have spoken about are relatively easier to implement using service providers such as IBM[1], Google[2], and AWS[3] and are also a popular choice of industry practitioners over custom code writing.

---

[1] https://www.ibm.com/blogs/research/2016/10/entity-linking/
[2] https://cloud.google.com/natural-language/docs/analyzing-entities
[3] https://docs.aws.amazon.com/comprehend/latest/dg/how-entities.html

7.1.1 Named entity recognition (NER)

Named entity recognition has many alternate names, such as entity extraction, entity chunking, and entity identification. It is a sub-task of information extraction for extracting named entities from unstructured text. Examples include automatic identification of locations, organizations, person names, etc. from the text. See Figure 7.1 as an example.

Nina Smith from Barclay's lives in Dubai.
PERSON   ORGANIZATION   LOCATION

FIGURE 7.1 Named entity recognition (NER) on a sentence.

There are different ways you can implement NER.

- For simple problems, a rule-based approach can work well.

- There are several pre-trained open-source models and tools that you can directly use for NER. Service providers also offer such services at some cost.

- You can also train models for your own entities using your own data and the available tool's training pipelines.

- Furthermore, if you wanted to build a custom model from scratch using custom machine learning techniques, you could do that as well with the help of existing libraries in Python.

> *TIP*
>
> Often, in practical scenarios, you may need to combine multiple techniques to build your NER algorithm, i.e., pattern matching, rule-based look-ups, pre-trained models, and your own models.

Let's explore some options below.

7.1.1.1 Rule-based approaches

For many tasks, a rule-based approach works very well. For example, extracting email IDs from free-form text can be solved using `regex` because email IDs typically follow a pattern.

```
import re

# \S matches any non-whitespace character
# @ for its occurrence in the emaIl ID,
# . for the period after @
# + for when a character is repeated one or more times
re.findall('\S+@\S+\.\S+', text)

# >> text = "send to j_2.4-dj3@xyz.co.net for queries."
# >> ['j_2.4-dj3@unknowndomain.co.net']

# >> text = "follow me on twitter@jyotikasingh_."
# >> []
```

The above code can also be found in section5/ner-regex.ipynb.

Imagine you have a giant list of names of people. Using that, you could find their presence in the text to recognize the entity - person. This solution can perform well as a baseline model, especially if your application expects names that are present in your look-up list and does not contain much ambiguity. However, if you ever encounter a new name within your text, your look-up-based model would not be able to identify it. Furthermore, this method would not be able to distinguish between ambiguous words. For example, 'Olive' can be a person's name but also a food item. For this reason, using a different model that can learn from patterns in the data is a preferred approach for such tasks.

Other rule-based NER solutions comprise a list of patterns that depend on word tokens and POS (part-of-speech) tags. For instance, two consecutive proper nouns in a sentence could imply the presence of a person's first and last name. spaCy's EntityRuler provides functionalities to implement custom rule-based NER[4].

7.1.1.2 Open-source pre-trained models

spaCy
spaCy offers PERSON, ORG, LOCATION, DATES, and many more entities. The full list includes the following entities.

```
['CARDINAL', 'DATE', 'EVENT', 'FAC', 'GPE', 'LANGUAGE', 'LAW',
'LOC', 'MONEY', 'NORP', 'ORDINAL', 'ORG', 'PERCENT', 'PERSON',
'PRODUCT', 'QUANTITY', 'TIME', 'WORK_OF_ART']
```

For NER, popular spaCy's pre-trained models include en_core_web_sm, en_core_web_md, en_core_web_lg, and en_core_web_trf. For example, en_core_web_sm is a small English pipeline trained on written web text (blogs, news, comments), that includes vocabulary, syntax, and entities. spaCy also has a news genre other than the web genre.

spaCy's NER system was reported to feature a sophisticated word embedding strategy using sub-word features and 'Bloom' embeddings, a deep convolutional neural network with residual connections, and a novel transition-based approach to named entity parsing [80].

Using one of spaCy's pre-trained models, you can load the model and perform entity recognition as follows.

---

[4]https://spacy.io/usage/rule-based-matching#entityruler

To download the `en_core_web_lg` model, run the following in your Jupyter notebook. To run it in bash, remove the !.

```
! pip install spacy
! python -m spacy download en_core_web_lg

import spacy

nlp = spacy.load("en_core_web_lg")
raw_text = ""

doc = nlp(raw_text)

for word in doc.ents:
  print(word.text,word.label_)
```

Input raw_text:

> *The Mars Orbiter Mission (MOM), informally known as Mangalyaan, was launched into Earth orbit on 5 November 2013 by the Indian Space Research Organisation (ISRO) and has entered Mars orbit on 24 September 2014. India thus became the first country to enter Mars orbit on its first attempt. It was completed at a record low cost of $74 million.*

Output:

```
The Mars Orbiter Mission (MOM) PRODUCT
Mangalyaan PERSON
Earth LOC
5 November 2013 DATE
the Indian Space Research Organisation ORG
ISRO ORG
Mars LOC
24 September 2014 DATE
India GPE
first ORDINAL
Mars LOC
first ORDINAL
$74 million MONEY
```

`Displacy` is a component of `spaCy` where the output can be printed in an easier-to-read representation. It is shown in Figure 7.2.

```
from spacy import displacy
displacy.render(doc, style="ent", jupyter=True)
```

NLTK

NLTK offers a pre-trained model that recognizes PERSON, ORG, GPE entities. The function can be accessed by `nltk.ne_chunk()` and it returns a nested `nltk.tree.Tree` object, so you have to traverse the Tree object to get to the named entities. Additionally, it accepts a parameter `binary`. If `binary` is set to `True`, then named entities are just tagged as NE (i.e., if an entity was detected or not); otherwise, the classifier adds category labels (PERSON, ORGANIZATION, and GPE).

FIGURE 7.2 spaCy NER output with displacy.

In code, it looks as follows.

You need to run the below only once.

```
! pip install nltk
from nltk import download
download('averaged_perceptron_tagger')
download('maxent_ne_chunker')
download('words')
download('punkt')
```

Then, you have the needed models and can get entities as follows.

```
from nltk.tokenize import word_tokenize, sent_tokenize
from nltk.tag import pos_tag
from nltk import ne_chunk

doc = pos_tag(word_tokenize(raw_text))

NLTK_LABELS = ["PERSON", "ORGANIZATION", "GPE"]

tagged_doc = []
for sent in sent_tokenize(raw_text):
  tagged_doc.append(pos_tag(word_tokenize(sent)))

entities = []
for sent in tagged_doc:
  trees = ne_chunk(sent)
  for tree in trees:
    if (
      hasattr(tree, "label")
      and tree.label() in NLTK_LABELS
    ):
      entities.append((
        " ".join([
          entity
          for (entity, label) in tree
          # filter for non-entities
          if (
            # removing noise, if it is a URL or empty
            "http" not in entity.lower()
```

```
            and "\n" not in entity.lower()
            and len(entity.strip()) > 0
        )
    ]), tree.label(),
    ))
print(entities)
```

Passing in the same input as in the previous example, here is the output.

[('Mars', 'ORGANIZATION'), ('MOM', 'ORGANIZATION'), ('Mangalyaan', 'GPE'), ('Earth', 'GPE'), ('Indian', 'GPE'), ('Space Research Organisation', 'ORGANIZATION'), ('ISRO', 'ORGANIZATION'), ('Mars', 'PERSON'), ('India', 'GPE'), ('Mars', 'PERSON')]

spaCy transformers

spaCy 3, in particular, has prebuilt models with HuggingFace's `transformers`. The `en_core_web_trf` model is a RoBERTa-based English language transformer pipeline. Its various components include a transformer, tagger, parser, ner, attribute_ruler, and lemmatizer. Using this model right out of the box can be done as follows.

```
! pip install spacy-transformers
! python -m spacy download en_core_web_trf

import spacy
from spacy import displacy

nlp = spacy.load("en_core_web_trf")

doc = nlp(raw_text)

displacy.render(doc, style="ent", jupyter=True)
```

Displacy output is shown in Figure 7.3.

The Mars Orbiter Mission (MOM) PRODUCT , informally known as Mangalyaan PRODUCT , was launched into Earth LOC orbit on 5 November 2013 DATE by the Indian Space Research Organisation ORG (ISRO ORG) and has entered Mars LOC orbit on 24 September 2014 DATE . India GPE thus became the first ORDINAL country to enter Mars LOC orbit on its first ORDINAL attempt. It was completed at a record low cost of $74 million MONEY .

FIGURE 7.3 spaCy transformer (RoBERTa) NER output with displacy.

Transformers

You can also use the transformers library directly to perform NER.

```
! pip install transformers
```

We discussed transformers and the difference between pre-trained and fine-tuned transformer models. We have chosen the `bert-base-NER` model which is a fine-tuned BERT model for NER and achieves state-of-the-art performance for the NER task. This model is a `bert-base-cased` model fine-tuned on the English version of the standard CoNLL-2003 Named Entity Recognition dataset [146]. A larger version of this model is `BERT-large-NER`.

It can recognize the four entities - location (LOC), organizations (ORG), person (PER), and Miscellaneous (MISC).

```
from transformers import pipeline

ner = pipeline(
  "ner",
  model="dslim/bert-base-NER",
  grouped_entities=True
)


print(ner(raw_text))
```

The output is as follows.

['entity_group': 'MISC', 'score': 0.7344227, 'word': 'Mars Orbiter Mission', 'start': 4, 'end': 24,
'entity_group': 'MISC', 'score': 0.6008748, 'word': 'MOM', 'start': 26, 'end': 29,
'entity_group': 'LOC', 'score': 0.43170515, 'word': 'Man', 'start': 52, 'end': 55,
'entity_group': 'MISC', 'score': 0.5044298, 'word': '##gal', 'start': 55, 'end': 58,
'entity_group': 'LOC', 'score': 0.47212577, 'word': '##ya', 'start': 58, 'end': 60,
'entity_group': 'MISC', 'score': 0.48969588, 'word': '##an', 'start': 60, 'end': 62,
'entity_group': 'LOC', 'score': 0.75420374, 'word': 'Earth', 'start': 82, 'end': 87,
'entity_group': 'ORG', 'score': 0.99907124, 'word': 'Indian Space Research Organisa-tion', 'start': 120, 'end': 154,
'entity_group': 'ORG', 'score': 0.9986104, 'word': 'ISRO', 'start': 156, 'end': 160,
'entity_group': 'LOC', 'score': 0.99694604, 'word': 'Mars', 'start': 178, 'end': 182,
'entity_group': 'LOC', 'score': 0.99982953, 'word': 'India', 'start': 211, 'end': 216,
'entity_group': 'LOC', 'score': 0.99614346, 'word': 'Mars', 'start': 256, 'end': 260]

Many additional models can be used for NER with the transformers library. Refer to[5] and use the tag of the model that you want to use against the `model=` argument above in the `pipeline()` function.

The code demonstrated in this section can be found in the notebook section5/ner-pretrained.ipynb.

We can see how each model can have its own drawbacks in terms of quality of results. The biggest limitations of the pre-trained models is the limited number of entities it can recognize.

---

[5]`https://huggingface.co/models?language=en&pipeline_tag=token-classification& sort=downloads`

> *TIP*
>
> With so many pre-trained (and fine-tuned for transformers) models to choose from, how do you choose your model for NER?
>
> This process can be experimental in nature. Different models can perform differently based on the dataset. Trying a few options and testing a sample of results can help with the selection process. Another consideration factor is the time it takes to use these different models.
>
> In the above implementations, it took 137.67 seconds to load the spaCy model, 57.36 seconds to load bert-base-NER, and 4 seconds to load NLTK models. Once the model was loaded, it took approximately 0.02 seconds to get entities for the sample text for both NLTK and spaCy, and 0.22 seconds to get entities using **transformers**.

7.1.1.3 *Training your own model*

Pre-trained models and available entities may not work for your use case. This can be the case when the data that the model was built with differs from the data you are dealing with, or when the entities you need are not offered by the pre-trained models. For such applications, you can create your own model using some of the tools discussed below. For this task, you'll need a dataset with labeled entities.

Training your own model using spaCy

spaCy pipeline

To begin with, arrange your entity-labeled data in the format below. In this example, we want to label the entities - main ingredient and spice.

```
train_data = [
(
    'Chef added some salt and pepper to the rice.',
    {'entities': [
        (16, 20, 'SPICE'),
        (25, 31, 'SPICE'),
        (39, 43, 'INGREDIENT')
    ]}
),
(
    'The pasta was set to boil with some salt.',
    {'entities': [
        (4, 9, 'INGREDIENT'),
        (36, 40, 'SPICE')
    ]}
),
```

```
(
    'Adding egg to the rice dish with some pepper.',
    {'entities': [
        (7, 10, 'INGREDIENT'),
        (18, 22, 'INGREDIENT'),
        (38, 44, 'SPICE')
    ]}
)
]
```

We start by creating a blank model, adding *ner pipe*, and addding our entities to the *ner pipe*.

```
! pip install spacy

import spacy

nlp = spacy.blank("en")
print("Created a blank en model")

nlp.add_pipe('ner', last=True)
ner = nlp.get_pipe("ner")
print("pipe_names", nlp.pipe_names)

for _, annotations in train_data:
  for ent in annotations.get("entities"):
    ner.add_label(ent[2])

# begin training
optimizer = nlp.begin_training()
```

Then, we update the model with the training data.

```
import random
from spacy.training.example import Example

n_iter = 100
pipe_exceptions = ["ner", "trf_wordpiece", "trf_tok2vec"]
other_pipes = [
  pipe
  for pipe in nlp.pipe_names
  if pipe not in pipe_exceptions
]
with nlp.disable_pipes(*other_pipes):
  for _ in range(n_iter):
    random.shuffle(train_data)
    losses = {}
    for batch in spacy.util.minibatch(
      train_data, size=2
    ):
      for text, annots in batch:
        doc = nlp.make_doc(text)
        nlp.update(
          [Example.from_dict(doc, annots)],
          drop=0.5,
          sgd=optimizer,
          losses=losses
        )
    print("Losses", losses)
```

Trying out the model as follows.

```
def get_entities(raw_text):
    doc = nlp(raw_text)
    result = []
    for word in doc.ents:
        result.append((word.text,word.label_))
    return result

print(get_entities("Add water to the spaghetti"))
print(get_entities("Add some paprika on top to your pasta."))
```

[('water', 'INGREDIENT'), ('spaghetti', 'INGREDIENT')] [('paprika', 'SPICE'), ('pasta', 'INGREDIENT')]

This is not a highly accurate model and is built to demonstrate the functionality alone. Adding more training data will help train a better model. The complete code can be found at section5/training-ner-spacy.ipynb.

A model can be saved to disk for future use as follows.

```
nlp.to_disk(output_dir)

# to load back

nlp = spacy.load(output_dir)
```

Sequence classifier training

NER is a sequence labeling problem. What does that mean? The context of the sentence is important for tasks like NER.

There are rule-based methods that can work as a sequence labeling model. Additionally, NER can be done using a number of sequence labeling methods. Popular ones include Linear Chain Conditional Random Fields (Linear Chain CRF), Maximum Entropy Markov Models, and Bi-LSTM.

CRF

CRF stands for conditional random fields and is used heavily in information extraction. The principal idea is that the context of each word is important in addition to the word's meaning. One approach is to use the two words before a given word and the two words following the given word as features.

We can use `sklearn-crfsuite` to accomplish training a custom NER model. To begin with, we need data that is annotated in a given format. The labels follow a *BIO* notation where *B* indicates the beginning of an entity, *I* indicates the inside of an entity for multi-word entities, and *O* for non-entities. An example can be seen below. *PER* stands for person and *LOC* stands for location.

```
Jessie I-PER
Johnson I-PER
went O
to O
Dubai B-LOC
. O
```

Once we have annotated data, we can perform feature extraction and classifier training.

The feature extraction logic used should depend on the task at hand. In a typical scenario, looking at the POS (part-of-speech) tag of words before and after a word is helpful. A complete demo code can be found at[6].

7.1.1.4 Fine-tuning on custom datasets using transformers

As we discussed in Chapter 4 (Section 4.2.3), you can find many fine-tuned transformer models in Hugging Face[7] for a specific task and type of data. But what if your data is custom and no fine-tuned model is working for you? You can take a pre-trained model using transformers and fine-tune in on any custom dataset. We will see an example of this below.

We will use the WNUT 17: Emerging and Rare entity recognition dataset [4] to demonstrate transformer fine-tuning. You can download this data as follows.

```
! pip install transformers
! python -m pip install wget
! wget http://noisy-text.github.io/2017/files/wnut17train.conll
```

To read the text and tags, the following code can be used.

```
from pathlib import Path
import re

def split_into_tokens(raw_text):
    raw_docs = re.split(r'\n\t?\n', raw_text)
    token_docs = []
    tag_docs = []
    for doc in raw_docs:
        tokens = []
        tags = []
        for line in doc.split('\n'):
            row = line.split('\t')
            if len(row) == 1:
                token = row[0]
                tag = None
            else:
                token, tag = line.split('\t')
            tokens.append(token)
            tags.append(tag)
        token_docs.append(tokens)
        tag_docs.append(tags)

    return token_docs, tag_docs

def read_wnut(file_path):
    file_path = Path(file_path)

    raw_text = file_path.read_text().strip()
```

---

[6]https://medium.com/data-science-in-your-pocket/training-custom-ner-system-using-crfs-146e0e922851

[7]https://huggingface.co/models

```
token_docs, tag_docs = split_into_tokens(raw_text)

return token_docs, tag_docs

texts, tags = read_wnut('wnut17train.conll')

print(texts[0][10:17], tags[0][10:17], sep='\n')
```

' This is what the data looks like.

> ['for', 'two', 'weeks', '.', 'Empire', 'State', 'Building']
>
> ['O', 'O', 'O', 'O', 'B-location', 'I-location', 'I-location']

'O' indicates that the token does not correspond to any entity. 'location' is an entity. 'B-' indicates the beginning of the entity and 'I-' indicates consecutive positions of the same entity. Thus, 'Empire', 'State', and 'Building' have tokens 'B-location', 'I-location', and 'I-location'.

Next, we split the data into training and validation samples and initialize a pre-trained DistilBert tokenizer using the model distilbert-base-cased. Our data has split tokens rather than full sentence strings, thus we will set is_split_into_words to True. We pass padding as True and truncation as True to pad the sequences to be the same length.

```
from sklearn.model_selection import train_test_split
train_texts, val_texts, train_tags, val_tags = train_test_split(
   texts, tags, test_size=.2
)

from transformers import DistilBertTokenizerFast

tokenizer = DistilBertTokenizerFast.from_pretrained(
   'distilbert-base-cased'
)
train_encodings = tokenizer(
   train_texts,
   is_split_into_words=True,
   return_offsets_mapping=True,
   padding=True,
   truncation=True
)
val_encodings = tokenizer(
   val_texts,
   is_split_into_words=True,
   return_offsets_mapping=True,
   padding=True,
   truncation=True
)
```

We can tell the model to return information about the tokens that are split by the WordPiece tokenization process.

WordPiece tokenization is the process by which single words are split into multiple tokens such that each token is likely to be in the vocabulary. Some words may not be in the vocabulary of a model. Thus the model splits the word into sub-words/tokens.

Since we have only one tag per token, if the tokenizer splits a token into multiple sub-tokens, then we will end up with a mismatch between our tokens and our labels. To resolve this, we will train on the tag labels for the first subtoken of a split token. We can do this by setting the labels we wish to ignore to -100.

```
import numpy as np

unique_tags = set(tag for doc in tags for tag in doc)
tag2id = {tag: id for id, tag in enumerate(unique_tags)}
id2tag = {id: tag for tag, id in tag2id.items()}

def encode_tags(tags, encodings):
  labels = [[tag2id[tag] for tag in doc] for doc in tags]
  encoded_labels = []
  for doc_labels, doc_offset in zip(
    labels, encodings.offset_mapping
  ):
    # create an empty array of -100
    doc_enc_labels = np.ones(len(doc_offset),dtype=int) * -100
    arr_offset = np.array(doc_offset)

    # set labels whose 1st offset position is 0 and the 2nd is not 0
    doc_enc_labels[
      (arr_offset[:,0] == 0) & (arr_offset[:,1] != 0)
    ] = doc_labels
    encoded_labels.append(doc_enc_labels.tolist())
  return encoded_labels

train_labels = encode_tags(train_tags, train_encodings)
val_labels = encode_tags(val_tags, val_encodings)

print(
  f"""There are total {len(unique_tags)} entity tags in the data:
  {unique_tags}"""
)
```

There are total 13 entity tags in the data: dict_keys(['I-corporation', 'I-product', 'I-person', 'I-group', 'B-location', 'O', 'I-location', 'B-creative-work', 'B-group', 'I-creative-work', 'B-person', 'B-product', 'B-corporation'])

Next, we will create a dataset object.

```
import tensorflow as tf

train_encodings.pop("offset_mapping")
val_encodings.pop("offset_mapping")

train_dataset = tf.data.Dataset.from_tensor_slices(
  (dict(train_encodings), train_labels)
)
val_dataset = tf.data.Dataset.from_tensor_slices(
  (dict(val_encodings), val_labels)
)
```

Now we load in a token classification model and specify the number of labels. Then, our model is ready for fine-tuning.

```
from transformers import TFDistilBertForTokenClassification
model = TFDistilBertForTokenClassification.from_pretrained(
  'distilbert-base-cased',
  num_labels=len(unique_tags)
)
```

To fine-tune the model, the following code is used.

```
from transformers import TFDistilBertForSequenceClassification

optimizer = tf.keras.optimizers.Adam(learning_rate=5e-5)
# you can also use any keras loss fn
model.compile(optimizer=optimizer, loss=model.compute_loss)
model.fit(
  train_dataset.shuffle(1000).batch(16), epochs=3, batch_size=16
)
```

You can check the model config by running `model.config`.

Now your model is fine-tuned on a custom dataset. You can call it as follows to get entities as output.

```
from transformers import pipeline

custom_ner = pipeline(
  "ner",
  model=model,
  tokenizer=tokenizer,
  aggregation_strategy="simple"
)
output = custom_ner("""
  Ella Parker purchased a Samsung Galaxy s21+ from Elante mall.
""")

print(output)
```

The resultant output has entity group labels as 'LABEL_0', 'LABEL_1', etc. You can map it to your label names using **id2tag** or the mapping available in **model.config**.

The output is as follows.

['entity_group': 'B-person', 'score': 0.97740185, 'word': 'Ella', 'start': 65, 'end': 69,

'entity_group': 'I-person', 'score': 0.97186667, 'word': 'Parker', 'start': 70, 'end': 76,

'entity_group': 'O', 'score': 0.9917011, 'word': 'purchased a', 'start': 77, 'end': 88,

'entity_group': 'B-product', 'score': 0.39736107, 'word': 'Samsung', 'start': 89, 'end': 96,

'entity_group': 'I-product', 'score': 0.65990174, 'word': 'Galaxy', 'start': 97, 'end': 103,

'entity_group': 'O', 'score': 0.77520126, 'word': 's21 + from', 'start': 104, 'end': 113,

'entity_group': 'B-location', 'score': 0.41146958, 'word': 'El', 'start': 114, 'end': 116,

'entity_group': 'I-corporation', 'score': 0.23474006, 'word': '##ante', 'start': 116, 'end': 120,

'entity_group': 'O', 'score': 0.87043536, 'word': 'mall.', 'start': 121, 'end': 126]

The full code along with outputs can be found in section5/transformers-ner-fine-tuning.ipynb.

> **TIP**
>
> With so many ways to train a customer NER model, how do you decide which one to proceed with?
>
> It is a common practice to first find existing models that can be leveraged for your use case. If none exist, you will need some labeled data to get started. If you are already using spaCy pipelines for other projects, it may make sense to start with spaCy. It is common to evaluate the model based on training and inference time in addition to model accuracy. If you have labeled dataset but your custom model isn't doing as well as you need it to, or if your goal is to get the more accurate results, you may need to curate more labeled data of good quality. If you are not using a transformer model already, fine-tuning a transformer can help with better results at the cost of longer training time and model size.

7.1.2 Keyphrase extraction (KPE)

Keyphrase extraction, or KPE, is the task of identifying words and phrases that communicate important information within a piece of text. Unsupervised approaches work fairly well for KPE and are popularly used in practice. A supervised approach is possible too, but it would require a lot of labeled data, which can be time-consuming and strenuous.

A popular unsupervised approach is a graph-based algorithm where words or phrases are represented as nodes in a weighted graph based on the importance of the phrase in the text, often determined by the frequency of occurrence. The most important nodes are returned as keyphrases.

Let's look at a few approaches below that work well and can be implemented quickly with the help of open-source tools.

We'll run a demo on the sample document below.

> text = 'Natural language processing (NLP) is a subfield of linguistics, computer science, and artificial intelligence concerned with the interactions between computers and human language, in particular how to program computers to process and analyze large amounts of natural language data. The goal is a computer capable of 'understanding' the contents of documents, including the contextual nuances of the language within them. The technology can then accurately extract information and insights contained in the documents as well as categorize and organize the documents themselves.'

7.1.2.1   textacy

This library is built on top of **spaCy** and contains implementations of multiple graph-based approaches for extracting keyphrases. It includes algorithms such as TextRank, SGRank, YAKE, and sCAKE.

Summarized notes on TextRank, SGRank, YAKE, and sCAKE

TextRank algorithm is based on a graph-based approach where each node is a word, and the edges between the nodes represent the relationship between the words using a co-occurrence measure. The document is tokenized and annotated with part-of-speech (POS) tags. An edge is created if words co-occur within a window of N-words to obtain an unweighted undirected graph. The words are then ranked using TextRank. The most important words are selected, and any adjacent keywords are combined to form multi-word keywords. The algorithm is inspired by PageRank which was originally used by Google to rank websites.

YAKE [41] is not a graph-based approach. It is a statistical algorithm where the importance of words is determined by word frequencies and other measures, such as how much a given word resembles a stop word, for example [25] [a].

The sCAKE (Semantic Connectivity Aware Keyword Extraction) [68] and SGRank (Statistical and Graphical) [58] algorithms rely on a hybrid approach and use both graphical and statistical methods to generate an importance score.

---
[a]http://yake.inesctec.pt/demo.html

```
! pip install textacy==0.9.1
! python -m spacy download en_core_web_sm

from textacy import load_spacy_lang, make_spacy_doc
from textacy.ke import sgrank, textrank

en = load_spacy_lang(
 "en_core_web_sm", disable=("parser",)
)
doc = make_spacy_doc(text, lang=en)

# TextRank
tr = textrank(doc, normalize="lemma", topn=5)

# SGRank
sg = sgrank(doc, topn=5)


print("\n\n TextRank keyphrases \n ", [kp for kp, _ in tr])
print("\n\n SGRank keyphrases \n ", [kp for kp, _ in sg])
```

Here are the top 5 keywords.

TextRank keyphrases

['natural language processing', 'natural language datum', 'computer capable', 'computer science', 'human language']

SGRank keyphrases

['natural language datum', 'natural language processing', 'artificial intelligence', 'human language', 'computer science']

7.1.2.2 rake-nltk

Rapid Automatic Keyword Extraction, or RAKE, is a domain-independent keyword extraction algorithm. The logic analyzes the frequency of word appearance and its co-occurrence with other words in the text. Many open-source contributors have implemented RAKE. Usage of one such RAKE implementation with NLTK is as follows.

```
! pip install rake-nltk==1.0.6

from rake-nltk import Rake

# Considers nltk english stopwords and punctuations
r = Rake()

r.extract_keyqwords_from_text(text)

# top 5 keyphrases
print(r.get_ranked_phrases()[:5])
```

The output is as follows.

['artificial intelligence concerned', 'analyze large amounts', 'accurately extract information', 'natural language processing', 'natural language data']

7.1.2.3 KeyBERT

KeyBERT implements a keyword extraction algorithm that leverages sentence-BERT (SBERT) embeddings to create keywords and keyphrases that are most similar to the input document.

The logic involves the generation of document embeddings using SBERT model, followed by the extraction of n-gram phrases from the embeddings. Then, cosine similarity is used to measure the similarity of each keyphrase to the document. The most similar words can then be identified as the terms that best describe the entire document and are considered keywords and keyphrases.

```
! pip install keybert==0.5.1

from keybert import KeyBERT

# any model from sbert.net/docs/pretrained_models.html
# can be specified below
# default model = all-MiniLM-L6-v2
```

```
kw_model = KeyBERT()

keywords = kw_model.extract_keywords(text)

keywords = kw_model.extract_keywords(
  text, keyphrase_ngram_range=(1, 3),
  stop_words=None, highlight=True
)
```

Here is the output.

> [('processing nlp', 0.7913), ('language processing nlp', 0.7629), ('processing nlp is', 0.7527), ('natural language processing', 0.7435), ('of natural language', 0.6745)]

There are many other ways to get keyphrase extraction in Python. Some other libraries include `MultiRake` (multilingual rake), `summa` (TextRank algorithm), `Gensim` (`summarization.keywords` in version 3.8.3), and `pke`.

In general, preprocessing of the text, what 'n' to choose in n-grams, and which algorithm to use are factors that can change the outcome of the KPE model that you construct and are worth experimenting with to fine-tune your model.

> *TIP*
>
> Some common problems in results include overlapping keyphrases, for example, 'stock price' and 'buy stock price'. Post-extraction cleaning works well to clean up the result set. A cosine similarity measure between returned keyphrases can help identify some duplicates. KPE is also sensitive to sentence structure. Post-processing of the results to clean them up can help with most issues and improve overall results.

> *TIP*
>
> Most KPE algorithms are sensitive to the length of your text and can take a long time to run. To shorten the time, one approach that is sometimes applied is trimming the content to the first few and last few sentences. This works well if a good gist of the content can be assumed to be at the beginning (introduction) and at the end (conclusion).

The code used for KPE can be found in section5/KPE.ipynb.

7.2   TEXT SUMMARIZATION

Many industries are researching and using text summarization applications, such as insurance and legal. When you have large documents, searching through them all can be a time-consuming and low-efficiency application. Text summarization can help with the shortening of documents that can make search operations faster.

Broadly, text summarization is of two types.

1. Extractive summarization
   Certain phrases or sentences from the original text are identified and extracted. Together, these extractions form the summary.

2. Abstractive summarization
   New sentences are generated to form the summary. In contrast to extractive summarization, the sentences contained with in the generated summary may not be present at all in the original text.

7.2.1   Extractive summarization

This is the most popular summarization that finds applications across industries. Typically, graph-based sentence ranking approaches are popularly adopted to solve this problem. Different open-source tools can be leveraged to implement extractive summarization. The overall principle is as follows - each sentence in a document is assigned a score based on its relationship with every other sentence in the document. The scoring can be different based on the model/library you use. Finally, the sentences with the top scores together form the summary of the document. As you might be able to sense from the approach, summarizers can be sensitive to overall document length, and it can be a low-efficiency computation. As a solution, practitioners sometimes run a summarization on only some parts of the document rather than the entire document. If you expect the main information of your document to be embedded towards the start and the end, you can trim the document down before passing it through summarization for faster performance.

7.2.1.1   Classic open-source models

sumy

The most common algorithm for this use case is called TextRank. TextRank is a graph-based ranking model for text processing that can be used to find keywords and the most relevant sentences in text. Open-source library **sumy** can be used to implement text summarization based on Textrank.

```
! pip install sumy==0.11.0
! pip install nltk

# You will need to run this one time
import nltk
nltk.download("punkt")
```

We'll use the text from the Wikipedia page on 'Data Science' as the document we want to summarize.

```
from sumy.parsers.html import HtmlParser
from sumy.nlp.tokenizers import Tokenizer
from sumy.summarizers.text_rank import TextRankSummarizer

url = "https://en.wikipedia.org/wiki/Data_science"
parser = HtmlParser.from_url(url, Tokenizer("english"))
summarizer = TextRankSummarizer()
for sentence in summarizer(parser.document, 4):
  print(sentence)
```

The above results in the following summary.

> Turing Award winner Jim Gray imagined data science as a 'fourth paradigm' of science (empirical, theoretical, computational, and now data-driven) and asserted that 'everything about science is changing because of the impact of information technology' and the data deluge. [20] Later, attendees at a 1992 statistics symposium at the University of Montpellier II acknowledged the emergence of a new discipline focused on data of various origins and forms, combining established concepts and principles of statistics and data analysis with computing. [24]'Data science' became more widely used in the next few years: in 2002, the Committee on Data for Science and Technology launched Data Science Journal. [24] In 2014, the American Statistical Association's Section on Statistical Learning and Data Mining changed its name to the Section on Statistical Learning and Data Science, reflecting the ascendant popularity of data science.

Gensim

Gensim, another open-source library in Python, implements an improvised version of TextRank and can be used to get document summaries as well. This support was removed in Gensim 4.0 onwards, but you can still use the functionality by installing Gensim 3.8. [8]

```
! pip install gensim==3.8.3
```

Let's define the variable *text* as the contents of the Wikipedia webpage on 'Data Science'.[9]

```
from gensim.summarization import summarize

text = "" # replace with the text you want to summarize

# ratio param can help us specify the proportion
# of sentences to retain
gensim_summary = summarize(text, ratio=0.055)

print(gensim_summary)
```

The above leads to the following result.

> A data scientist is someone who creates programming code and combines it with statistical knowledge to create insights from data.[7] Data science is an interdisciplinary

---

[8]https://github.com/RaRe-Technologies/gensim/wiki/Migrating-from-Gensim-3.x-to-4#12-removed-gensimsummarization

[9]https://en.wikipedia.org/wiki/Data_science

field focused on extracting knowledge from data sets, which are typically large (see big data), and applying the knowledge and actionable insights from data to solve problems in a wide range of application domains.[8] The field encompasses preparing data for analysis, formulating data science problems, analyzing data, developing data-driven solutions, and presenting findings to inform high-level decisions in a broad range of application domains.

7.2.1.2 Transformers

We discussed transformer models in Chapter 4. Library `bert-extractive-summarizer` can be used for document summarization using transformer models like BERT, GPT-2, and XLNet. Each of these models comes in different sizes.

Let's look at their implementation in code below. We'll use the same value for variable *text* as above, i.e., the Wikipedia page on 'Data Science'.

```
! pip install transformers
! pip install bert-extractive-summarizer==0.10.1

# BERT
from summarizer import Summarizer

bert_model = Summarizer()
bert_summary = ''.join(
    bert_model(text, min_length=60, max_length=500)
)
print(bert_summary)
```

You can control the `min_length` and `max_length` of the summary. BERT summarization results in the following.

> Data science is an interdisciplinary field that uses scientific methods, processes, algorithms and systems to extract knowledge and insights from noisy, structured and unstructured data,[1][2] and apply knowledge and actionable insights from data across a broad range of application domains. Data science is a 'concept to unify statistics, data analysis, informatics, and their related methods' in order to 'understand and analyze actual phenomena' with data.[3] It uses techniques and theories drawn from many fields within the context of mathematics, statistics, computer science, information science, and domain knowledge.[4] However, data science is different from computer science and information science. Further information: Statistics Âǧ Methods
> Linear regression
> Logistic regression
> Decision trees are used as prediction models for classification and data fitting.

Other transformer models can be called as below.

```
# GPT2
from summarizer import TransformerSummarizer

gpt2_model = TransformerSummarizer(
    transformer_type="GPT2",
    transformer_model_key="gpt2-medium"
)
gpt2_summary = ''.join(
    gpt2_model(text, min_length=60, max_length=500)
```

```
)
print(gpt2_summary)


# XLNet
from summarizer import TransformerSummarizer

xlnet_model = TransformerSummarizer(
  transformer_type="XLNet",
  transformer_model_key="xlnet-base-cased"
)
xlnet_summary = ''.join(
  xlnet_model(text, min_length=60, max_length=500)
)
print(xlnet_summary)
```

GPT-2 summarization results in the following.

> Data science is an interdisciplinary field that uses scientific methods, processes, algorithms and systems to extract knowledge and insights from noisy, structured and unstructured data,[1,2] and apply knowledge and actionable insights from data across a broad range of application domains. He describes data science as an applied field growing out of traditional statistics.[18] In summary, data science can be therefore described as an applied branch of statistics. The decision tree structure can be used to generate rules able to classify or predict target/class/label variable based on the observation attributes.

XLNet summarization results in the following.

> Data science is an interdisciplinary field that uses scientific methods, processes, algorithms and systems to extract knowledge and insights from noisy, structured and unstructured data,[1,2] and apply knowledge and actionable insights from data across a broad range of application domains. Support-vector machine (SVM)
> Cluster analysis is a technique used to group data together. Naive Bayes classifiers are used to classify by applying the Bayes' theorem.

The code used in this section can be found in the notebook section5/extractive-summarization.ipynb.

7.2.2 Abstractive summarization

Abstractive text summarization (ATS) has been primarily dominant in the field of research and is not yet an application that is widely implemented in the industry other than in organizations focused on research. ATS has been gaining prominence in recent years and there now exist a few options to implement these models.

1. Service provider Google offers an abstractive summarization tool [10].

2. Hugging Face offers transformers fine-tuned for summarization [11]. We'll look into T5, BART, and PEGASUS.

---

[10]https://cloud.google.com/ai-workshop/experiments/abstractive-document-summarization

[11]https://huggingface.co/course/chapter7/5?fw=pt#models-for-text-summarization

7.2.2.1 Transformers

T5

We can use a sequence-to-sequence model like T5 [137] [12] for abstractive text summarization. We'll pass in the same text we did for the previous section.

```
! pip install transformers

from transformers import pipeline

summarizer = pipeline(
  "summarization",
  model="t5-base",
  tokenizer="t5-base",
  framework="tf"
)


summary = summarizer(
  text, min_length=50, max_length=500
)
print(summary)
```

The above results in the following abstract summary. The bold text represents the sentences formed by the model that were not present in this exact form in the input document.

> **data science is an interdisciplinary field that uses scientific methods, processes, algorithms and systems . many statisticians, including Nate Silver, have argued that it is not a new field, but another name for statistics . a data scientist creates programming code and combines it with statistical knowledge .**

BART

BART models come in different sizes that can be found on Hugging Face's website[13]. The following code sample uses **bart-base** model for abstractive summarization.

```
from transformers import pipeline

bart_summarizer = pipeline(
  "summarization",
  model="facebook/bart-base",
  tokenizer="facebook/bart-base"
)


bart_summary = bart_summarizer(
  text,
  min_length=50,
  max_length=500,
  truncation=True
)
print(bart_summary)
```

---

[12]https://huggingface.co/docs/transformers/model_doc/t5
[13]https://huggingface.co/docs/transformers/model_doc/bart

Below are the first few sentences from the returned abstract summary. The bold text represents the new sentences formed by the model.

> Data science is an interdisciplinary field that uses scientific methods, processes, algorithms and systems to extract knowledge and insights from noisy, structured and unstructured data,[1][2] and apply knowledge and actionable insights from data across a broad range of application domains. Data science is related to data mining, machine learning and big data. The term 'data science' has been traced back to 1974, when Peter Naur proposed it as an alternative name for computer science.[4] However, data science is different from computer science and information science. **Turing Award winner Jim Gray imagined data science as a 'concept to unify statistics, data analysis, informatics, and their related methods' in order to 'understand and analyze actual phenomena' with data.[3] It uses techniques and theories drawn from many fields within the context of mathematics, statistics, computer science, information science, technology, engineering, and domain knowledge.[4][5]**

PEGASUS

PEGASUS is currently the state-of-the-art for abstractive summarization on many benchmark datasets. For our demo, we will use the fine-tuned model google/pegasus-xsum.

```
from transformers import pipeline

p_summarizer = pipeline(
  'summarization',
  model='google/pegasus-xsum',
  tokenizer='google/pegasus-xsum'
)

p_summary = p_summarizer(
  text,
  min_length=50,
  max_length=500,
  truncation=True
)
print(p_summary)
```

The bold text represents the new sentences formed by the model.

> **Data science is an emerging field that uses scientific methods, processes, algorithms and systems to extract knowledge and insights from noisy, structured and unstructured data, and apply knowledge and actionable insights from data across a broad range of application domains, according to the American Statistical Association.**

The code used in this section can be found at section5/abstractive-summarization.ipynb.

Many other fine-tuned models based on PEGASUS, BART, and T5 are available to use from Hugging Face. You can find a complete list of fine-tuned transformer models for summarization at [14].

---

[14]https://huggingface.co/models?language=en&pipeline_tag=summarization&sort=downloads

For this task, it is common to use a solution option that already exists with the available fine-tuned models. You can also fine-tune your own models on custom datasets [15]. This solution can be time-consuming and requires labeled data with summaries. Due to lack of labeled data, this option is primarily explored by industry practitioners with a primary focus on research or domain-specific datasets.

7.3 LANGUAGE DETECTION AND TRANSLATION

Language translation is an important application across several industries, especially global businesses reaching customers across the world. Here, we will look at implementations of language detection and language translation (also called machine translation). Most state-of-the-art machine translation tools contain and offer language detection capabilities.

7.3.1 Language detection

Language detection is helpful if you do not know what language your text is in. Here's a quick solution for detecting language using the open-source library `langdetect`. The code can also be found in section5/language-detection.ipynb.

```
! pip install langdetect==1.0.9

from langdetect import detect

detect("Hello. How are you?") # English
# >> 'en'

detect("Hogy vagy ma?") # Hungarian
# >> 'hu'
```

7.3.2 Machine translation

Machine translation refers to language translation for text or speech data. It is considered a sub-field of computational linguistics.

7.3.2.1 Paid services

The state-of-the-art solutions for machine translation are neural learning-based models. It forms a popular subject in research and the big industrial players like Google [16], Amazon [17], Microsoft [18], and IBM [19] offer state-of-the-art translations via an API. The charge is typically per-use and may be the best option for reliable translation.

---

[15] https://huggingface.co/docs/transformers/tasks/summarization
[16] https://cloud.google.com/translate
[17] https://aws.amazon.com/translate/
[18] https://www.microsoft.com/en-us/translator/
[19] https://www.ibm.com/cloud/watson-language-translator

Table 7.1 lists out a comparison of the machine translation offerings by different industry leaders. [20]

TABLE 7.1 State-of-the-art translation services.

Service	URL	Cost	Number of supported languages
Amazon Translate	docs.aws.amazon.com/ translate/	Pay-as-you-go based on the number of characters of text that you processed + special offers	75
Google Cloud translation	cloud.google.com/translate	Based on monthly usage + special offers	>100
Watson Language Translator	www.ibm.com/cloud /watson-language-translator	Differs with the various pricing plans options	>75
Azure translator	azure.microsoft.com/en-us/services/cognitive-services/translator/	Pay as you go	>100

7.3.2.2 Labeled open-source

Translate

As for free open-source options, the `translate` library provides free translations from MyMemory [21] as the default, which is a translation memory i.e., a database that stores sentence-like units that have previously been translated. Since individual contributors aid in creating translations without strong correctness checks, some results may not be reliable. Moreover, free, anonymous usage is limited to 5000 chars/day. There are options for increasing the limit in their documentation. Per this tool's setup, exceeding the limitation will not throw an error in translations, but overwrite the return variable supposed to hold the actual translation with the error message as follows.

MYMEMORY WARNING: YOU USED ALL AVAILABLE FREE TRANSLATIONS FOR TODAY. NEXT AVAILABLE IN 10 HOURS 07 MINUTES 34 SECONDS VISIT HTTPS://MYMEMORY.TRANSLATED.NET/DOC/USAGELIMITS.PHP TO TRANSLATE MORE

```
! pip install translate==3.6.1

from translate import Translator
```

---

[20]https://learn.vonage.com/blog/2019/12/10/text-translation-api-comparison-dr/
[21]https://mymemory.translated.net/

```
en_hi_translator = Translator(
  from_lang="english", to_lang="hindi"
)
translation = en_hi_translator.translate("How are you today?")
print(translation)
```

>> Aj abhi aap bhi kha lo (This is not a correct translation.)

```
translation = en_hi_translator.translate("How are you?")
print(translation)
```

>> क्या हाल है? (This is a correct translation.)

```
hu_hi_translator = Translator(
  from_lang="hungarian", to_lang="hindi"
)
translation = hu_hi_translator.translate("Hogy vagy ma?")
print(translation)
```

>> आप कैसे हैं? (This is a correct translation.)

The code can be found at section5/language-translation-translate.ipynb.

While this may not be a production-friendly tool, it can be helpful if you are working on a prototype and want to get some quick translations using Python.

7.3.2.3 *Transformers*

You can also perform language translation using Hugging Face **transformers** library.

The following example converts English to French. The default model for the pipeline is t5-base.

```
from transformers import pipeline

en_fr_translator = pipeline("translation_en_to_fr")
print(en_fr_translator("Is this true?"))
```

  Est-ce vrai?

The below example converts Spanish to English.

```
from transformers import pipeline

es_en_translator = pipeline(
  "translation", model="Helsinki-NLP/opus-mt-es-en"
)
print(es_en_translator("Me gusta esto muchisimo"))
```

  I like this so much.

The above code can be found in section5/language-translation-transformers.ipynb.

The complete list of transformer models for language translation can be found here.[22]

---

[22]https://huggingface.co/models?pipeline_tag=translation&sort=downloads

> *TIP*
>
> Using service providers is popular for language translation among businesses. This is a convenient option for companies where you don't require a workforce with a data science background to implement the solution. For companies with research teams building custom models, transformers perform well for language translation tasks. In general, models do better with more training data for such applications.

## CHAPTER 8

Text Categorization and Affinities

In this chapter, we will implement topic modeling, text similarity, and text classification including sentiment classification.

8.1 TOPIC MODELING

Topic modeling refers to statistical modeling for discovering abstract topics in a collection of documents. It is used for unsupervised classification or clustering of data. Imagine you have a massive list of books and have a few sentences of description for each. How would you club or categorize books around similar topics together without having to manually look at every title? A solution to such a problem can be implemented using topic modeling. Such algorithms help find natural groups of topics when we don't already know all the ones our corpus contains. The main application areas include searching, summarizing, understanding, and organizing documents.

8.1.1 Latent dirichlet allocation (LDA)

Let's see how we can implement topic modeling using Latent Dirichlet Allocation (LDA) in Python with open-source tools. The full code can be found at section5/LDA-topic-modeling.ipynb.

One popular way to go about it is using the library `Gensim`.

In our example, we have four documents, where each document is the description of a different textbook as seen in Figure 8.1.

To clean the data, we'll remove stop words, punctuation, and lemmatize the words.

```
! pip install gensim

from nltk.corpus import stopwords
from nltk.stem.wordnet import WordNetLemmatizer
import string

documents = [doc1, doc2, doc3, doc4]

# Text preprocessing as discussed in book's Part 2
```

DOI: 10.1201/9781003264774-8

FIGURE 8.1 Books whose descriptions were used to build our LDA model. Source doc1 [23], doc2 [82], doc3 [90], doc4 [76].

```python
stop = set(stopwords.words('english'))
exclude = set(string.punctuation)
lemma = WordNetLemmatizer()
def clean(doc):
  stop_free = " ".join(
    [i for i in doc.lower().split() if i not in stop]
  )
  punc_free = "".join(
    [ch for ch in stop_free if ch not in exclude]
  )
  normalized = " ".join(
    lemma.lemmatize(word) for word in punc_free.split()
  )
  return normalized

processed_docs = [
  clean(doc).split() for doc in documents
]
```

Next, we use `Gensim` to index each term in our corpus and create a bag-of-words matrix.

```python
import gensim
from gensim import corpora

# Creating the term dictionary of our corpus,
# where every unique term is assigned an index.
dictionary = corpora.Dictionary(processed_docs)
```

```
# Filter infrequent or too frequent words.
#dictionary.filter_extremes(no_below=10, no_above=0.5)
# Converting a list of documents (corpus) into
# Document-Term Matrix using dictionary prepared above.
doc_term_matrix = [
  dictionary.doc2bow(doc) for doc in processed_docs
]
```

Finally, we create the LDA model. Some trial and error on the number of topics is required.

```
# Creating the object for LDA model using gensim library
lda = gensim.models.ldamodel.LdaModel
# Running and Training LDA model on the
# document term matrix for 3 topics
lda_model = lda(
  doc_term_matrix,
  num_topics=3,
  id2word=dictionary,
  passes=20
)
# Results
for itm in lda_model.print_topics():
  print(itm)
  print("\n")
```

The output is as follows.

(0, '0.048*"management" + 0.043*"revenue" + 0.012*"book" + 0.012*"spectrum" + 0.012*"emerging" + 0.012*"business" + 0.012*"organization" + 0.012*"give" + 0.012*"practice" + 0.012*"particular"')

(1, "0.032*"learning" + 0.022*"machine" + 0.018*"sport" + 0.015*"ai" + 0.015*"method" + 0.015*"data" + 0.015*"net" + 0.013*"deep" + 0.013*"neural" + 0.010*"scientist"")

(2, '0.043*"influence" + 0.032*"social" + 0.017*"process" + 0.017*"research" + 0.012*"theory" + 0.012*"role" + 0.012*"phenomenon" + 0.012*"behavior" + 0.012*"strategy" + 0.012*"volume"')

A topic model returns a collection of keywords per topic. It is up to human interpretation as to what each topic represents in the LDA model. Here, we can see three distinct topics - revenue & management, machine learning / deep learning, and social influence.

Now, let's pass an unseen book description from the book seen in Figure 8.2 to this model and see which topic it gets assigned. unseen_document in our example is the description of the book shown in Figure 8.3.

```
unseen_document = ""#
bow_vector = dictionary.doc2bow(
  clean(unseen_document).split()
)
for index, score in sorted(
  lda_model[bow_vector], key=lambda tup: -1*tup[1]
):
  print("Score: {}\t Topic: {}\n".format(
    score, lda_model.print_topic(index, 5))
  )
```

FIGURE 8.2 The book used to test our LDA model. Source [188].

Book description

Organizations spend huge resources in developing software that can perform the way a human does. Image classification, object detection and tracking, pose estimation, facial recognition, and sentiment estimation all play a major role in solving computer vision problems.

This book will bring into focus these and other deep learning architectures and techniques to help you create solutions using Keras and the TensorFlow library. You'll also review mutliple neural network architectures, including LeNet, AlexNet, VGG, Inception, R-CNN, Fast R-CNN, Faster R-CNN, Mask R-CNN, YOLO, and SqueezeNet and see how they work alongside Python code via best practices, tips, tricks, shortcuts, and pitfalls. All code snippets will be broken down and discussed thoroughly so you can implement the same principles in your respective environments.

Computer Vision Using Deep Learning offers a comprehensive yet succinct guide that stitches DL and CV together to automate operations, reduce human intervention, increase capability, and cut the costs.

FIGURE 8.3 The book description to test our LDA model.

The log is as follows.

Score: 0.7505645155906677 Topic: 0.032*"learning" + 0.022*"machine" + 0.018*"sport" + 0.015*"ai" + 0.015*"method"

Score: 0.18311436474323273 Topic: 0.043*"influence" + 0.032*"social" + 0.017*"process" + 0.017*"research" + 0.012*"theory"

Score: 0.06632108241319656 Topic: 0.048*"management" + 0.043*"revenue" + 0.012*"book" + 0.012*"spectrum" + 0.012*"emerging"

We can see it got bucketed with the highest score on the topic of machine learning / deep learning.

> *TIP*
>
> This model was built for demonstration. We only used a handful of samples. In a practical scenario, you would train this model on a much larger corpus to extract meaningful topics from the data.

8.2   TEXT SIMILARITY

Text similarity is the determination of how close two pieces of text are. There are many different types of text similarities. Similarity is determined by the distance between two documents or words. We have discussed many numerical representations of text and distance metrics in Chapter 3 (Section 3.4) and Chapter 4 (Section 4.1).

Semantic similarity refers to the context similarity between two documents. Examples include words or phrases that are related to each other conceptually such as *car* and *truck* are both vehicles, *car* is related to *driving* and *road*, etc.

Finding numerical representation of two documents followed by using an appropriate distance metric can be used to find similarities between two documents. Cosine distance is used most popularly as it is not impacted by magnitude of numerical vectors and helps with finding directionally and contextually similar vectors (the smaller the distance, the higher the similarity).

> *TIP*
>
> Another approach to finding similar documents is using clustering approaches. We looked at using LDA for topic modeling above. That model can also be used to group similar documents.

Let's dive into different ways of implementing text similarity below.

8.2.1   Elasticsearch

If you have your data housed in Elasticsearch, you can write a query to find similar records to a record or any piece of text. Its underlying principle works by computing TF-IDF followed by cosine distance. To find records similar to some custom text, use the field *like*. All the fields to consider for computing similarity are listed under *fields*. You can define several other parameters to tune the model. The documentation lists out the different inputs accepted[1].

An example query is as follows.

```
{
 "query": {
    "more_like_this" : {
        "fields" : ["title"],
        "like" : "elasticsearch is fast",
        "min_term_freq" : 1,
        "max_query_terms" : 12
    }
 }
}
```

---

[1]https://www.elastic.co/guide/en/elasticsearch/reference/current/query-dsl-mlt-query.html

8.2.2   Classic TF-IDF approach

One of the oldest and still very popular approaches is computing the TF-IDF of the documents followed by finding the cosine distance between documents to find similar ones.

We can preprocess the text before computing TF-IDF to get rid of noise elements depending on how our dataset looks.

Let's look at a code sample. Here, we'll use `sklearn` to get the cosine similarity metric.

```
! pip install scikit-learn

from sklearn.feature_extraction.text import TfidfVectorizer
from sklearn.metrics.pairwise import cosine_similarity

# this is your corpus
docs_list = [
  "I like cold soda",
  "hot chocolate is filling",
  "ice cream is cold",
  "burger tastes best when hot"
] # replace with text items in a list

# this is the item you want to find similar items to
sample = "hot meal"
```

Fit the vectorizer and transform your data

```
vect = TfidfVectorizer()
# get tfidf of all samples in the corpus
tfidf = vect.fit_transform(docs_list)

# get tfidf vector for sample document
selected_itm = vect.transform([sample])
```

Next, use cosine similarity to get the results.

```
# similarity between sample doc & the rest of the corpus
cosine_sim = [
  cosine_similarity(selected_itm, itm)[0][0]
  for itm in tfidf
]

# top matches with scores
inxs = sorted(
  range(len(cosine_sim)),
  key=lambda i: cosine_sim[i],
  reverse=True
)
for i in inxs:
  print(docs_list[i], cosine_sim[i])
```

hot chocolate is filling 0.4377912310861148

burger tastes best when hot 0.3667390112974172

I like cold soda 0.0

icecream is cold 0.0

This code can be found in section5/text-similarity-tfidf.ipynb.

8.2.3 Pre-trained word embedding models

Another popular way of solving this problem is using word embeddings. This can be done by calculating the word vectors for each document. Having that for the two different documents, you can calculate the distance between their vectors using cosine distance.

> *TIP*
>
> Using pre-trained models is especially useful when you don't yet have a corpus. When you have a lack of data, a pre-trained model can help get you moving.

We discussed many word embedding models in Chapter 3 (Section 3.4.4) with code samples, advantages, and disadvantages. Any method can be used for the application of text similarity in conjunction with cosine similarity. Let's look at code samples for some of them below.

spaCy

Here's a code sample of computing text similarity with spaCy using an existing model. You can choose from any of the available pre-trained models with this library.

```
! pip install spacy
! python -m spacy download "en_core_web_lg"

import spacy

nlp = spacy.load("en_core_web_lg")

docs = [
  nlp(u"I like cold soda"),
  nlp(u"hot chocolate is filling"),
  nlp(u"ice cream is cold"),
  nlp(u"burger tastes best when hot")
]

sample = nlp(u"hot meal")

for doc in docs:
  print(doc, "<>", sample, "->", doc.similarity(sample))
```

The results are as follows.

I like cold soda <> hot meal -> 0.6526761073589249

hot chocolate is filling <> hot meal -> 0.7840665641430987

ice cream is cold <> hot meal -> 0.6564778194706912

burger tastes best when hot <> hot meal -> 0.8263906754007433

Gensim

Another way of getting cosine similarty is using the `Gensim` library as follows.

```
! pip install gensim
```

```
import gensim.downloader as api
corpus = api.load('word2vec-google-news-300')

print(
  corpus.n_similarity(
    ['hot', 'meal'],
    ['burger', 'tastes', 'best', 'when', 'hot']
  )
)
# >> 0.674938
print(
  corpus.n_similarity(
    ['hot', 'meal'],
    ['I', 'like', 'cold', 'soda']
  )
)
# >> 0.46843547
```

Transformers

We will use the **sentence-transformers** library [142] with the model name specified as below to get word embeddings. This library uses Hugging Face **transformers** behind the scenes. Then, we will use cosine similarity to measure text similarity. The full list of available models can be found at[2].

```
! pip install transformers
! pip install sentence-transformers
```

```
from sentence_transformers import SentenceTransformer, util
import numpy as np

model = SentenceTransformer('stsb-roberta-base')
doc1 = "hot chocolate is filling"
doc2 = "ice cream is cold"
samp = "hot meal"

# encode sentences to get their embeddings
embedding1 = model.encode(doc1, convert_to_tensor=True)
embedding2 = model.encode(doc2, convert_to_tensor=True)
samp_embedding = model.encode(samp, convert_to_tensor=True)

# compute similarity scores of two embeddings
cosine_scores = util.cos_sim(embedding1, samp_embedding)
print("Similarity score:", cosine_scores.item())
# >> Similarity score: 0.3480038046836853

cosine_scores = util.cos_sim(embedding2, samp_embedding)
print("Similarity score:", cosine_scores.item())
# >> Similarity score: 0.11001470685005188
```

---

[2]https://www.sbert.net/docs/pretrained_models.html

Replacing the model with `bert-base-nli-mean-tokens`, we get the following results.

```
bert_model = SentenceTransformer('bert-base-nli-mean-tokens')

# encode sentences to get their embeddings
embedding1 = bert_model.encode(doc1, convert_to_tensor=True)
embedding2 = bert_model.encode(doc2, convert_to_tensor=True)
samp_embedding = bert_model.encode(samp, convert_to_tensor=True)

# compute similarity scores of two embeddings
cosine_scores = util.cos_sim(embedding1, samp_embedding)
print("Similarity score:", cosine_scores.item())
# >>Similarity score: 0.7925456762313843

cosine_scores = util.cos_sim(embedding2, samp_embedding)
print("Similarity score:", cosine_scores.item())
# >> Similarity score: 0.30324894189834595
```

The code used can be found at section5/text-similarity-embeddings.ipynb.

8.3 TEXT CLASSIFICATION

Text classification refers to the task of categorizing data into different types or classes. Usually, these classes/categories are known or pre-defined. There are several ways to leverage machine learning for solving text classification tasks.

8.3.1 Off-the-shelf content classifiers

Text classification has been popular for many years. Researchers and practitioners have been able to create and benchmark text classifiers that classify data into popular categories. If your use case feels like something that someone may have already done in the past, it is worth checking existing tools that you can leverage. An example of common text classification includes sentiment classification, which is the task of classifying a piece of text into positive, negative, or neutral categories. There are multiple open-source tools, such as **VADER** and **TextBlob**, that can be leveraged for sentiment analysis without needing to train custom models. Outside of open-source options, most major service providers including Google, Amazon, and Microsoft, serve sentiment analysis APIs with varying payment plan options. We'll discuss sentiment analysis in more detail later in this Section 8.4.

In general, for any text classification task, you can consider using existing APIs if they serve your classification needs. For instance, the Google Cloud Natural Language provides off-the-shelf content classification models that can identify approximately 700 different categories of text[3].

8.3.1.1 Zero-shot classification

If your labels are known, you can use zero-shot classification so you don't have to rely on the labels of an available pre-trained model. Zero-shot learning is the ability

---

[3]https://cloud.google.com/natural-language/docs/classifying-text

to complete a task without any training examples. Hugging Face `transformers` can be used for zero-shot classification using any one of their models offered for this task. You can choose from the various models fine-tuned for this task at[4]. Here's how it would look like in Python with the model `distilbert-base-uncased-mnli`.

```
from transformers import pipeline

classifier = pipeline(
  "zero-shot-classification",
  model="typeform/distilbert-base-uncased-mnli"
)

classifier(
  "This is a book about Natural Language Processing.",
  candidate_labels=["education", "politics", "business"],
)
```

    'sequence': 'This is a book about Natural Language Processing.',

    'labels': ['education', 'politics', 'business'],

    'scores': [0.421528697013855, 0.32243525981903076, 0.2560359835624695]

```
classifier(
  "I saw a large python crawing in the jungle behind the house.",
  candidate_labels=["animal", "programming"]
)
```

    'sequence': 'I saw a large python crawing in the jungle behind the house.',

    'labels': ['animal', 'programming'],

    'scores': [0.6283940076828003, 0.3716059923171997]

```
classifier(
  "NLP applications can be implemented using Python.",
  candidate_labels=["animal", "programming"],
)
```

    'sequence': 'NLP applications can be implemented using Python.',

    'labels': ['programming', 'animal'],

    'scores': [0.9994968175888062, 0.0005031615728512406]

These classifiers may not work well for all use cases, such as the below example.

```
classifier(
  "I wanna order a medium pizza for pick up at 6pm.",
  candidate_labels=["delivery", "pickup"],
)
```

    'sequence': 'I wanna order a medium pizza for pick up at 6pm.',

    'labels': ['delivery', 'pickup'],

    'scores': [0.9513348937034607, 0.04866514727473259]

The code can be found at section5/text-classification-zero-shot.ipynb.

---

[4]https://huggingface.co/models?language=en&pipeline_tag=zero-shot-classification&sort=downloads

8.3.2 Classifying with available labeled data

In the event you are required to build a custom classification model, the following example will walk you through the steps involved in building such a model and the considerations to keep in mind.

Let's consider the spam/not-spam(called ham here) dataset.[5] This dataset contains text documents and an associated label for each document.

The typical flow of steps is as follows.

1. Removing any bad samples (Null, too short, etc.) from your data

2. Cleaning / preprocessing text

3. Forming features (numerical representations)

4. Passing through a supervised learning model

5. Model hyperparameter tuning, cross-validation evaluation, and testing

Now, let's build a *spam vs ham* classifier.

8.3.2.1 Classic ML

```
! pip install nltk
! pip install pandas
! pip install scikit-learn
import nltk
nltk.download('wordnet')

import pandas as pd

# Read dataset
df = pd.read_csv("spam.csv", encoding ='latin1')

# Rename columns, remove unused columns
df.rename(
  columns={'v1': 'class', 'v2': 'text'},
  inplace=True
)
drop_columns = [
  col
  for col in df.columns
  if col not in ['class', 'text']
]
df.drop(drop_columns, axis=1, inplace=True)

print(df['class'].value_counts(normalize=True))
# >>  ham     0.865937
# >>  spam    0.134063
```

86.5% of the data belongs to class ham. There is a high class imbalance.

---

[5]http://archive.ics.uci.edu/ml/machine-learning-databases/spambase/.

> TIP
>
> In class imbalance cases as above, once we build the model, looking at the overall accuracy, precision, and/or F1 score would not be enough to understand how the model would work on unseen data. Looking at evaluation metrics per class is important.

Exploring the text by manually checking samples, we find some informal language and excess punctuation. Now, let's preprocess the text by removing stop words, punctuation, and lemmatizing the words. You can experiment further here by adding and removing other cleaning steps, such as removing specific words, stemming, etc.

```python
import string
import random
from nltk.corpus import stopwords
from nltk.stem.wordnet import WordNetLemmatizer

stop = set(stopwords.words('english'))
exclude = set(string.punctuation)
lemma = WordNetLemmatizer()

def clean(doc):
    """
    Removes stopwords, punctuation, and lemmatizes input.
    """
    stop_free = " ".join(
        [i for i in doc.lower().split() if i not in stop]
    )
    punc_free = "".join(
        [ch for ch in stop_free if ch not in exclude]
    )
    normalized = " ".join(
        lemma.lemmatize(word)
        for word in punc_free.split()
    )
    return normalized

data = df.values.tolist()
cleaned_data = [
    (clean(doc), label) for label, doc in data
]
cleaned_data = [
    (d, l) for d, l in cleaned_data in len(d) > 5
]
random.shuffle(cleaned_data)
x = [itm[0] for itm in cleaned_data]
y = [itm[1] for itm in cleaned_data]
```

Next, we'll build features and split the data into training and testing sets. Here, we will build TF-IDF features from the text data. The min_df, max_df, and `max_features` parameters can be experimented with to find the right values for your dataset.

You can build other features and experiment further with your model. We described some of the other feature options in Chapter 3.

```python
from sklearn.model_selection import train_test_split
from sklearn.feature_extraction.text import TfidfVectorizer

train_x, valid_x, train_y, valid_y = train_test_split(x, y)

vectorizer = TfidfVectorizer(
  max_df=0.9, min_df=0.01, max_features=5000
)

# fitting on training samples only
X_train = vectorizer.fit_transform(train_x)

# transforming using the vectorizer that was fit on training data
X_valid = vectorizer.transform(valid_x)
```

Here, we will try the MultinomialNB classification model, which is known to do well on text data.

TIP

MultinomialNB classifier has a hyperparameter called `alpha`. Different values of `alpha` may yield different results. You can compare results for different hyperparameter values to select the best option.

We write a function to train the model and return evaluation scores for the model.

```python
import numpy
from sklearn.naive_bayes import MultinomialNB
from sklearn.metrics import precision_recall_fscore_support

def multinomialBN_model(
  X_train, train_y, X_valid, valid_y, alpha=1.0
):
  model = MultinomialNB(alpha=alpha).fit(
    X_train.todense(), train_y
  )
  y_pred = model.predict(X_valid.todense())
  prec, recall, f1, class_size = precision_recall_fscore_support(
    valid_y,
    y_pred,
    average=None,
    labels=model.classes_
  )
  scores = {
    "class_order": model.classes_,
```

```
    "precision": prec,
    "recall": recall,
    "f1": f1,
    "avg prec": numpy.mean(prec),
    "avg recall": numpy.mean(recall),
    "avg f1": numpy.mean(f1)
  }
  return model, scores
```

Next, we train models for different `alpha` values and save all scores in the variable `models`. We also find the maximum F1 score.

We have discussed methods from tools like `sklearn` in Chapter 4 for grid searching as we implemented here. We could replace this implementation with the `sklearn` one. The reason for demonstrating it this way is the simplicity of the problem (only one hyperparameter with a limited set of values), small model size, the flexibility to experiment with the choice for the best model based on different evaluations metrics, and having multiple models to experiment with as needed. For instance, is the model with the best accuracy the same as the model with the best F1? This type of implementation can help analyze multiple resultant models.

```
models = {}
f1_max = 0
for alpha in [0.1, 0.2, 0.4, 0.6, 0.8, 1.0]:
  models[alpha] = multinomialBN_model(
    X_train, train_y, X_valid, valid_y, alpha=alpha
  )

# Get model with best f1 score
f1_max = max([models[alpha][1]["avg f1"] for alpha in models])
```

We find the model corresponding to the maxmimum F1 score and print the results.

```
best_alpha, best_model, best_score, y_pred = [
  (
    alpha, models[alpha][0],
    models[alpha][1],
    models[alpha][2]
  )
  for alpha in models
  if models[alpha][1]["avg f1"] == f1_max
][0]
print(f"""
  Best alpha      : {best_alpha}
  Avg. Precision  : {best_score["avg prec"]}
  Avg. Recall     : {best_score["avg recall"]}
  Avg. F1         : {best_score["avg f1"]}"""
)
print(f"""
  \nPer class evaluation :
  Classes         : {best_score["class_order"]}
  Precision       : {best_score["precision"]}
  Recall          : {best_score["recall"]}
  F1              : {best_score["f1"]}"""
)
```

Output is as follows.

```
Best alpha : 0.4
Avg. Precision : 0.954273785981103
Avg. Recall : 0.8729883813235189
Avg. F1 : 0.9080138649208602


Per class evaluation
Classes : ['ham' 'spam']
Precision : [0.96260163 0.94594595]
Recall : [0.99328859 0.75268817]
F1 : [0.97770438 0.83832335]
```

We also compute the confusion matrix to further understand the model results.

```
from sklearn.metrics import confusion_matrix, ConfusionMatrixDisplay

# Compute and print the confusion matrix
cm = confusion_matrix(
  valid_y, y_pred, labels=best_model.classes_
)
disp = ConfusionMatrixDisplay(
  confusion_matrix=cm, display_labels=best_model.classes_
)
disp.plot()
```

The confusion matrix image can be seen in Figure 8.4.

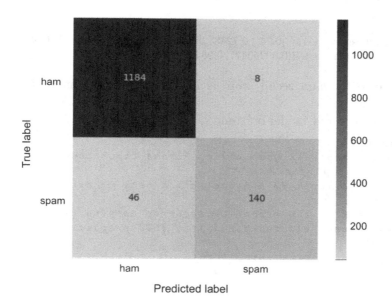

FIGURE 8.4 Confusion matrix for spam vs ham classification model using Multinomial Naive Bayes classifier.

We observe the recall score for spam class to be 75.2%, which is a lot lower than that of class ham which is at 99.3%. We already know of class imbalance. Having less data for the spam class is one likely large factor. Now let's check the 5-fold cross validation score per class to check for variance in recall.

```
# Checking cross validation recall scores per class

from sklearn.metrics import make_scorer
from sklearn.metrics import recall_score
from sklearn.model_selection import cross_validate

vect = TfidfVectorizer(
  max_df=0.9, min_df=0.01, max_features=5000
)

scoring = {
  'recall_spam': make_scorer(
    recall_score, average=None, labels=["spam"]
  ),
  'recall_ham': make_scorer(
    recall_score, average=None, labels=["ham"]
  )
}

cross_validate(
  MultinomialNB(alpha=best_alpha),
  vect.fit_transform(x),
  y,
  scoring=scoring,
  cv=5
)
```

'test_recall_spam': array([0.74 , 0.72483221, 0.75838926, 0.65100671, 0.68666667])
'test_recall_ham': array([0.99265477, 0.98426023, 0.9884575 , 0.99370409, 0.99369748])

The variance for *ham* recall score is low. On the other hand, the *spam* recall variance is high.

Running the created model on some samples below.

```
new_samples = [
  """You have completed your order. Please check your email for a
    refund receipt for $50.""",
  """Win lottery worth $2 Million! click here to participate for free
    .""",
  """Please send me the report by tomorrow morning. Thanks.""",
  """You have been selected for a free $500 prepaid card."""
]
sample_vects = vectorizer.transform(
  [clean(doc) for doc in new_samples]
)

print(
  "Predicted class for samples: ",
```

```
    best_model.predict(sample_vects)
)
print(
    "Probabilities: \n",
    best_model.classes_, "\n",
    best_model.predict_proba(sample_vects)
)
```

Predicted class for samples: ['ham' 'spam' 'ham' 'spam']

Probabilities: ['ham' 'spam']

[0.70874105 0.29125895]

[0.10782766 0.89217234]

[0.94339795 0.05660205]

[0.37811938 0.62188062]

The complete script can be found in section5/ham-spam-clasiifier-MultinomialNaive Bayes.ipynb.

How can you tell if you need more data?

Check cross-validation evaluation. If the variance is high, more data could help your model. You can also increase training data in small increments and keep increasing it until you reach a point where the incremental improvement of the evaluation metric (recall/F1/precision) gets minimal.

What is your goal?

If the goal is to correctly identify spam as spam, at the cost of missing some spam detections, then a high precision value for spam will give you the desired result. If both the classes are equally important, then the evaluation of both classes remains important.

How can you resolve class imbalance?

Let's assume that you have a model where the output is always 'ham'. For a random sample of this dataset, the overall model accuracy would be at 85.5% (because 85.5% of the data belongs to class 'ham'). That would not be a good model, even though the score may appear satisfactory. Thus looking at evaluation metrics per class can be helpful. One method to resolve class imbalance is randomly removing excess data for the class that has more data. However, this can at times impact your model and yield a higher (worse) variance in cross-validation accuracy for the class for which you removed samples. It can make the data representation in that class weaker. In such cases, the ideal solution is to add more data for the class that lacks samples by manually labeling more data, finding open-sourced labeled data samples that might be relevant to your use case, or by artificially synthesizing data using augmentation techniques where applicable as discussed in Chapter 3 (Section 3.3).

What else can you try to improve your model?

Try more classification models. Try other feature generation techniques. Try other text preprocessing/cleaning methods.

8.3.2.2 Deep learning

CNN and RNN models can be used instead of Naive Bayes or other classic ML models for text classification. For tasks where classic ML models don't perform as per the requirement, deep learning approaches can do better.

We have looked at CNNs at a high-level in Chapter 4 (Section 4.2.2). Let's implement it for the same ham-spam classification problem.

First, we tokenize the data using `keras` text tokenizer. An important step is to ensure each sample sequence is of the same length. We pad them with 0's if the length is short to make it even.

```
! pip install keras
! pip install tensorflow
! pip install nltk
```

```
! pip install scikit-learn
! pip install pandas
! pip install matplotlib

import numpy as np
from keras.preprocessing.text import Tokenizer
from keras.utils import pad_sequences
from sklearn.preprocessing import LabelEncoder
from keras.utils import to_categorical

MAX_SEQUENCE_LENGTH = 200
MAX_NB_WORDS = 10000

tokenizer = Tokenizer(num_words=MAX_NB_WORDS)
tokenizer.fit_on_texts(train_x)

train_sequences = tokenizer.texts_to_sequences(train_x)
test_sequences = tokenizer.texts_to_sequences(valid_x)

train_data = pad_sequences(
  train_sequences, maxlen=MAX_SEQUENCE_LENGTH
)
test_data = pad_sequences(
  test_sequences, maxlen=MAX_SEQUENCE_LENGTH
)
print(
  "train and test data shapes",
  train_data.shape, test_data.shape
)
# >> train and test data shapes (4133, 200) (1378, 200)
```

Next, we label encode the output as follows.

```
#label encoding
le = LabelEncoder()
le.fit(train_y)
train_labels = le.transform(train_y)
test_labels = le.transform(valid_y)
labels = le.transform(le.classes_)
print(f"{le.classes_=} -> {labels=}")
# >> le.classes_=array(['ham', 'spam']) -> labels=array([0, 1])

labels_train = to_categorical(np.asarray(train_labels))
labels_test = to_categorical(np.asarray(test_labels))
```

Then, we start adding different layers to build our model. First, we add an Embedding layer.

```
# Model training
from keras.layers import (
  Dense,
  Embedding,
  Conv1D,
  MaxPooling1D,
  Flatten,
  Dropout
)
```

```
from keras.models import Sequential

EMBEDDING_DIM = 100

print("Training CNN\n")

model = Sequential()
model.add(Embedding(
  MAX_NB_WORDS,
  EMBEDDING_DIM,
  input_length=MAX_SEQUENCE_LENGTH
))
model.add(Dropout(0.5))
```

Dropout layers prevent overfitting on the training data.

Next, we add two Convolutional and Pooling layers with Dropout layers, followed by a hidden Dense layer, and Output Dense layer. We described more details on these layers in Chapter 4.

```
model.add(Conv1D(128, 5, activation="relu"))
model.add(MaxPooling1D(5))
model.add(Dropout(0.5))
model.add(Conv1D(128, 5, activation="relu"))
model.add(MaxPooling1D(5))
model.add(Dropout(0.5))

model.add(Flatten())
model.add(Dense(128, activation="relu"))
model.add(Dense(2, activation="softmax"))
```

Then, the model is ready to be compiled and trained.

```
model.compile(
  loss="categorical_crossentropy",
  optimizer="rmsprop",
  metrics=["accuracy"]
)
history = model.fit(
  train_data, labels_train,
  batch_size=64,
  epochs=10,
  validation_data=(test_data, labels_test)
)
```

Now, we can get the metrics of this model on the test data using the following code.

```
from sklearn.metrics import precision_recall_fscore_support as sc
from sklearn.metrics import classification_report

predicted = model.predict(test_data)

# evaluation
precision, recall, fscore, _ = sc(labels_test, predicted.round())

print(labels, "->", le.classes_)
print(f"{precision=}")
print(f"{recall=}")
print(f"{fscore=}")
```

```
print(classification_report(labels_test, predicted.round()))
```

The CNN model evaluation is as follows for ['ham', 'spam'] classes.

precision=array([0.97981497, 0.96825397])
recall=array([0.99487617, 0.88405797])
fscore=array([0.98728814, 0.92424242])

We can also visualize the training and testing accuracy and loss by epoch by using the following code.

```
import matplotlib.pyplot as plt

# training data
plt.plot(history.history["accuracy"])
plt.xlabel("Epochs")
plt.ylabel("Training accuracy")
plt.show()
plt.plot(history.history["loss"])
plt.xlabel("Epochs")
plt.ylabel("Training loss")
plt.show()

# validation data
plt.plot(history.history["val_accuracy"])
plt.xlabel("Epochs")
plt.ylabel("Validation accuracy")
plt.show()
plt.plot(history.history["val_loss"])
plt.xlabel("Epochs")
plt.ylabel("Validation loss")
plt.show()
```

The resultant plots are shown in Figure 8.5.

Running this model on sample text as below, we get the following result.

```
new_samples = [
  """You have completed your order. Please check your email for a
     refund receipt for $50.""",
  """Win lottery worth $2 Million! click here to participate for free
     .""",
  """Please send me the report by tomorrow morning. Thanks.""",
  """You have been selected for a free $500 prepaid card."""
]
sample = pad_sequences(
  tokenizer.texts_to_sequences(
    [clean(doc) for doc in new_samples]
  ),
  maxlen=MAX_SEQUENCE_LENGTH
)
for result in model.predict(sample):
  max_index = np.where(result == max(result))
  print(
    "classification: ", le.classes_[max_index],
    "scores: ", result
  )
```

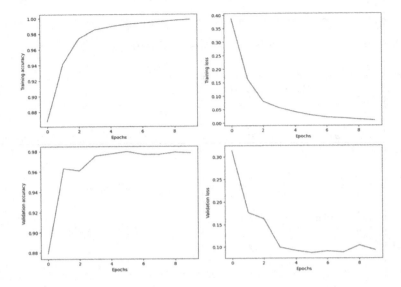

FIGURE 8.5 Training and validation accuracy and loss for ham/spam CNN model.

classification: ['ham'] scores: [0.87511957 0.12488045]
classification: ['spam'] scores: [0.0937926 0.90620744]
classification: ['ham'] scores: [0.99514043 0.00485962]
classification: ['spam'] scores: [0.00934407 0.99065596]

We see a higher score for the second and fourth sentence in `new_samples` for class *spam*, and a higher score for the first and third sentence for the class *ham*. The complete script can be found in section5/ham-spam-classifier-CNN.ipynb.

Similarly, you can use the code from Chapter 4 to train LSTM or BiLSTM by adding relevant layers to the model for this problem.

> **TIP**
>
> Time taken to train the Multinomial Naive Bayes model including grid search was 0.46 seconds, compared to 30.66 seconds to train the CNN. The ham-spam dataset is relatively small and the time taken would be higher as the model layers and dataset size change.
>
> In this case, deep learning did better in terms of result, but is surely not as lightweight and fast to train as the Naive Bayes model. Also, a deep learning model is not likely to always give you better results than classic machine learning models. Hence, it is common to try simpler approaches first.
>
> Occam's razor is a scientific and philosophical rule that entities should not be multiplied unnecessarily which is interpreted as requiring that the simplest of competing theories be preferred to the more complex or that explanations of unknown phenomena be sought first in terms of known quantities [118].

8.3.3 Classifying unlabeled data

What to do if you have data that you want to classify into different categories, but you don't have the data labeled? This is a very common problem with multiple solution options.

8.3.3.1 Solution 1: Labeling

A popular solution is to hand label the data to get started. You can also leverage data labeling services using Mechanical Turk[6], Google Cloud Platform (GCP)[7], or AWS[8] to get your data labeled faster. Some teams prefer hiring an additional workforce to help with the process.

It is recommended to use multiple people for a task requiring humans to label a dataset. This aids in alleviating any individual-level mistakes and biases. Taking the majority vote for a sample's label gives more confidence in the label's quality.

8.3.3.2 Solution 2: Clustering

Algorithmic approaches such as data clustering can help organize data into categories. Clustering algorithms (as discussed in Chapter 4) automatically find traits in your data samples and group similar samples together. One thing to keep in mind is that the nature of this step is experimental and iterative. The number of clusters to try and group your data into is often experimental. You may try with 5 clusters, and if none make sense, increase or decrease the number of clusters and try again. Sometimes, only one or a few clusters make sense. One practice is to note the data samples that belong to a cluster that looks good, i.e., looks like it represents one of your classes well. Like this, if you can find relevant clusters for all your classes from different runs, they can form a baseline labeled dataset that you can start with to build a supervised classification model. Figure 8.6 illustrates the process. You can also manually verify the data labels which would be faster than hand labeling from scratch.

A popular way to check clusters is through word cloud visualizations as described in Chapter 3 (Section 3.2).

In Chapter 10, we will build a topic classification model on hotel review comments and look at a couple of different approaches while working with unlabeled data with code samples.

8.3.3.3 Solution 3: Hybrid approach

Once you hand-label/curate a few hundred samples, you can train a classification model. It may be weak at first, but you can pass unlabeled data through it and manually verify their classifications, followed by adding them to your pool of labeled data. It is often easier to check the correctness of labels rather than manually assign labels for each sample.

---

[6]https://www.mturk.com/
[7]https://cloud.google.com/ai-platform/data-labeling/docs
[8]https://aws.amazon.com/sagemaker/data-labeling/

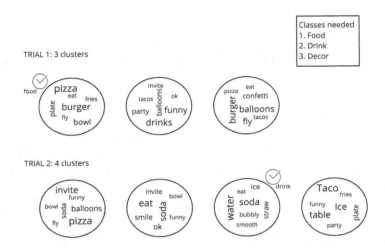

FIGURE 8.6 Curating labeled data using clustering experiments.

8.4 SENTIMENT ANALYSIS

Sentiment analysis is the ability to categorize text into a sentiment - positive, negative, or neutral. An extension to sentiment analysis is emotion classification, where classification models break down the happy sentiment to an underlying emotion such as love and joy, and similarly break down negative sentiment into negative emotions.

In the industry, sentiment analysis is highly valuable in understanding how an audience responds to a product, service, or topic. Businesses often draw insights to improve and create products based on the sentiment understanding.

Sentiment analysis is a task for which the available open-source options do fairly well. In most cases, it eliminates the need to create custom models and practitioners spend the majority of their time developing ways to clean text prior to passing through the sentiment analysis model.

For certain domains where the language is unlike the public documents that the open-sourced models are trained on, the need for training a custom sentiment classifier might be required. If you do need to create your own model, labeling sentences with different sentiments, computing numerical representations using methods described in Chapter 3, and passing through a classification model will be a good starting point. The code demonstrated below can be found in section5/sentiment.ipynb.

8.4.1 Classic open-source models

TextBlob

TextBlob is a library for processing textual data. TextBlob uses NLTK and is capable of multiple text processing operations. It goes beyond just sentiment analysis and is able to do part-of-speech tagging, noun phrase extraction, tokenization, and more.

The sentiment property returns a named tuple of the form `Sentiment(polarity, subjectivity)`.

Polarity depicts the sentiment; the higher the polarity score, the higher the strength of the sentiment. The scores range between -1 and 1. Lower values indicate a negative sentiment, and higher values indicate a positive sentiment. As a common practice, negative scores are labeled with negative sentiment, positive scores with positive sentiment, and 0 with neutral.

Subjectivity score depicts the subjectivity of the input text. The values range between 0 and 1, where 0 is objective and 1 is subjective.

Here's how getting sentiment using `TextBlob` looks like.

```
! pip install textblob

from textblob import TextBlob

sent = TextBlob("Textblob is great to use.")
print(sent.sentiment)

#>> Sentiment(polarity=0.8, subjectivity=0.75)
```

This tool does fairly well in terms of accuracy of the predicted sentiment.

Like any probabilistic tool, there are areas of ambiguity where models fail. One such example is as follows.

'Who wouldn't love a headache?' = Sentiment(polarity=0.5, subjectivity=0.6)

`TextBlob` sentiment analysis identifies the above as positive sentiment.

VADER

VADER stands for Valence Aware Dictionary and sEntiment Reasoner. It is a lexicon and rule-based sentiment analysis tool that is specifically attuned to sentiments expressed in social media [83].

The model returns a dictionary with scores for *pos, neg, neu,* and *compound.*

The compound score is computed by combining the valence/polarity scores of each word in the lexicon, with the final values normalized between -1 and 1. -1 stands for most negative, and +1 stands for most positive. This metric is the most used for scenarios where a single measure of sentiment of a given sentence is desired, i.e., positive, negative, or neutral. Threshold reported by the library is as follows.

Positive sentiment: compound score $>= 0.05$

Neutral sentiment: (compound score > -0.05) and (compound score < 0.05)

Negative sentiment: compound score $<= -0.05$

The scores assigned to pos, neg, and neu are the ratios for proportions of text that fall in each category. These are useful if you want to understand the context and presentation of how sentiment is conveyed in rhetoric for a given sentence. An example reported by the library - *'some writing styles may reflect a penchant for strongly flavored rhetoric, whereas other styles may use a great deal of neutral text while still conveying a similar overall (compound) sentiment'.*

Here's how to get sentiment using **Vader**.

```
! pip install vaderSentiment==3.3.2

from vaderSentiment.vaderSentiment import SentimentIntensityAnalyzer

sid_obj = SentimentIntensityAnalyzer()
sentiment_dict = sid_obj.polarity_scores(
  "Vader works well !"
)
print(sentiment_dict)
#>> {'neg': 0.0, 'neu': 0.556, 'pos': 0.444, 'compound': 0.3382}
```

Trying the model on an ambiguous sample below.

> 'Who wouldn't love a headache?' = 'neg': 0.457, 'neu': 0.543, 'pos': 0.0, 'compound': -0.5216

Vader classifies our sample 'Who wouldn't love a headache?' as negative sentiment.

Depending on the nature of the dataset, one tool may do better than the other.

> *TIP*
>
> *How to choose the open-source solution for your application?*
> Manually label 100 documents, and see which tool does better on your data subset to make the choice.

8.4.2 Transformers

Sentiment analysis can also be performed using the `transformers` library. We have seen a demo of Hugging Face `transformers` for some other NLP tasks. Let's look at how to use it for sentiment analysis.

```
! pip install transformers

from transformers import pipeline

sentiment_analysis = pipeline("sentiment-analysis")

result = sentiment_analysis(
  "Transformers are great for many tasks."
)[0]

print(result)
# >> {'label': 'POSITIVE', 'score': 0.9994866847991943}
```

As the default, the `transformers` library uses a DistilBERT [148] model fine-tuned on the Stanford Sentiment Treebank v2 (SST2) [145] task from the GLUE Dataset [190]. Using any different model or tokenizer is possible by passing it in on instantiation of the pipeline. The full list of available models can be found here[9].

---

[9]`https://huggingface.co/models?other=sentiment-analysis&sort=downloads`

Passing the same ambiguous sample sentence through this model, the results are as follows.

'Who wouldn't love a headache?' = 'label': 'NEGATIVE', 'score': 0.9960442781448364

8.4.3 Paid services

Several other options are available to compute sentiment. Top service providers offer APIs returning sentiment for input text.

Google Cloud Natural Language API[10] is an option that can be a quick implementation if your organization already subscribes to other Google Cloud services.

A sample response is as follows.

```
{
  "documentSentiment": {
    "magnitude": 0.8, "score": 0.8
  },
  "language": "en",
  "sentences": [
    {
      "text": {
        "content": "Enjoy your vacation!",
        "beginOffset": 0
      },
      "sentiment": {
        "magnitude": 0.8, "score": 0.8
      }
    }
  ]
}
```

Amazon Lex[11] and Watson Natural Language Understanding[12] offer sentiment analysis as well.

> *TIP*
>
> TextBlob and Vader are the most popularly used tools for getting sentiment analysis across many companies computing sentiment on text. These tools do well on a variety of datasets and are quick to implement. Transformers are relatively new and hence more popularly used in companies focussed on research. Training custom classifiers for sentiment analysis is the least popular method unless the nature of the language in the dataset is unique and domain-specific.

---

[10] https://cloud.google.com/natural-language/docs/analyzing-sentiment
[11] https://docs.aws.amazon.com/lex/latest/dg/sentiment-analysis.html
[12] https://www.ibm.com/cloud/watson-natural-language-understanding

Windup

In this Section, we implemented several advanced NLP applications. We discussed IE (Information Extraction), specifically implementations for NER and keyphrase extraction using open-source tools and pre-trained models. These applications typically form an important part of larger NLP projects, such as personally identifiable information (PII) recognition and chatbots.

We examined topic modeling as a unsupervised approach to club similar documents together. Topic modeling is a popular approach to cluster data where certain overlap is expected between clusters. This method is also used to curate data labels and understand data patterns.

Then, we looked at different types of text similarity measures and explored implementations of semantic text similarity. This finds use in building recommendation systems that measure similarity between search terms and content, or between two pieces of content.

Summarization of documents is helpful in reducing the size of the data, enabling faster search, and generating a summary to sift through documents rather than having to go through full documents manually. Many applications exist in different industry domains, such as in Healthcare to summarize patient visit notes, and in Legal and Research. We discussed extractive and abstractive text summarization and shared implementations using a variety of models. The need to implement these solutions from scratch is rare for practitioners working in an enterprise setting. Many available tools can be used to implement such solutions, which we discussed in this section.

We also looked at language detection and translation along with the options of service providers as well as some open-source tools. This is particularly useful for businesses with users across the globe. It is most common to opt for service providers for this application.

We looked at many ways of approaching a text classification problem and demonstrated them using the ham/spam dataset. Finally, we discussed sentiment analysis and implementing it using open-source pre-trained models. Since, this problem is common and has been implemented and made available, the need to build custom sentiment analysis models is rare, unless the dataset is domain-specific containing many jargons.

Throughout this section, we looked at classic approaches, API services, and the latest transformer-based approaches. Each of these applications are directly valuable for many use cases in the industry. Other times, multiple such applications have to be combined to satisfy an industry application. How does it all fit into projects around text data in a company? We'll build some real-world industrial projects in Section VI using the techniques and concepts discussed thus far. We will explain an NLP project in the context of company goals and build solutions using Python. We will also share some practical tips and solutions to common industrial problems.

VI

Implementing NLP Projects in the Real-World

An enterprise is a firm or a combination of firms that engages in economic activities which can be classified into multiple industries. We'll be using the terms industry and enterprise interchangeably throughout this section, referring to work that happens in a company rather than an educational setting. The primary reason for this focus is that the kind of projects you typically work on during advanced degrees, courses, or boot camps are very different in nature compared to real-world projects. On the academic front, there is a heavier focus on the concepts, models, and features which are highly relevant skills. But there are also expectations of available data sources and little visibility into considerations and impacts of building NLP solutions in enterprise settings. In this section, we will look at these projects in a real-world sense to give you a glimpse of how it all works in the enterprise.

In Section V, we implemented the most common advanced applications of NLP including information extraction, topic modeling, text summarization, language translation, text classification, and sentiment analysis. In this section, we'll build some real-world applications of NLP using the concepts and implementations presented in the previous chapters. We will discuss and build around business goals and data challenges commonly faced in practice. We'll build the following projects.

- Chatbots

- Customer review analysis and classification

- Social media post recommendation system

- Next word prediction

How do you know it is the right call to build a data science solution for your company and what it should be? These decisions are typically driven by key performance indicators (KPIs), which are a type of performance measurement that evaluate the success of an organization. The KPIs drive business objectives for a company. The business objectives then inform action plans, which may contain data science modeling. Figure 8.7 illustrates this flow. In this section, we'll share examples of such a flow for every project that we implement to increase the understanding of the impact of such NLP projects in an industrial setting and where they fit in.

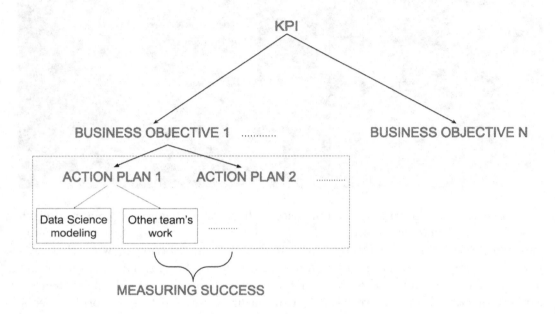

FIGURE 8.7 Where data science modeling fits within a business's goal and its driving factors.

## CHAPTER 9

Chatbots

A chatbot is also known as a chatterbot, virtual assistant, virtual agent, conversational agent, interactive agent, and artificial conversation agent. It is a tool that can converse with a human. Chatbots are widely deployed applications across several industries, especially in the last decade. Chatbots can be voice-based and/or text-based. For the scope of this section, we'll focus on text-based chatbots.

9.1 TYPES OF CHATBOTS

There are many types of chatbots. The two main distinctions for chatbots that leverage NLP are as follows.

1. Fixed response chatbots

   Fixed response chatbots have a fixed set of capabilities. The responses returned are all predefined. An example would be rule-based chatbots that follow a set of rules to respond to the user. Such chatbots are able to decipher the user's input as a fixed selection or free-form text, and maps it to the appropriate response. Figure 9.1 shows an example where you can ask the chatbot anything but the chatbot can identify only some types of questions based on the data it has been fed. It matches the user's message to one of the known questions. For questions outside the bot's understanding that match with low confidence to the known list of questions, it forwards the chat to a human representative. In such chatbots, a user message-response pair is often independent within a conversation. Such chatbots provide enhanced search capability in a conversational form. The key components of such chatbots are automated intent interpretation and similarity-based matching.

   The most common type of fixed response chatbot in the enterprise is the Q&A chatbot. Examples include chatbots by e-commerce brands like Zara and H&M.

2. Conversational chatbots

   These can be either goal-oriented, such as allowing users to place a pizza order over chat, or more open-ended such as having a normal human-like conversation

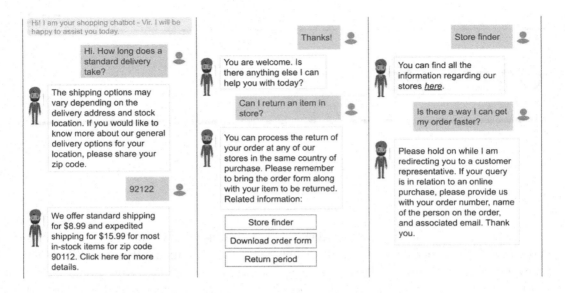

FIGURE 9.1 E-commerce chatbot conversation (left to right).

with no end goal. The key components are natural language generation to generate responses to users and adaptive state memory (does the bot need to have a history of 10 recent messages or 20?) because the user message-response pairs may not be independent.

In December 2022, OpenAI (an AI research and deployment company) released ChatGPT[1], a chatbot that converses with humans to help write code, debug code, compose essays, recommend places to visit, summarize a long document, make up stories, and give you ideas for questions like 'How do I decorate my room?' . Shortly after, Google announced Bard and Meta announced LLaMA. These chatbots decipher a user's requests and then call different models for different tasks they want to perform. For example, a different model is called if the request requires document summarization versus paraphrasing. These are some well-known examples of conversational chatbots that rely on large language models (LLMs) and integrate different fine-tuned models to perform a variety of different tasks.

In the enterprise, the most common type of conversational chatbot is the goal-oriented chatbot, where there is typically an end goal associated with the conversation. Examples include placing orders, booking movie tickets, and Cortana[2] by Microsoft.

---

[1]https://openai.com/blog/chatgpt/
[2]https://support.microsoft.com/en-us/topic/chat-with-cortana-54a859b0-19e9-cc13-c044-3b2db29be41e

9.2 COMPONENTS OF A CHATBOT

The important components of a chatbot are as follows.

Intent identification allows the chatbot to understand what the user wants. For example, is the user asking a question that needs an answer? Or is the user message giving some information?

Entity extraction allows retrieving relevant information needed to complete the conversation.

A **response generation** mechanism handles what the bot's message should be in response to the user's message. These can be basic template-based sentences, a look-up to defined FAQ (frequently asked questions) answers, or deep learning based machine-generated (more common in no-goal conversational chatbots).

Additionally, the system may need to maintain the state of the conversation.

Let's understand the components by looking at some examples below.

USER: Hi

                  BOT: Hello! How can I help you?

USER: what time does the store open?

        BOT: The store is open from 8am to 9pm PST every day.
        It is closed on public holidays.

USER: what is the store address?

        BOT: xyz St, Los Angeles, CA, 91***

USER: Do you sell cupcakes?

        BOT: Sorry, we are unable to answer your query.
        Please call +1(800)****** for assistance.

In the example above, we need a system to map a user's message to either timing, address, greeting, or something else. We call this the user intent. Identification of intent helps the chatbot generate an appropriate response.

Let's complicate our example and include the ability to get all information necessary to order a pizza from a store. Now we not only need to know the user's intent but also entities such as pizza size, toppings, etc. We need all these entities to place a pizza order. Hence if the user's first message does not contain all the required information, the chatbot will need to maintain a state and ask the user the follow-on questions in order to get all the required information.

Example 1

> *USER: I want to order a pizza* - Intent: order pizza.
>
> *BOT: What toppings would you like?*
>
> *USER: Chicken* - needed topping information (entity) to fulfill user intent

Example 2

> *USER: I want to order a chicken pizza.*
> - gives both the intent and the entity needed to fulfill the intent

In a practical scenario, we would need to connect the information to a query engine/API call to complete any required action, such as placing an order in an ordering system. The chatbot may additionally need access to a knowledge base like a pizza menu, a user identification mechanism such as a rewards number matching, location/timezone detection to estimate delivery availability, and sentiment analysis to sense if the user is angry.

Figure 9.2 contains a high-level block diagram of a chatbot system.

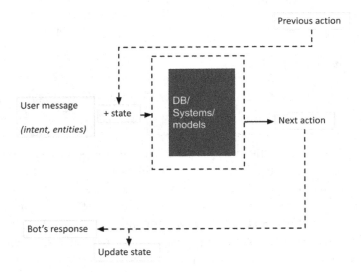

FIGURE 9.2   Chatbot system overview.

9.3   BUILDING A RULE-BASED CHATBOT

Figure 9.3 represents an example of why such a chatbot is of interest to a company.

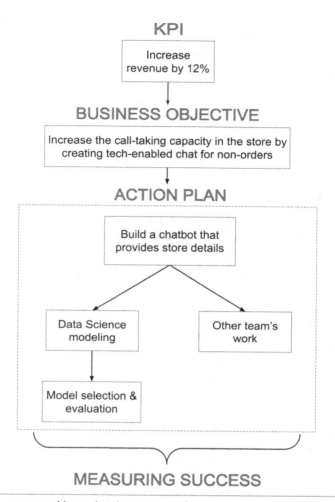

FIGURE 9.3 Building a chatbot from a company KPI perspective.

Action plan

You are tasked with creating a chatbot for a business that runs a store. The goal is to build a simple chatbot prototype that can chat with customers and tell them about store timing and address. The chatbot should be able to direct the users to a customer service representative for advanced questions.

Concepts

A chatbot implementation need not be complex if your use case is simple.

Rule-based or Q/A are the easiest to build and understand. Imagine your business sells certain services to its customers. You want to create a chatbot for your customers to be able to get answers to commonly asked questions. As a default, if the chatbot is unable to find an answer, it can either connect the customer to a human agent or ask the customer to call a customer service number.

Solution

This chatbot will present options to the user and respond with an answer.

```python
def get_responses(user_message):
    """
    Returns a list of responses based on user input message.
    """
    output = []
    if "timing" in user_message:
        output.append("""
        The store is open from 8am to 9pm PST every day.
        It is closed on public holidays.
        """)
    if "address" in user_message:
        output.append("xyz St, Los Angeles, CA, 91***")

    if len(output) > 0:
        return output
    else: # If user_message doesn't match 'timing' or 'address'
        return ["""
        Sorry, we are unable to answer your query.
        Please call +1(800)****** for assistance."""
        ]

print("""
Hi! I can help you with store information.
Type 'timing' to know about the store timings.
Type 'address' to learn about the store address.
""")
user_input = input().lower()
print("\n".join(get_responses(user_input)))
```

Sample output is as follows.

Example 1

> BOT: Hi! I can help you with store information.
> Type 'timing' to know about the store timings.
> Type 'address' to learn about the store address.
>
> USER: timing
>
> BOT: The store is open from 8am to 9pm PST every day.

Example 2

> *BOT: Hi! I can help you with store information.*
> *Type 'timing' to know about the store timings.*
> *Type 'address' to learn about the store address.*
>
> *USER: timing address*
>
> *BOT: The store is open from 8am to 9pm PST every day.*
> *It is closed on public holidays.*
>
> *BOT: xyz St, Los Angeles, CA, 91****

The code can also be found at section6/simple-chatbot-1.ipynb.

Easy, right?

But now, what if you want your users to be able to type in their questions in free-form text, and interpret their questions as 'timing' or 'address'? Below is an example that this simple rule-based bot can not handle.

> *USER: store time*
>
> *BOT: Sorry, we are unable to answer your query.*
> *Please call +1(800)****** for assistance.*

The following implementation accounts for one of the ways for better handling free-form text questions by matching them to a fixed set of questions. This approach uses synonyms.

```
import re
from nltk.corpus import wordnet

# Building a list of Keywords
words_dict = {
  "greet": ["hello", "hi", "hey"],
  "timings": ["timings", "open"],
  "address": ["address", "location", "where"],
  "exit": ["bye"]
}
syns = {}
# adding synonyms to each word above
for key in words_dict:
  synonyms = []
  for word in words_dict[key]:
    for syn in wordnet.synsets(word):
      for lem in syn.lemmas():
        # Remove special characters from synonym strings
        lem_name = re.sub(
          "[^a-zA-Z0-9 \n\.]", " ", lem.name()
        )
        synonyms.append(".*\\b" + lem_name + "\\b.*")
```

```
    synonyms.append(".*\\b" + word + "\\b.*")
  syns[key] = set(synonyms)
```

Next, we create a keywords to intent map and populate it with keywords.

```
keywords_dict={}
for intent, keys in syns.items():
  # Joining with OR (/) operator
  keywords_dict[intent] = re.compile("|".join(keys))
```

Next, we define fixed responses for every intent identified.

```
responses = {
  "greet": "Hello! How can I help you?",
  "timings": """
    The store is open from 8am to 9pm PST every day.
    It is closed on public holidays.
  """,
  "address": """
    The store is located at xyz St, Los Angeles, CA, 91***.
  """,
  "fallback": """
    Sorry, we are unable to answer your query.
    Please call +1(800)****** for assistance.
  """,
  "exit": "Bye!",
}
```

Then, we put it all together.

```
print("\n\nWelcome to Jo's store. How may I help you?")
while True:
  # Takes the user input
  user_input = input().lower()
  matched_intent = []
  # Note: this implementation matches one intent at a time
  for intent, pattern in keywords_dict.items():
    # Using the regular expression
    if re.search(pattern, user_input):
      # select intent on keyword match
      matched_intent.append(intent)
  # The fallback intent is selected by default
  if len(matched_intent) == 0:
    matched_intent.append("fallback")
  for intent in matched_intent:
    if intent in responses:
      # Prints response that matches the selected intent
      print(responses[intent])
  # Defining the Chatbot's exit condition
  if "exit" in matched_intent:
    break
```

Here is a sample conversation.

> *USER: Hi*
>
> *BOT: Hello! How can I help you?*
>
> *USER: what time does the store open? where is it located?*
>
> *BOT: The store is open from 8am to 9pm PST every day.*
> *It is closed on public holidays.*
> *The store is located at xyz St, Los Angeles, CA, 91***.*
>
> *USER: Do you sell cupcakes?*
>
> *BOT: Sorry, we are unable to answer your query.*
> *Please call +1(800)****** for assistance.*

The notebook can be found at section6/simple-chatbot-2.ipynb.

Components that can be further improved include understanding the user's free-form text better. Intent classification can help understand a user's intent better once some data is collected. If you have a FAQ sheet, and you want to map a user's question to one of the FAQ sheet's questions, you can use text similarity and interpret the questions. We saw options for implementing text similarity in Chapter 8 (Section 8.2). Another option is to use the zero-shot classification using fine-tuned transformer models available with Hugging Face as we saw in Chapter 8. The transformer models are comparatively larger in size than other classic/traditional models.

Rule-based chatbots are limited in what they can accomplish, but can still be very useful depending on the requirement.

9.4   BUILDING A GOAL-ORIENTED CHATBOT

Figure 9.4 represents an example of why such a chatbot is of interest to a company.

Action plan

You are tasked with building a chatbot for a pizza shop. The goal is to build a prototype that can assist customers to place orders for pickup.

Concepts

You want your customer to be able to place an order for a pizza by chatting with your chatbot. First, two things need to be identified from an NLP perspective-intent and entities. The intent will help you differentiate between - does the customer wants to place an order, is the customer just inquiring about the pizza toppings available, or just ask for store timings. If you have an entity classification and intent classification, that seems to solve some of the big requirements to implement a chatbot. The intent and entities are likely different for different industries or use cases of the chatbot.

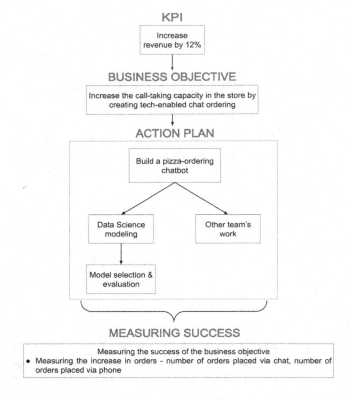

FIGURE 9.4 Building a pizza-ordering chatbot from a company KPI perspective.

Biggest challenge - where do you get the data from?

It is important to first define the range of possible intents that your chatbot will need to identify. Secondly, it is also important to define a list of entities your model will need to identify. For training any such models, you should first look for any available datasets you can leverage for the use case that can give you a labeled list of predefined entities or intents. If none of these exist, start by manually generating a few samples, and then using augmentation techniques to build your dataset up. You can also use data labeling services like the ones offered by AWS, Google, or Mechanical Turk.

How to manually generate data samples?

This is where a combination of creative and hacky methods can help kick-start a data science solution. Often, when there is no data available, many practitioners may not know how to proceed and might deem the project unfit for data science work. Putting in some creative thinking can help gather data to solve the problem. Think of it this way - if you could have all the data available, what data would you need and where from? And then backtrack into ways of generating those given the current situation.

In this pizza ordering example, one could transcribe phone conversations for order placements to generate datasets or go to the store to place an order and record or take notes of the dialogs.

Once you have some labeled data, you can train an intent classification model and an entity recognition model using tools and techniques discussed in Section V. There are also other options for building a chatbot using your labeled data. One such option is to leverage prebuilt services such as Google's Dialogflow[3] to implement the chatbot. Most service providers like AWS, IBM, etc. have options you can use to build and deploy your chatbot. Another option is using the RASA chatbot framework [37] if you want to build your own components. We'll look into both these options in this section.

The reason many industry practitioners do not build complete chatbot pipelines from scratch is the complexities outside of the intent and entity models. In addition, you will need a response generation mechanism, a service that talks to your database, and other systems that can successfully trigger an action, such as placing an order. You'll also need a way to deploy the chatbots on your website as well as chat platforms such as Facebook Messenger, Slack, etc.

Solution

For this demonstration, we will build a pizza-ordering chatbot using RASA. Before that, we'll highlight some other solution options as well.

9.4.1 Chatbots using service providers

Some existing tools can be leveraged for a quick implementation. One such example is Dialogflow. The usage is simple with a lot of guides available to help you through the process. Dialogflow requires you to enter your data samples and labels in their interface, and they train models using their own algorithms that you can't modify.

---

[3]https://cloud.google.com/dialogflow/docs

> These types of solution options are also called a 'black box'. A black box is a system where the input and output are known, but the knowledge of the inner workings is not known. The advantages include zero maintenance or understanding/expertise in the workings of the black box. The disadvantages include the lack of flexibility to customize the black box.

There are many other options offered by different service providers. Table 9.1 provides some high-level details, differences, and pricing. Since the costs are subject to change, we denote expensiveness in the number of dollar signs compared to the other vendors in the table. Even then, a vendor might be cheaper for your company than the others based on any existing contracts which may include free credits.

9.4.2 Create your own chatbot

If you find the need to build your own custom models for the different chatbot components, you can create the individual models using methods described in Section III and Section V, and integrate them into your framework. A popular choice in such cases is to build entity recognition and intent classification models that are tuned and specialized for your use case. If you are using RASA's framework, you can leverage their different model options to train models. You can also build your own spaCy models and integrate them with RASA. We will build models with RASA in the next section. Before we do that, the following demonstrates building a custom entity recognition model for the pizza-ordering system using spaCy.

Entity recognition

Entities are often unique to a business problem or domain. In such cases, we do not find pre-trained models that we can leverage. Here we want to detect entities such as TOPPING and PIZZASIZE. Let's leverage `spaCy` to build a custom NER model.

We begin with a hand-curated sample of labeled data that looks like the format shown in Figure 9.5. Since we'll be using `spaCy`, we will structure it in the format acceptable by spaCy.

We start by creating a blank model, add *ner pipe*, and add your entities to the *ner pipe*. Then, update the model with the training data. We use the same code as the one used in Chapter 7 (Section 7.1.1.3). The only difference is the training data. The full file script can be found in section6/pizza-entity-spacy-model.ipynb (Figure 9.5).

Testing it out, we have the results as shown in Figure 9.6.

You can build an intent classification model using models for text classification discussed in Chapter 8 (Section 8.3).

TABLE 9.1 Chatbot service providers.

Provider	Languages	Integrations	Channels	Cost
Google Dialogflow	20+ languages (English, Spanish, French, Hindi, Portuguese, Chinese, etc.)	Google Assistant, websites, Slack, Facebook Messenger, Skype, Twitter, Viber, Twilio, and many others	Voice, Text	($$$) -> Free with trail edition -> Essentials Edition (ES Agent) charges USD 0.002 per request -> CX Agent Edition charges USD 20 per 100 chat sessions and USD 45 per 100 voice sessions
Amazon Lex	US English	Facebook, Kik, Slack, Twilio, SMS	Voice, Text	($$) -> 10K text & 5K voice requests per month free for first year -> USD 0.004 per voice request -> USD 0.00075 per text request
Azure bot services (LUIS)	Multiple languages (English, French, German, Spanish, etc.)	Web, Facebook, Skype, Microsoft Teams, Slack, Telegram, Kik, Twilio etc.	Voice, Text	($) -> Free 10k messages per month -> USD 0.5 for 1000 messages
IBM	10+ languages (mostly in BETA) (English, Spanish, Japanese, Italian, Chinese, etc.)	Facebook Messenger, Slack, Voice Agent (Telephony), WordPress, and custom applications through APIs	Voice, Text	($$$) -> Free lite plan -> Plus plan at USD 140 per month

9.4.3 Using RASA

RASA is an open-source framework for chatbots. It allows you to choose from various model options for entity recognition and intent classification or connect with your custom-built models. It also provides users with data labeling interfaces and chatbot integrations with social media.

You can run RASA locally and run multiple instances. RASA can be a good option if you don't want vendor lock-in (a vendor lock-in means that you are tied to the vendor contract in place and the integrations it supports). The main downside is

```
[('I would like pizza with pepproni and mushrooms.',
  {'entities': [(24, 32, 'TOPPING'), (37, 46, 'TOPPING')]}),
 ('I would like a medium crust pizza with chicken and mushroom.',
  {'entities': [(15, 21, 'PIZZASIZE'),
    (39, 46, 'TOPPING'),
    (51, 59, 'TOPPING')]}),
 ('Can I have a large chicken and pepproni pizza please?',
  {'entities': [(13, 18, 'PIZZASIZE'),
    (19, 26, 'TOPPING'),
    (31, 39, 'TOPPING')]}),
 ('I want to order a chicken pizza, make it large with lots of pepproni.',
  {'entities': [(18, 25, 'TOPPING'),
    (41, 46, 'PIZZASIZE'),
    (60, 68, 'TOPPING')]}),
 ('I would like to place an order for a chicken and pepproni pizza. Thanks.',
  {'entities': [(37, 44, 'TOPPING'), (49, 57, 'TOPPING')]}),
 ('chicken on the pizza', {'entities': [(0, 7, 'TOPPING')]}),
 ('pepproni and mushroom',
  {'entities': [(0, 8, 'TOPPING'), (13, 21, 'TOPPING')]}),
 ('large', {'entities': [(0, 5, 'PIZZASIZE')]}),
 ('medium', {'entities': [(0, 6, 'PIZZASIZE')]}),
 ('mushroom pizza', {'entities': [(0, 8, 'TOPPING')]})]
```

FIGURE 9.5 Training data for building a custom NER model with spaCy.

that it could be complex for beginners and a fair understanding of chatbots and how the tool works would need to be acquired.

Let's build a small prototype for a pizza-ordering chatbot and demonstrate the usage.

Running this demo in a virtual environment would help ensure there remain fewer dependency conflicts with what you may have installed on your machine. We use conda[4] to create a Python 3.8 environment using *bash* commands below.

```
conda create -n rasademo python=3.8
```

Enter *y* on the prompts. Once done, run the following command to activate. Then, install rasa and create a project.

```
conda activate rasademo
pip install rasa
```

> pip version $>= 20.3$ and < 21.3 can make the install very slow. It is due to the dependency resolution backtracking logic that was introduced in pip v20.3. v21.3 appears to no longer have the same issue. If your install is taking long, check your pip version. Upgrade your pip as follows to resolve the issue, and run the rasa install command again.
>
> ```
> pip install --upgrade pip==21.3
> ```

Then, running the following command will prompt the user to create a sample RASA project We used RASA version 3.1.

---

[4]https://www.anaconda.com/products/distribution

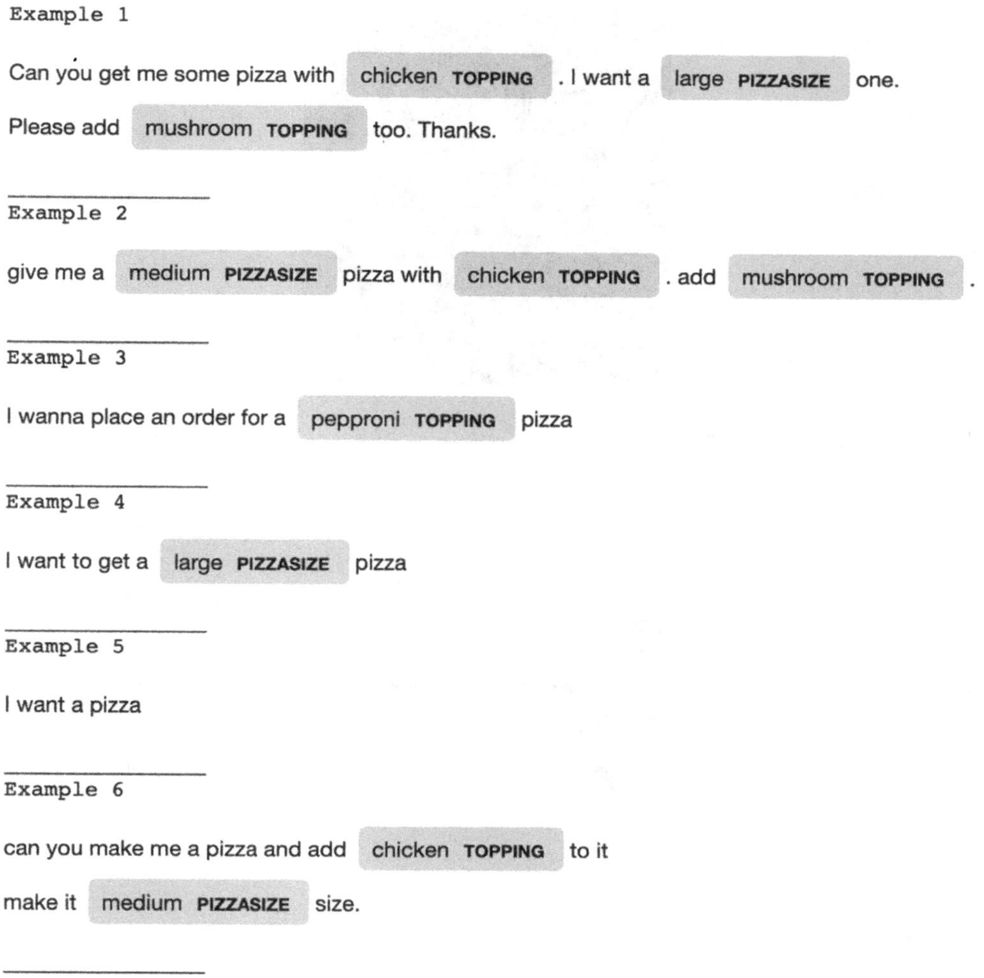

Example 1

Can you get me some pizza with   chicken **TOPPING**   . I want a   large **PIZZASIZE**   one.

Please add   mushroom **TOPPING**   too. Thanks.

_____

Example 2

give me a   medium **PIZZASIZE**   pizza with   chicken **TOPPING**   . add   mushroom **TOPPING**   .

_____

Example 3

I wanna place an order for a   pepproni **TOPPING**   pizza

_____

Example 4

I want to get a   large **PIZZASIZE**   pizza

_____

Example 5

I want a pizza

_____

Example 6

can you make me a pizza and add   chicken **TOPPING**   to it

make it   medium **PIZZASIZE**   size.

_____

FIGURE 9.6 Test results for our custom NER model built using spaCy for entities related to pizza attributes.

```
rasa init
```

Enter the path you want to create your project in. You'll notice some files are created as in Figure 9.7.

To configure a chatbot, you will need to understand what some of the files contain. At a high-level, Figure 9.8 shows where these files sit within the chatbot system seen earlier in Figure 9.2. Let's look at the files one by one.

nlu.yml : This file contains intents. You can add a new intent by following the format you already see there. In our case, we want to add the intent of ordering a pizza. The intent names should not be duplicated. See Figures 9.9 and 9.10 for how we defined our intents in the file *nlu.yml*.

actions.py : You'll see a class Action and two methods - *name* and *run*. To create your own actions, create a child of Action.

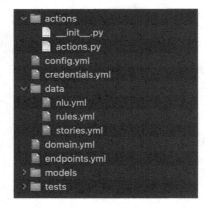

FIGURE 9.7 RASA folder.

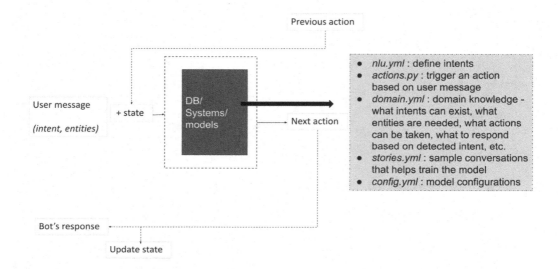

FIGURE 9.8 RASA components for a chatbot system.

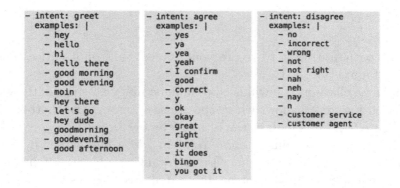

FIGURE 9.9 nlu.yml intents related to greeting, user agreement, and user disagreement.

```
- intent: order_pizza_topping_size
  examples: |
    - I would like a [medium](pizzasize) crust pizza with [chicken](topping) and [mushroom](topping)
    - Can I have a [large](pizzasize) [chicken](topping) and [pepperoni](topping) pizza please?
    - I want to order a [chicken](topping) pizza, make it [large](pizzasize) with lots of [pepperoni](topping)
- intent: order_pizza_topping
  examples: |
    - [chicken](topping) pizza
    - Can I get a [mushroom](topping) pizza
    - Please give me a [chicken](topping) and [mushroom](topping) pizza
    - I want to order a [mushroom](topping) pizza
    - I would like to place an order for a [chicken](topping) and [pepproni](topping) pizza. Thanks
    - I would like pizza with [pepproni](topping) and [mushrooms](topping)
    - [pepperoni](topping)
    - [mushroom](topping)
- intent: order_pizza_size
  examples: |
    - [medium](pizzasize) pizza
    - Can I get a [large](pizzasize) pizza
    - [large](pizzasize) pizza
    - [large](pizzasize) size
    - [medium](pizzasize) base
- intent: order_pizza
  examples: |
    - order a pizza
    - get a pizza
    - I would like pizza
    - Can I have a pizza
    - pizza please
```

FIGURE 9.10 nlu.yml intents related to pizza ordering.

domain.yml : This file contains the domain knowledge needed by the chatbot in terms of what to respond or do to what people ask. Add your custom actions, responses, entity slots, and intents to this file. More on domain.yml can be found here[5]. Here's how we structured it.

```
intents:
  - greet
  - order_pizza
  - order_pizza_topping_size
  - order_pizza_topping
  - order_pizza_size
  - agree
  - disagree

entities:
  - topping
  - pizzasize

slots:
  topping:
  type: list
  mappings:
    - type: from_entity
    entity: topping
  pizzasize:
  type: text
  mappings:
    - type: from_entity
```

---

[5]https://rasa.com/docs/rasa/domain/

```
    entity: pizzasize
```

For defining responses, you can have multiple responses under each action utterance. The bot will randomly select one of those in chats. See utter_greet below as an example. You can also customize responses with values from entities. See how we defined some of our responses for utter_order_placed as an example. The full file can be found in section6/rasademo/domain.yml.

```
responses:
  utter_greet:
  - text: "Hey! How can I help you?"
  - text: "Hello! Which pizza would you like to order?"

  utter_order_pizza:
  - text: "Can you tell me what toppings you'd like and
  the size of the pizza?"

  utter_order_pizza_topping:
  - text: "Can you tell me what toppings you'd like?"

  utter_order_pizza_size:
  - text: "Can you tell me what pizza size you'd like?
  We have medium and large."

  utter_order_pizza_topping_size:
  - text: "Thank you. We are getting ready to place
  your order for pizza size: {pizzasize} with toppings
  {topping}. Does the order look correct?"

  utter_disagree:
  - text: "Sorry that we were unable to help you on
  chat. Kindly call +1(800)xxx-xxxx and they'll assist
  you right away."

  utter_order_placed:
  - text: "Good news, your order has been placed! Your
  {pizzasize} pizza with {topping} will be ready in
  30 mins!"
```

'actions' in domain.yml need to contain a list of every possible action your bot can take. This includes responses and actions (such as updating a database, etc.).

```
actions:
 - utter_greet
 - utter_disagree
 - action_order_pizza
 - utter_order_pizza
 - utter_order_pizza_topping
 - utter_order_pizza_size
 - utter_order_pizza_topping_size
 - utter_order_placed
```

Next, *stories.yml* helps tie all the pieces together. This file contains sample sequences of events in sample conversations. Here are a few examples of how we defined our stories for this demo. The full script can be found in section6/ rasademo/data/stories.yml.

```
version: "3.1"

stories:

- story: pizza ordering with no info
  steps:
  - intent: greet
  - action: utter_greet
  - intent: order_pizza
  - action: utter_order_pizza
  - intent: order_pizza_topping_size
  - action: utter_order_pizza_topping_size
  - intent: agree
  #- action: action_order_pizza
  - action: utter_order_placed

- story: pizza ordering with size info
  steps:
  - intent: greet
  - action: utter_greet
  - intent: order_pizza_size
  entities:
  - pizzasize: medium
  - action: utter_order_pizza_topping
  - intent: order_pizza_topping
  entities:
  - topping: chicken
  - action: utter_order_pizza_topping_size
  - intent: agree
  #- action: action_order_pizza
  - action: utter_order_placed
```

For this demo, we will be testing this sample without a defined action. Hence, we comment out action_order_pizza in the stories section.

Run `rasa data validate` to ensure there are no errors with your data changes/additions.

Now, you can train your model.

```
rasa train
```

To run this in shell, run the following command.

```
rasa shell
```

Figure 9.11 shows sample chats with our chatbot.

You can also build this on localhost by running **rasa run**. This command exposes a REST endpoint at 5005 port in the localhost.

The model appears to deal well with small typing errors as seen in Figure 9.12.

This prototype was built on smaller data for the demo. Some obvious failures are as seen in Figure 9.13.

We have not included any unknown input handling or fallbacks, hence we observe certain undesirable outcomes. Here's more information on setting the behavior per your requirements.[6]

---

[6]`https://rasa.com/docs/rasa/unexpected-input`

User input -> Hi
Hey! How can I help you?
User input -> Can i get a pizza?
Can you tell me what toppings you'd like and the size of the pizza?
User input -> give me chicken and pepperoni
Can you tell me what pizza size you'd like? We have medium and large.
User input -> large
Thank you. We are getting ready to place your order for pizza size: large with toppings ['chicken', 'pepperoni']. Does the order look correct?
User input -> yes
Good news, your order has been placed! Your large pizza with ['chicken', 'pepperoni'] will be ready in 30 mins!

User input -> can i get a large pizza?
Can you tell me what toppings you'd like?
User input -> chicken, pepperoni, and mushroom
Thank you. We are getting ready to place your order for pizza size: large with toppings ['chicken', 'pepperoni', 'mushroom']. Does the order look correct?
User input -> sounds good
Good news, your order has been placed! ! Your large pizza with ['chicken', 'pepperoni', 'mushroom'] will be ready in 30 mins!

User input -> hello
Hey! How can I help you?
User input -> Can I get a large pizza with chicken and mushroom?
Thank you. We are getting ready to place your order for pizza size: large with toppings ['chicken', 'mushroom']. Does the order look correct?
User input -> correct
Good news, your order has been placed! ! Your large pizza with ['chicken', 'mushroom'] will be ready in 30 mins!

User input -> hey
Hey! How can I help you?
User input -> can i get a mushroom and chicken pizza?
Can you tell me what pizza size you'd like? We have medium and large.
User input -> medium
Thank you. We are getting ready to place your order for pizza size: medium with toppings ['mushroom', 'chicken']. Does the order look correct?
User input -> ok
Good news, your order has been placed! Your medium pizza with ['mushroom', 'chicken'] will be ready in 30 mins!

FIGURE 9.11 RASA pizza-ordering chatbot - sample conversations.

Your input -> can i get a pizza with mushrom chicken and peproni
Thank you. We are getting ready to place your order for pizza size: large with toppings ['mushrom', 'chicken', 'peproni']. Does the order look correct?

FIGURE 9.12 RASA chatbot conversation with typos.

Your input -> can i get a pizza with olives
Can you tell me what toppings you'd like and the size of the pizza?
Your input -> olives and chicken
Can you tell me what pizza size you'd like? We have medium and large.
Your input -> large
Thank you. We are getting ready to place your order for pizza size: large with toppings ['chicken']. Does the order look correct?

Your input -> hi
Hello! Which pizza would you like to order?
Your input -> what's the weather?
Hey! How can I help you?
Your input -> Can you tell me the weather?
Hello! Which pizza would you like to order?

FIGURE 9.13 RASA chatbot bad conversation samples.

Several options can improve your chatbot besides adding more relevant training data and fine-tuning rasa rules, domain, nlu, and stories.

Notes on customization options

Model options

There are several options available with RASA that you can choose from for your models. In the file *config.yml*, the commented lines specify the default selections in the pipeline. You can uncomment and alter the pipeline. To learn more about different components of the pipeline, here is a good resources.[7]

Summarized notes of RASA pipeline components

A pipeline usually consists of five main parts[a]:
- Tokenization
- Featurization using pre-trained word embeddings or Supervised Embeddings
- Intent Classification
- Response Selector
- Entity Extraction

Rasa NLU offers several entity recognition components as follows.
- Entity recognition with SpaCy language models: ner_spacy
- Rule-based entity recognition using Facebook's Duckling: ner_http_duckling
- Training an extractor for custom entities: ner_crf [b]

You can also configure Tensorflow[c].

---

[a]https://rasa.com/docs/rasa/tuning-your-model/
[b]https://rasa.com/blog/rasa-nlu-in-depth-part-2-entity-recognition/
[c]https://rasa.com/docs/rasa/tuning-your-model/#configuring-tensorflow

---

The default selection uses DIETClassifier, which is Dual Intent Entity Transformer (DIET) used for both intent classification and entity extraction.

Summarized notes on DIET
DIET is a transformer-based architecture.
- *entity*: A sequence of entity labels is predicted through a Conditional Random Field (CRF) tagging layer on top of the transformer output sequence corresponding to the input sequence of tokens.
- *intent*: The transformer output for the complete utterance and intent labels are embedded into a single semantic vector space. They use the dot-product loss to maximize the similarity with the target label and minimize similarities with negative samples. Reference document[a].

---

[a]https://rasa.com/docs/rasa/components/#dietclassifier

---

[7]https://rasa.com/docs/rasa/components/

Here is an example of altering *config.yml* to use Logistic Regression for intent classification and CRFEntityExtractor for entity extraction.

```
pipeline:
  - name: WhitespaceTokenizer
  - name: LexicalSyntacticFeaturizer
  - name: CountVectorsFeaturizer
  - name: CountVectorsFeaturizer
  analyzer: char_wb
  min_ngram: 1
  max_ngram: 2
  - name: LogisticRegressionClassifier
  - name: CRFEntityExtractor
```

Integrating custom models

You can also build your own entity recognition model and pass it into RASA. To use your own spaCy model for NER, compile and package your model and alter the config.yml. Further details on the exact steps to follow can be found here[8]. To only test your component model, `rasa shell nlu` lets you experiment with different inputs.

Testing

You can test various components of your chatbot with rasa. You can write sample test stories and run `rasa test`. As a default, the command runs tests on stories from any files with names starting with 'test_'. You can provide a specific test stories file or directory with a `-stories` argument.

Writing sample stories for testing when you don't have real conversational data can come in handy to kick-start the tool. A good practice would be to add new stories as your chatbot grows and learns.

> *TIP*
>
> When you start generating real chat data for your bot, manually go through some of it to label and save as test data for your chatbot. This way, you'll be able to run tests on real conversations.

You can also test different components of your chatbot in addition to complete test stories. You can test your NLU (natural language understanding) model using the command `rasa data split nlu`, which will shuffle and split your data into training and testing samples. `rasa test nlu -nlu data/nlu.yml -cross-validation` is a sample command you can use to run a full NLU evaluation using cross-validation.

To test the intent and entity models, run

```
rasa shell nlu
```

---

[8]https://rasa.com/blog/custom-spacy-components/

The model we built in this demonstration recognized order_pizza_topping as the intent with a score of 0.996, and entities 'pepperoni' and 'chicken' with a score of 0.999 and 0.999 respectively. The full result file can be found in the code repository at section6/rasa-nlu-diet-peproni-pizza-with-extra-chicken.json.

There are several other ways you can test the different components. RASA documentation[9] provides other good examples of how you can do that.

Integrations

You can integrate your chatbot[10] with any website, Facebook Messenger, Slack, Telegram, Twilio, Microsoft Bot Framework, Cisco Webex Teams, RocketChat, Mattermost, and Google Hangouts Chat. You can also connect the chatbot to other platform by creating a custom connector.

9.5   CLOSING THOUGHTS

There are many other steps you can follow to make your chatbot more robust. For example, it may make sense to get confirmation on the user's order before placing it and include logic to correct any misinformation based on the user's response. It also may be a good idea to list a phone number and alternate chat routing for the customer to get in touch with a human in case the order could not be placed successfully. Furthermore, for a menu with fixed options on toppings and pizza size, you can add rule-based matching to the chatbot's entity recognition. Since typing errors can be expected from customers, you should add commonly expected typos in the list of possible pizza toppings and add a reference back to the spellings on the menu. Further actions we add should check your dB of available inventory and communicate to the user if their requested item is unavailable. All of that together is a recipe for making a good prototype / first version. In a typical scenario in the industry, a prototype tool is first set up and tested by internal team members to rule out any obvious failures. Once the performance feels reasonable, it is then deployed in production and integrated with websites, messengers, etc.

---

[9]https://rasa.com/docs/rasa/testing-your-assistant/
[10]https://rasa.com/docs/rasa/connector

What can make the chatbot better?
More training data samples will help make the intent classification model perform better. You can also experiment with different NLP processes and ML models to tune your intent classifier. More training data also helps the entity recognition task. There are several options available with RASA that can help you define specifications for tuning your model.

Aside from the models, an important aspect of the chatbot is the ability to handle input that it isn't prepared for. Diverting customers accordingly to handle such input creates a good customer experience.

Learning how customers are using your chatbot and where it fails will further help you create a better-performing tool. The chatbot can learn from its experiences. Thus, log all customer conversations together with metadata - if they order the pizza, your chatbot worked, but failed orders can help you identify where your bot needs work.

Just like RASA models, Dialogflow gets better with more data. However, some complex examples that fail with Dialogflow are where multiple pieces of information are present in the same sentence.

I have a chicken with me, what can I cook with it besides chicken lasagna?

Give me a recipe for a chocolate dessert that can be made in just 10 minutes instead of the regular half an hour.

In a RASA pipeline with custom models, such adversarial examples can be added for the model to learn to identify correct entities and their values.

## CHAPTER 10

Customer Review Analysis

Understanding aspects of customer reaction to a product or a service is one of the most common applications of NLP across various industry domains including e-commerce, hospitality, and travel. Tasks such as text visualization, sentiment analysis, information extraction, topic modeling, and text classification find use in review analysis depending on the business use case.

10.1 HOTEL REVIEW ANALYSIS

Figure 10.1 represents an example of why such analysis is of interest to a company.

Action plan

Your customer strategy team has a few different requirements.

- They want to understand comment sentiment.

- They want to understand themes in the positive and negative sentiment comments without having to manually read all the comments.

- Once they gain more visibility into the popular themes, they want to select a few themes that make sense from a business standpoint and also from a data standpoint.

- Then, they want you to build a model that can detect the presence of the selected themes within any comments.

This will eventually allow the business to show the classification on their website so users can sift through reviews around a particular theme of interest, such as 'staff and service'.

Dataset

We will build our analysis and models for comments on hotels from the OpinRank Review Dataset available at the UCI Machine Learning Repository.[1]

We'll select New York based hotels for our analysis.

The total number of reviews is 50656

Shortest review length: 10 characters

Longest review length: 793 characters

Mean review length: 981 characters

---

[1]`https://archive.ics.uci.edu/ml/datasets/opinrank+review+dataset`

DOI: 10.1201/9781003264774-10

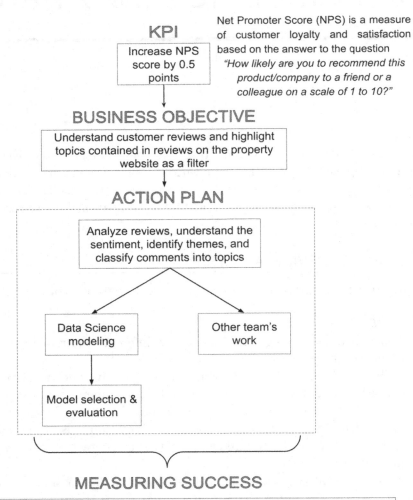

KPI

Increase NPS
score by 0.5
points

Net Promoter Score (NPS) is a measure
of customer loyalty and satisfaction
based on the answer to the question
*"How likely are you to recommend this
product/company to a friend or a
colleague on a scale of 1 to 10?"*

BUSINESS OBJECTIVE

Understand customer reviews and highlight
topics contained in reviews on the property
website as a filter

ACTION PLAN

Analyze reviews, understand the
sentiment, identify themes, and
classify comments into topics

Data Science
modeling

Other team's
work

Model selection &
evaluation

MEASURING SUCCESS

Measuring the success of the business objective
- Increase in the NPS score
- Number of clicks on reviews topic filters on the website
- Increase in bookings for properties with review filters versus others
- Number of issues identified by Product and Operations using model results on negative reviews compared to past times when the analysis was not available
- Time savings in going through comments manually

FIGURE 10.1 Performing comment review analysis from a company KPI perspective.

Median review length: 19846 characters

The size of the dataset here is good for producing a data-driven analysis.

> *TIP*
>
> In a real-world use case, if you have only < 100 comments that get produced in a few months, it may not be worth investing time and resources in such an analysis as it may be quicker to manually sift through the comments to understand what the users are saying. Once the number of comments becomes larger such that it is not feasible to understand the data in a relatively short amount of time by manually looking at it, then it is likely the right time to explore automation via NLP.

Solution

From a data science perspective, the steps that we will go through are shown in Figure 10.2.

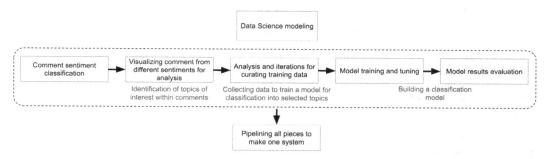

FIGURE 10.2 Data science tasks breakdown for customer review analysis project.

10.1.1   Sentiment analysis

We visited a few different options to perform sentiment analysis on text in Chapter 8. Vader appears to do better on social media data [83]. Since the language in our reviews looks more formal, we start with **TextBlob**. The **textblob.sentiments** module contains two sentiment analysis implementations, **PatternAnalyzer** (based on the **pattern** library) and **NaiveBayesAnalyzer** (an NLTK classifier trained on a movie reviews corpus)[2]. The default implementation is **PatternAnalyzer**. Here, we will assign the review of positive for polarity score > 0 and negative for polarity score < 0.

---

[2]https://textblob.readthedocs.io/en/dev/advanced_usage.html

> TIP
> How to select between the available tools?
> Take a random sample of 100 comments from your data and pass through the different sentiment classification models. Compare the differences and choose the tool that is more accurate.

```
! pip install textblob

from collections import Counter
from textblob import TextBlob

sentiment = {}
for rev_id, rev in id_review.items():
  pol = TextBlob(rev).sentiment.polarity
  if pol > 0:
    sent = "pos"
  elif pol < 0:
    sent = "neg"
  else:
    sent = "neu"
  sentiment[rev_id] = {"class": sent, "polarity": pol}
```

Let's find the overall sentiment distribution.

```
sent_classes = [
  sent["class"] for _, sent in sentiment.items()
]
print(Counter(sent_classes))
# >> {"pos": 47976, "neg": 2618, "neu": 62}
```

We notice that majority of the comments are positive. Let's look at a few samples from each sentiment class.

- Positive:
  '*We were given an overnight stay at the St. Regis as an anniversary present and were treated to elegant luxury. The accommodations were plush, clean and first class. The location to the theater district was convenient as well as many choices of restaurants. For an overnight in the City, do not hesitate to enjoy the St. Regis.*'
  '*I was on a trip looking for sites to hold business meetings in New York City. Everyone at the St. Regis, from the front desk to security to the housekeeping and butlers were friendly, helpful and went out of their way to provide anything I requested. The rooms were spacious (for New York) and quiet and the sheets on the bed were Pratesi. What more could someone ask for? Oh yes, they also provided butler service.*'
  '*I've stayed at the St. Regis on several occasions and had a wonderful experience each time. The guest rooms are spacious, quiet, well decorated and functional, with comfortable beds and big marble bathrooms. Public areas are elegant. The staff is cheerful and professional. Room service is prompt and the food is tasty. Ideal location. Overall, a lovely hotel.*'

- Neutral:
  'could not fault this hotel, fab location, staff and service... will definitely stay there again'
  'If you like animals - cockroaches - this is the hotel for you!Stayed here in june and it was cockroaches all over the placein the bathroom and under the bed - not nice.....But if you like animals this is the hotel for you!I don't recommend this hotel at all!!'
  'STAY HERE! But choose the river view, not the twin towers view.'

- 'Negative: While this hotel is luxurious, I just spent my second night on the fourth floor and was woken up at two by garbage trucks outside which loaded and beeped for an hour. My colleague got bumped up to a suite when she complained about her room. Avoid any rooms on low floors facing the street and you might get some sleep.'
  'room smelled like mold....you could see mold in the tub...when i checked in on saturday agent failed to tell me the following day there would be a festival that would on shut down all street including the one in front of the hotel making it impossible to get a taxi to anywhere. The deorative pillows on the bed were so filthy i have to put them on the floor. I would never stay here again even for half the price.'
  'We must have had the worst room at the hotel compared to the other ratings. Our windows faced a brick wall, the windows wouldn't open properly which we wanted because the airconditioning system wouldn't regulate properly. The room was small and because of the windows facing the wall, the room was dark and dreary. Never saw the sun. It was like staying in a closet. The staff were a bit put off and arrogant. Not friendly. The only positive about this hotel is the location. There are better choices. We will not stay here again.'

We notice that neutral sentiment analysis fails when abbreviations are used to describe the stay, such as 'fab'. Furthermore, any sarcasm present in the comments leads to further incorrect classification.

On manually checking 100 random comments per class, the neutral class had the most incorrect classifications with 60% correct classifications. We noticed 80% accurate results for the positive class and 100% accurate results for the negative class.

For our purpose, we want to understand the negative and positive comments further. These results overall seem satisfactory.

> In the event we wanted to re-purpose this model with a heavy focus on neutral sentiment, we would have needed to access whether 60% accuracy would be satisfactory by discussing with the team intending to use the outcome.

With this, we just finished the highlighted task in Figure 10.3.

10.1.2 Extracting comment topic themes

Let's further look into positive and negative reviews. The goal is to understand common themes around positive comments and negative comments. We start by plotting word clouds for each of the two sentiments. In the word cloud representation, the more often a word appears in the corpus, the bigger it is in the figure.

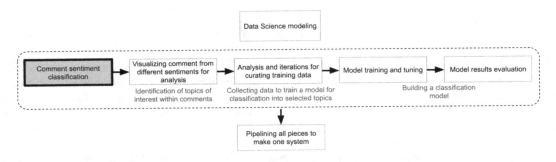

FIGURE 10.3 Data science tasks breakdown for customer review analysis project (sentiment analysis).

We clean the comments to remove stop words that aren't going to give us any meaningful insights, words such as to, at, a, etc. We also remove punctuation and lemmatize the words.

```
! pip install nltk
! pip install wordcloud

import string
from matplotlib import pyplot as plt
from nltk.corpus import stopwords
from nltk.stem.wordnet import WordNetLemmatizer
from wordcloud import WordCloud


STOP = set(stopwords.words('english'))
PUNCT = set(string.punctuation)
LEMMA = WordNetLemmatizer()
WC = WordCloud(
  mode = "RGBA",
  collocations = False,
  background_color = None,
  width=1500,
  height=1000
)


def clean(doc):
  """Revove stop words, punctuations, and lemmatize."""
  stop_free = " ".join(
    [i for i in doc.lower().split() if i not in STOP]
  )
  punc_free = "".join(
    [ch for ch in stop_free if ch not in PUNCT]
  )
  normalized = " ".join(
    LEMMA.lemmatize(word) for word in punc_free.split()
  )
  return " ".join([i for i in normalized.split() if len(i)>1])


def plot_wc(text_list):
  """Plots word cloud using a list of string values"""
```

```
word_cloud = WC.generate(" ".join(text_list))
plt.figure( figsize=(30,20) )
# Display the generated Word Cloud
plt.imshow(word_cloud, interpolation="bilinear")
plt.axis("off")
plt.show()

negatives = []
positives = []

for rev_id in sentiment:
  if sentiment[rev_id]["class"] == "neg":
    negatives.append(rev_id)
  if sentiment[rev_id]["class"] == "pos":
    positives.append(rev_id)

plot_wc([clean(id_review[i]) for i in positives])
plot_wc([clean(id_review[i]) for i in negatives])
```

The above result in plots shown in Figures 10.4 and 10.5.

FIGURE 10.4 Word cloud for positive comments.

FIGURE 10.5 Word cloud for negative comments.

The largest common themes in both positive and negative sentiments appear to be around room and hotel. These word clouds have multiple words that do not give us information about the theme, such as 'one', 'really', etc. Thus, we will pass the data through another cleaning function to retain only nouns and plot word clouds again. We'll also remove the words 'room' and 'hotel' for studying other themes for the two sentiment classes and compare them.

```python
from nltk import word_tokenize
from nltk import pos_tag


def noun_clean(x):
    """
    Retain only nouns and then pass through cleaning function
    """
    tokens = word_tokenize(x)
    tags = pos_tag(tokens)
    nouns = [
        word
        for word, pos in tags
        if (
            pos == 'NN'
            or pos == 'NNP'
            or pos == 'NNS'
            or pos == 'NNPS'
        )
    ]
    return clean(" ".join(nouns))


# positives
noun_pos = [noun_clean(id_review[rev_id]) for rev_id in positives]
# remove hand-selected words
clean_pos = [
    " ".join(
        [
            j for j in i.split()
            if j not in ["room", "hotel", "quot"] and len(j) >= 2
        ]
    ) for i in noun_pos
]
plot_wc(clean_pos)


# negatives
noun_neg = [noun_clean(id_review[rev_id]) for rev_id in negatives]
# remove hand-selected words
clean_neg = [
    " ".join(
        [
            j for j in i.split()
            if j.lower() not in ["room", "hotel", "quot"] and len(j) >= 2
        ]
    ) for i in noun_neg
]
plot_wc(clean_neg)
```

The above results in word clouds in Figures 10.6 and 10.7.

FIGURE 10.6 Word cloud for positive comments (nouns only).

FIGURE 10.7 Word cloud for negative comments (nouns only).

Let's first look at the positive reviews on the word cloud. In these plots, we observe the words time, staff, location, night, and several other room-related words such as door, bathroom, and bed. Bucketing some top words in general topical areas, we have

1. staff and service with other related words such as time, night, etc.

2. location, with other related words such as area, street, york, park, etc.

3. room-related words such as bathroom, floor, door, bed, etc.

4. food-related keywords such as breakfast, bar, and restaurant.

Next, let's explore the negative reviews word cloud. We see words such as night, staff, time, desk, day, bathroom, and service. Bucketing some top words in general topical areas, we have

1. staff and service with other related words such as time, night, desk (likely coming from front desk), manager, etc.

2. room-related words such as bathroom, floor, door, bed, etc.

There are fewer location-related and food-related words compared to the positive word cloud. In comparison, 'service' 'bathroom', and 'night' seem to be mentioned a lot more in negative reviews.

To understand which reviews contain what topics, we will create a classification model. The above topics identified from the word clouds can be a good baseline for classifying our comments. In reality, such decisions are made in conjunction with important stakeholders to satisfy the business applications.

Here, we choose *service & staff* (including hotel food services), *location*, and *room* as the topics with which we want to classify our comments. These three categories are also generally common from a business perspective for hotel review classification (see Google reviews classification for hotels).

This completes the highlighted task in Figure 10.8.

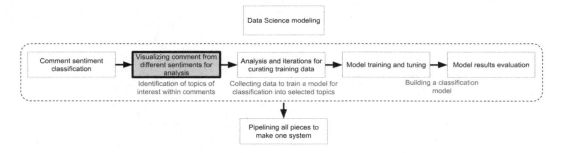

FIGURE 10.8 Data science tasks breakdown for customer review analysis project (identification of topics and themes).

10.1.3 Unlabeled comment classification into categories

First, we randomly select 75% of the data (37992 comments) that we will use for training purposes, and leave 25% of the data for testing later after finalizing a model.

```
import random

subset = set(
  random.sample(
    list(id_review.keys()), int(len(id_review)*0.75)
  )
)
```

Although it is possible to utilize a zero-shot transformers-based model (Section 8.3.1.1), the inference time would be substantial. Another approach is getting data labeled manually and then training a classification model. However, that process is often time-consuming. Some methods can help create a model without having to manually label each sample.

Note: The word 'document' refers to a text sample, and the word 'documents' refers to all samples in the corpus.

1. One method is to hand-curate a set of words that identify with a topic. We then plot word clouds for all the documents that contain our hand-curated word list but remove the words from our hand-curated set. This surfaces other words that co-occur with our initial set. We can then increase our initial set and add more words identified from the word cloud. Next, we assume all documents containing any of the words in the set belong to our topic. We repeat this for each topic. This process helps quickly gather some training data for the classification problem. The main downside is a potential bias that can get introduced in our model via the hand-curation process. A further step could be to remove the search word from the document that we append to our training dataset to limit the bias of this initial process if the test results are not satisfactory. Nonetheless, this can form a good baseline model that you can improve upon as a part of future iterations once you're able to curate more generalizable training data.

2. We can run a clustering algorithm such as LDA and inspect the resulting clusters for several runs with different num_topics. Whichever cluster seems relevant to a topic, we can manually check accuracy for a random 100 samples and add all documents that get assigned to that cluster to our training dataset for the topic if the accuracy is satisfactory. A similar approach can be used with any clustering algorithm such as K-means. We can also use zero-shot classification to refine data labels, followed by manual verification of the results. This strategy limits the high inference time to only the initial label curation process.

While approach number 1 may not seem like a conventional data science method of solving such a problem compared to approach number 2, it can work well and fast for a problem like this. For this exercise, we'll go with approach number 1 and evaluate our model. We'll also explore approach number 2 at the surface level using LDA before wrapping up this section for demonstration purposes.

Before we begin, we need to break down each review comment into segments. This is because the review comments in our data contain information about multiple topics in the same comment, and sometimes in the same sentence as well. Breaking down the comment into parts and sentences will help us segregate the data such that multiple topics are less likely to occur within the same sample.

'The rooms were very clean, service was excellent and useful. Location was outstanding' -> ['The rooms were clean', 'service was excellent and useful', 'Location was outstanding']

```
import re

SENT_SPLIT = ",|\.|\?|\!|\n"
```

```
new_id_docs = []
for rev_id, rev in id_review.items():
  if rev_id in subset:
    rev_split = re.split(SENT_SPLIT, rev)
    for phrase in rev_split:
      # get each word in the cleaned phrase
      phr_list = clean(phrase).split()
      # only select cleaned phrases
      # that contain more than 2 words
      if len(phr_list) > 2:
        new_id_docs.append((rev_id, phr_list))
```

Approach 1: Hand-curated words for creating training dataset

We begin with hand-curating some obvious words for each topic. We choose
- 'location' for the topic *location*;
- 'room', 'bed', 'bathroom', and 'bedroom' for the topic *room*;
- 'service' and 'staff' for the topic *service & staff*.

We then find all documents containing these words.

```
loc_set = {"location"}
room_set = {"room", "bed", "bathroom", "bedroom"}
serv_set = {"service", "staff"}

def filter_by_words(new_id_docs, word_set):
  return [
    itm for itm in new_id_docs
    if any(w in itm[1] for w in word_set)
  ]

location = filter_by_words(new_id_docs, loc_set)
room = filter_by_words(new_id_docs, room_set)
serv = filter_by_words(new_id_docs, serv_set)
```

Then we plot word clouds to see the top noun words in the documents. We remove overall top-occurring terms such as 'hotel' in addition to the initial hand-curated set.

```
remove_set = {"hotel"}

def clean_training_samples(id_words, remove_words):
  nouns = [
  noun_clean(
    " ".join([
      w for w in word_list
      if w not in remove_words
    ])
  ) for _, word_list in id_words
  ]
  return nouns

print("\nFor location\n")
plot_wc(clean_training_samples(
  location, set.union(remove_set, loc_set))
```

```
)
print("\nFor room\n")
plot_wc(clean_training_samples(
  room,  set.union(remove_set, room_set))
)
print("\nFor staff and service\n")
plot_wc(clean_training_samples(
  serv, set.union(remove_set, serv_set))
)
```

The word clouds produced are shown in Figures 10.9, 10.10, and 10.11. We curate more words by looking at the word clouds. Then, we select all comment segments containing any of our curated words per topic to form our training dataset.

FIGURE 10.9 Room-word cloud.

FIGURE 10.10 Location-word cloud.

For *location*,

```
loc_set = {
  "location", "subway", "walking", "street", "block",
  "distance", "walk", "park", "midtown", "manhattan",
  "empire", "avenue", "shop", "attraction"
}
loc_set_dual = {"time", "square"}
location_train = []
for rev_id, word_list in new_id_docs:
  for loc_word in loc_set:
    if loc_word in word_list:
```

FIGURE 10.11 Service and staff-word cloud.

```
    location_train.append(
      (
        rev_id, word_list
      )
    )
  if len(
    [w for w in loc_set_dual if w in word_list]
  ) == loc_set_dual:
    location_train.append(
      (
        rev_id, word_list
      )
    )
print(len(location), len(location_train))
# >> 18292 88196
```

For *room,*

```
room_set = {
  "bath", "floor", "shower", "window", "space",
  "room", "bed", "bathroom", "bedroom"
}
room_train = []
for rev_id, word_list in new_id_docs:
  for room_word in room_set:
    if room_word in word_list:
      room_train.append(
        (
          rev_id, word_list
        )
      )
print(len(room), len(room_train))
# >> (103584, 141598)
```

For *service & staff*,

```
serv_set = {
  "service", "staff", "reception", "concierge",
  "desk", "front", "helpful", "customer", "breakfast",
  "food", "restaurant", "problem", "polite", "help"
}
serv_train = []
for rev_id, word_list in new_id_docs:
  for serv_word in serv_set:
    if serv_word in word_list:
      serv_train.append(
        (
          rev_id,  word_list
        )
      )
print(len(serv), len(serv_train))
# >> (33749, 105870)
```

This completes the highlighted task in Figure 10.12.

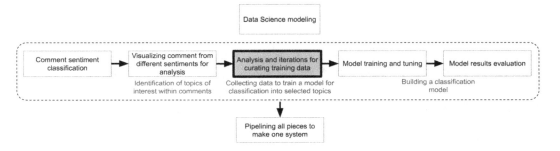

FIGURE 10.12 Data science tasks breakdown for customer review analysis project (curating training data).

Next, we put together this data, randomly shuffle, and create a baseline Multinomial Naive Bayes model as in Chapter 8.

```
cleaned_data = (
  [
    (" ".join(word_list), "staff_serv")
    for _, word_list in serv_train] + [
    (" ".join(word_list), "loc")
    for _, word_list in location_train] + [
    (" ".join(word_list), "room")
    for _, word_list in room_train
  ]
)
cleaned_data = [
  itm for itm in cleaned_data
  if len(itm[0].split()) > 2
]
random.shuffle(cleaned_data)
x = [itm[0] for itm in cleaned_data]
y = [itm[1] for itm in cleaned_data]
```

We'll use the same code used in Chapter 8 for training the model. The full script can be found in section6/comment-analysis-hotel-reviews.ipynb.

The model results are as follows.

Best alpha : 0.2
Avg. Precision : 0.905341376566488
Avg. Recall : 0.9027806534128331
Avg. F1 : 0.9039970523346635

Per class evaluation
Classes : ["loc" "room" "staff_serv"]
Precision : [0.91026637 0.90473806 0.9010197]
Recall : [0.90010843 0.92312715 0.88510638]
F1 : [0.9051589 0.9138401 0.89299215]

The confusion matrix can be seen in Figure 10.13.

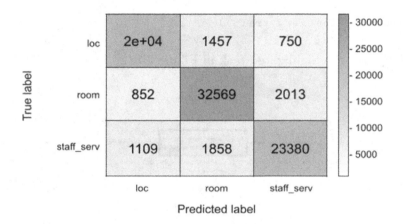

FIGURE 10.13 Confusion matrix for hotel review classification model.

This completes the highlighted task in Figure 10.14.

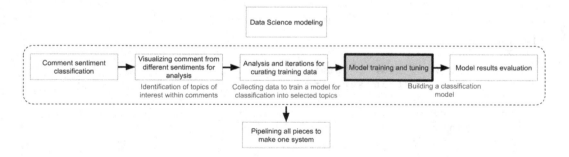

FIGURE 10.14 Data science tasks breakdown for customer review analysis project (training a classification model).

We want to identify the correct classifications in each comment segment. We'll use the `predict_proba` function to get probabilities of prediction per class and identify a good cut-off threshold score. This means any data that has a classification of 'location' with a probability > threshold will be deemed location-related. This is also useful in our case as a lot of comments may have segments that do not belong to any of the three topics we want to identify, e.g. 'I was traveling on Monday for a work trip.' from 'I was traveling on Monday for a work trip. The staff was very helpful in accommodating my late check in request.' However, our classifier will force each segment to the three classes defined. Thus by eliminating low-probability detections, we can disregard some of the classifications of comment segments that are irrelevant to our model.

Since we curated the data manually, testing this model is important so we can detect cases of bias and work on future iterations accordingly. Let's inspect some results below.

```
best_model.classes_
# >> array(["loc", "room", "staff_serv"]

# comment unrelated to our classes
best_model.predict_proba(vectorizer.transform([clean(
  "the parking was good"
)]))
# >> array([[0.26565376, 0.34722567, 0.38712057]])

# Default classification appears to be "room"
best_model.predict_proba(vectorizer.transform([clean(
  "booked this hotelfor a stay on friday"
)]))
# >> array([[0.11400537, 0.68869973, 0.1972949 ]])

# Room classification
best_model.predict_proba(vectorizer.transform([clean(
  "the bedroom was spacious"
)]))
# >> array([[0.01944015, 0.95802311, 0.02253675]])

# curated words not present in the sentence
# here we see a correct classification
best_model.predict_proba(vectorizer.transform([clean(
  "loved the size and view"
)]))
# >> array([[0.04832765, 0.92979582, 0.02187653]])

# curated words not present in the sentence
# here we see a correct classification
best_model.predict_proba(vectorizer.transform([clean(
  "comfortable sleep"
)]))
# >> array([[0.04661195, 0.88965958, 0.06372847]])

# downtown was not in our curated word set,
# here we see a correct classification
best_model.predict_proba(vectorizer.transform([clean(
```

```
    "very close to downtown"
)]))
# >> array([[0.73054746, 0.11439228, 0.15506026]])

# intentional typo, but correct classification
best_model.predict_proba(vectorizer.transform([clean(
    "the stfaf was very friendly"
)]))
# >> array([[0.02694535, 0.05471212, 0.91834252]])
```

The above results look satisfactory.

Next, on the subset of data we didn't consider for training (our test set), we took a random sample of 500 and manually verified the results. We did so by writing the results to excel and manually going through the rows. The results are as follows.

The samples with a classification probability score of >0.62 contain 94.3% accurate topic detections.

This completes the highlighted task in Figure 10.15.

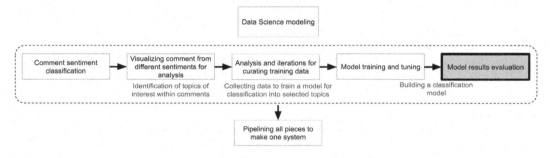

FIGURE 10.15 Data science tasks breakdown for customer review analysis project (model evaluation).

Using the above thresholds, we can now pass in new comments through our classifier and get sentiment and topics in each comment as follows.

```
clean_test = {}
for rev_id, rev in id_review.items():
  if rev_id not in subset:
    phrase_list = re.split(SENT_SPLIT, rev)
    clean_test[rev_id] = [
      clean(phr) for phr in phrase_list
    ]
print(f"{len(clean_test)} unseen test samples prepared")
# > A random sample was taken to identify a threshold
# Threshold of 0.62 was identified

# Next, we collect results using the identified threshold
classes_pred={}
for rev_id in clean_test:
  classes_pred[rev_id] = []
  for phr in clean_test[rev_id]:
    if len(phr.split()) >= 2:
      pred = best_model.predict_proba(
```

```
        vectorizer.transform([phr])
    )[0]
    if max(pred) >= 0.62:
      classes_pred[rev_id].append(
        best_model.classes_[
          np.where(pred == max(pred))[0][0]
        ]
      )

rand_sample = random.sample(list(classes_pred.keys()), 100)
results = []
for rev_id in rand_sample:
  results.append(
    [
      rev_id,
      id_review[rev_id],
      Counter(classes_pred[rev_id]).most_common(),
      sentiment[rev_id]["class"]
    ]
  )
```

Here is what a few samples look like. Format ([id, comment, topics, sentiment]).

[45522, 'Stayed here for 4 nights and really enjoyed it - staff were friendly and the rooms were lovely...had a real charm old school feeling. Don't be put off by the negative reviews here....we really did not have anything to complain about, it was great', [('staff_serv', 1)], 'pos']

[28126, 'Granted, the hotel has history, but trying to get a good nights sleep is a whole different story. The windows are single pane - I think they built a building next to us during the night. It was soo noisy you could hear honking and noises the entire evening. The room was tiny even for New York standards. The lampshade was actually torn and stained and looked like it belonged in a shady hotel(looked worse than a salvation army lampshade). This was evidence of how clean the overall room was with black hairs in the bathtub...yuk. The beds were small hard and uncomfortable. We changed hotels for the remainder of nights. Extremely disappointed, especially after the good reviews here.', [('room', 4)], 'neg']

This completes the final task of putting it all together as seen in Figure 10.16.

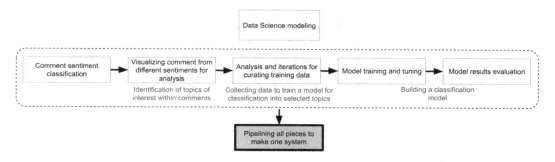

FIGURE 10.16 Data science tasks breakdown for customer review analysis project (pipeline).

Why not just look for the initial list of curated keywords to identify topics in comments? Why create a model?

Using the curated keywords to identify topics will work, but can fail to identify these topics from comment segments not containing the keywords. Building a model will take an algorithmic approach to identify other words that occur in these contexts.

To test this, we manually went through 100 correctly classified comment segments and found that >20% of them did not contain any of our originally curated keywords. This means we are getting about 25% more correct classifications by using this model.

- A potential bias that can be caused by the way we perform data curation. We are considering phrases containing certain keywords. However, based on our tests, it looks like the majority of comments in the dataset work well with the model and the model has successfully classified sentences with words not a part of our curated keywords set. Thus, it works fine for our application. Other ways to curate this data without manually labeling samples would be using a clustering approach or using zero-shot ready-to-use transformers classification model.

- Secondly, we split comments into segments by using a specific splitting technique. In addition to splitting sentences, we also split each sentence based on a comma. It successfully separates 'the hotel was great, the staff was good' into 'the hotel was great' and 'the staff was good'. However, it will fail to accurately split the sentence 'the service and the location was great' into a service-related phrase and a separate location-related phrase. Different splitting techniques can have different results and can be worth experimenting with for further enhancement.

- Thirdly, if we expect differences in the data we want to use the model for compared to the training and testing data, we should run tests on a sample from the expected input.

Approach 2: LDA-based training data curation

LDA can be used either in addition or instead of using the method we did for curating training data. This goes back to the data curation task as seen in Figure 10.17. Below, we demonstrate this method.

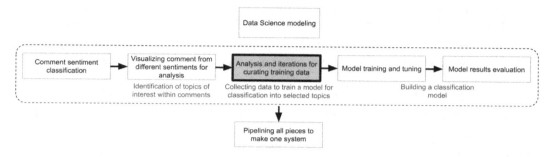

FIGURE 10.17 Data science tasks breakdown for customer review analysis project (curating training data).

We pass our data into LDA clustering and experiment using multiple runs with different number of clusters as follows. The complete code can be found in the notebook section6/comment-analysis-hotel-reviews.ipynb on GitHub.

```
from gensim import corpora, models
# Creating the object for LDA model using gensim library
lda = models.ldamodel.LdaModel

# Running and Training LDA model on
# the document term matrix for 2 topics.
lda_2 = lda(
    doc_term_matrix, num_topics=2,
    id2word=dictionary_pos, passes=10
)
# Results
for itm in lda_2.print_topics():
    print(itm, "\n")
```

The above results in the following 2 clusters.

(0, '0.053*"room" + 0.014*"staff" + 0.011*"bed" + 0.011*"u" + 0.009*"floor" + 0.009*"nice" + 0.008*"bathroom" + 0.008*"small" + 0.008*"clean" + 0.008*"service"')

(1, '0.054*"hotel" + 0.017*"time" + 0.016*"stay" + 0.016*"would" + 0.016*"great" + 0.015*"night" + 0.012*"new" + 0.012*"stayed" + 0.011*"location" + 0.009*"york"')

Here, cluster 0 appears to be related to the topics *room* and *service & staff*. Cluster 1 has aspects related to the topic *location*.

```
lda_3 = lda(
    doc_term_matrix, num_topics=3,
    id2word=dictionary_pos, passes=10
)
# Results
for itm in lda_3.print_topics():
    print(itm, "\n")
```

The above results in the following 3 clusters.

(0, '0.058*"hotel" + 0.023*"time" + 0.021*"stay" + 0.021*"would" + 0.021*"great" + 0.015*"stayed" + 0.015*"night" + 0.015*"location" + 0.010*"place" + 0.009*"good"')

(1, '0.085*"room" + 0.018*"bed" + 0.018*"new" + 0.015*"hotel" + 0.015*"floor" + 0.014*"york" + 0.014*"bathroom" + 0.014*"small" + 0.012*"clean" + 0.010*"like"')

(2, '0.023*"staff" + 0.019*"u" + 0.013*"breakfast" + 0.013*"service" + 0.011*"day" + 0.010*"desk" + 0.010*"friendly" + 0.009*"helpful" + 0.009*"front" + 0.008*"get"')

Here, cluster 2 looks strongly related to the topic *service & staff* and cluster 1 looks strongly related to the topic *room*. Cluster 0 has a few aspects that relate to *location*.

```
lda_4 = lda(
  doc_term_matrix, num_topics=4,
  id2word=dictionary_pos, passes=10
)
# Results
for itm in lda_4.print_topics():
  print(itm, "\n")
```

The above results in the following 4 clusters.

(0, '0.029*"staff" + 0.024*"u" + 0.022*"hotel" + 0.013*"service" + 0.013*"desk" + 0.012*"friendly" + 0.012*"helpful" + 0.011*"front" + 0.010*"could" + 0.009*"get"')

(1, '0.061*"hotel" + 0.031*"stay" + 0.028*"night" + 0.025*"would" + 0.023*"new" + 0.022*"stayed" + 0.017*"york" + 0.015*"nyc" + 0.014*"time" + 0.011*"city"')

(2, '0.108*"room" + 0.023*"bed" + 0.019*"floor" + 0.018*"nice" + 0.017*"bathroom" + 0.017*"small" + 0.016*"clean" + 0.012*"view" + 0.010*"comfortable" + 0.008*"shower"')

(3, '0.023*"hotel" + 0.022*"location" + 0.020*"time" + 0.018*"great" + 0.017*"breakfast" + 0.013*"square" + 0.012*"walk" + 0.012*"restaurant" + 0.011*"block" + 0.010*"around"')

Here, cluster 2 looks strongly related to the topic *room* and cluster 0 looks strongly related to the topic *service & staff*. Cluster 3 has aspects that relate to *location*.

```
lda_5 = lda(
  doc_term_matrix, num_topics=5,
  id2word=dictionary_pos, passes=10
)
# Results
for itm in lda_5.print_topics():
  print(itm, "\n")
```

The above results in the following 5 clusters.

(0, '0.032*"location" + 0.032*"great" + 0.025*"hotel" + 0.025*"time" + 0.019*"square" + 0.018*"walk" + 0.017*"street" + 0.016*"block" + 0.014*"subway" + 0.012*"central"')

(1, '0.047*"room" + 0.029*"hotel" + 0.023*"clean" + 0.023*"bed" + 0.020*"like"

+ 0.018*"bathroom" + 0.018*"well" + 0.015*"comfortable" + 0.015*"small" + 0.012*"review"')

(2, '0.059*"room" + 0.022*"good" + 0.019*"breakfast" + 0.016*"hotel" + 0.012*"price" + 0.011*"service" + 0.011*"great" + 0.010*"bed" + 0.009*"small" + 0.009*"one"')

(3, '0.048*"hotel" + 0.040*"stay" + 0.039*"would" + 0.036*"staff" + 0.029*"new" + 0.022*"york" + 0.015*"desk" + 0.015*"friendly" + 0.014*"helpful" + 0.013*"front"')

(4, '0.029*"night" + 0.029*"room" + 0.024*"u" + 0.023*"stayed" + 0.019*"day" + 0.017*"hotel" + 0.013*"one" + 0.013*"floor" + 0.010*"time" + 0.008*"get"')

Here, cluster 0 looks strongly related to the topic *location* and cluster 1 looks strongly related to the topic *room*. Clusters 2 and 4 also have aspects that relate to *room*. Cluster 3 has some hints of *service & staff*.

We see some of the resultant clusters look very relevant to our topics. Since cluster 0 of the lda_5 model is strongly related to *location*, we further explore the goodness of the data in the cluster.

We randomly sample 100 documents that belong to cluster number 0 for lda_5 and manually label them. We find that 72% of the documents are relevant to the class *location*. To further clean the document list, we can take the documents irrelevant to the topic *location*, find similar documents using text similarity (as discussed in Chapter 8), and remove them. The resultant accuracy will likely be higher and give you ready-to-use training data for the class *location*. A similar approach can be followed for the other two classes as well.

## CHAPTER 11

Recommendations and Predictions

11.1 CONTENT RECOMMENDATION SYSTEM

A recommendation system is a system that outputs recommended content most pertinent to a particular user. Recommendation systems are seen in a variety of places today. Ever noticed the 'more to consider' sections on e-commerce websites such as Amazon? How about the same behavior while browsing social media?

11.1.1 Approaches

Recommendation systems usually rely on a few different approaches.

1. Collaborative filtering

   Collaborative filtering is the process of getting recommendations for a user based on the interests of other users that have watched the same content.

2. Content-based filtering

   Content-based filtering gets recommendations for a user based on the user's preferences using content-based features. The recommendations are typically items similar to ones the user has expressed interest in previously.

3. Knowledge-based systems

   Another realm of recommendation systems includes knowledge-based systems, where contextual knowledge is applied as input by the user. Knowledge-based recommender systems are well suited to complex domains where items are not purchased very often. Examples include apartments, cars, financial services, digital cameras, and tourist destinations.

11.1.2 Building a social media post recommendation system

Figure 11.1 represents an example of why such recommendation systems are of interest to a company.

DOI: 10.1201/9781003264774-11

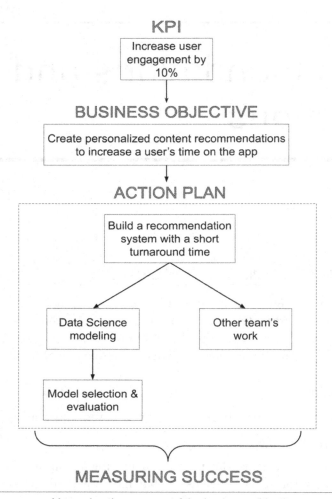

FIGURE 11.1 Building a recommendation system from a company KPI perspective.

Action plan

The goal is to build a recommendation system for videos. There is no user watch history available. The only known input is the title and description of the video that the user is currently watching. The goal is to recommend 8 videos similar to the one being watched. This is a part of a new product (with a user interface and platform) that is not fully built out yet. The goal is to work on building the model in parallel so the recommendation system can be launched with the product. You need to think of the best way to create the recommendation model prototype without having any data. The only known data detail is that it is in a video format with an attached text description.

The product team has evaluated use cases and would like to test them as follows for a proof of concept.

From a corpus of videos related to 'Python',
- get video recommendations for 'Python' the snake.
- get video recommendations for 'Python' the programming language.

Another requirement is to evaluate a few different options to accomplish the goal and choose the one with the best results for the homonym 'Python' example.

Dataset

Since the business is video-centric, we'll curate sample video data to build this prototype. We'll get data from YouTube using the YouTube API's 'search' endpoint. The keyword used to query this data is *python*.

To get the dataset, we'll use YouTube API as discussed in Section II. We'll use code from Chapter 2 (Section 2.2.7). The full code for this exercise can be found in the notebook section6/content-based-rec-sys.ipynb. We'll store YouTube video text in the yt_text variable which is a list of tuples containing video ID as the first element and video title + description as the second element. A total of 522 videos were grabbed using the API for the query search keyword = 'python'.

Concepts

Python is a homonym where on one hand it can refer to the snake, and on the other hand, it could refer to the popular programming language.

We may be serving video recommendations, but the underlying data is the text associated with the video title and description. We will build a recommendation model to get video recommendations based on an input video text. This will be the core component of a system that is able to recommend videos based on the video the user is looking at.

We will use some of the discussed approaches from the text similarity section of Chapter 8 (Section 8.2). We'll compare the results from a few different models to understand which model works well for the described application and data.

11.1.2.1 *Evaluating a classic TF-IDF method, spaCy model, and BERT model*

Solution

Approach 1: TF-IDF - cosine similarity

TF-IDF or Term Frequency - Inverse Document Frequency is a common and popular algorithm for transforming text into a numerical representation. It is a numerical statistic that intends to reflect how important a word is to a document in a corpus. The sklearn library offers a prebuilt TF-IDF vectorizer. Cosine similarity will be used to determine the similarity between the two documents.

We can preprocess the text before computing TF-IDF to get rid of noise elements within the text depending on how our dataset looks like. We can combine text from the title and description of the YouTube content into a single string variable and clean the data based on the observed noise. Removing URLs, stop words, and non-alphanumeric characters can be useful for social media data. However, here we'll proceed without cleaning the data but can always revisit it based on the results. Here's what a cleaning method to remove noise and unwanted elements from YouTube data could look like.

```python
import re
from nltk.corpus import stopwords

def clean_text(text):
    alpha_num = re.compile("[^a-zA-Z0-9]", re.X)
    link_pattern = re.compile(
        r"https?://\S+|www\.\S+", re.X
    )
    emoji_pattern = re.compile(
        "[\U00010000-\U0010ffff]", flags=re.UNICODE
    )
    cleaned_text = alpha_num.sub(" ", text.lower())
    cleaned_text = link_pattern.sub(" ", cleaned_text)
    cleaned_text = emoji_pattern.sub(" ", cleaned_text)
    cleaned_text = " ".join([
        word for word in cleaned_text.split()
        if word not in stopwords.words("english")
    ])

    return cleaned_text
```

We use `sklearn`'s built-in functionalities to get the cosine similarity metric.

```python
from sklearn.feature_extraction.text import TfidfVectorizer
from sklearn.metrics.pairwise import cosine_similarity

vect = TfidfVectorizer()
# get tfidf of all samples in the corpus
# yt_text is a list of video text - training data
tfidf = vect.fit_transform(yt_text)

# get tfidf vector for sample document
# sample_doc = our test sample
selected_itm = vect.transform([sample_doc])

# similarity between sample doc & the rest of the corpus
cosine_sim = [
    cosine_similarity(selected_itm, itm)[0][0]
    for itm in tfidf
]

# index of top 8 matches
indx_top8 = sorted(
    range(len(cosine_sim)),
    key=lambda i: cosine_sim[i],
    reverse=True
)[:8]
```

The top 8 recommendations can be seen in Figure 11.2.

Python Machine Learning Tutorial (Data Science). Python Machine Learning Tutorial - Learn how to predict the kind of music people like. Subscribe for more Python tutorials like ...

Ball python bite I decided to grab a snake out of its tank without asking, this was totally my fault. But now I can say I've been bit by a snake.

 Machine Learning With Python Full Course 2022 | Machine Learning Tutorial for Beginners| ...

 Pastave Ball Python. Pastave Ball Python ✓ ♥ #Snake #Reptile #Python...

 Scikit-Learn Course - Machine Learning in Python Tutorial. Scikit-learn is a free software machine learning library for the Python programming...

 rock python Anaconda snake.

 AI vs Machine Learning vs Deep Learning | Machine Learning Training with Python | ...

 Ball Pythons for Sale! Selling Some of my Holdbacks!. In this video I'll show you the rest of my 2021 ball pythons...

 Project 1: End To End Python ML Project (Complete)| Machine Learning Tutorials Using Python In Hindi...

 So tragic... Python Was Pierced By Impala's Sharp Horn And The Profiteer Was A Hyena...

 Practical Machine Learning Tutorial with Python Intro p.1. The objective of this course is to give you a holistic understanding of machine...

 Heading Back To Python Island Hunting Pythons With Moose. Heading Back To Python Island Hunting Pythons With Moose...

 Python Tutorial - Python Full Course for Beginners. Python tutorial - Python full course for beginners...

 Residents of Baringo shocked as python appears after the burial of a snake charmer. Residents of ..

 Machine Learning Tutorial Python - 13: K Means Clustering Algorithm. K Means clustering algorithm...

 Hyena Steal Python's Prey! Python Bite Hyena Mouth Off Because Of Its Brazenness - Python Vs Hyena...

 Machine Learning Tutorial Python - 8: Logistic Regression (Binary Classification). Logistic regression is used for classification problems...

 Python Was Pierced By Impala's Sharp Horns And The Profiteer Was Hyenas. Python Was Pierced ...

FIGURE 11.2 TF-IDF method: top 8 content recommendations.

Approach 2: Word embeddings using `spaCy`

spaCy offers many built-in pre-trained models which form a convenient way to get word embeddings quickly. We discussed further details in Chapter 3 (Section 3.4.4).

Let's load the `en_core_web_lg` model and get vectors for our data, followed by using cosine similarity to get similarity between the vectors.

```
! pip install spacy
! python -m spacy download en_core_web_lg

nlp = spacy.load("en_core_web_lg")

docs_spacy = [nlp("u'"+itm+"'") for itm in yt_text]
# add if itm in nlp.vocab to avoid out of vocab errors.

selected_itm = nlp("u'"+sample_doc+"'")

# Similarity between sample doc & the rest of the corpus
spacy_sim = [
    selected_itm.similarity(itm) for itm in docs_spacy
]

# index of top 8 matches
indx_top8 = sorted(
```

```
    range(len(spacy_sim)),
    key=lambda i: spacy_sim[i],
    reverse=True
)[:8]
```

Potential issues with a word embedding model as such are that processing a sentence with terms that are not in the pre-trained models can throw errors. To ensure a word is present and does not break your code, a check for presence can be added as seen above in the code comment.

The top 8 recommendations can be seen in Figure 11.3.

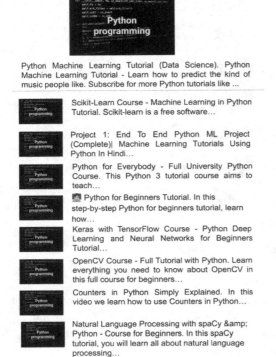

Python Machine Learning Tutorial (Data Science). Python Machine Learning Tutorial - Learn how to predict the kind of music people like. Subscribe for more Python tutorials like ...

Scikit-Learn Course - Machine Learning in Python Tutorial. Scikit-learn is a free software...

Project 1: End To End Python ML Project (Complete)| Machine Learning Tutorials Using Python In Hindi...

Python for Everybody - Full University Python Course. This Python 3 tutorial course aims to teach...

🐍 Python for Beginners Tutorial. In this step-by-step Python for beginners tutorial, learn how...

Keras with TensorFlow Course - Python Deep Learning and Neural Networks for Beginners Tutorial...

OpenCV Course - Full Tutorial with Python. Learn everything you need to know about OpenCV in this full course for beginners...

Counters in Python Simply Explained. In this video we learn how to use Counters in Python...

Natural Language Processing with spaCy & Python - Course for Beginners. In this spaCy tutorial, you will learn all about natural language processing...

Ball python bite I decided to grab a snake out of its tank without asking, this was totally my fault. But now I can say I've been bit by a snake.

Showing a Craigslist scammer who's boss using Python. Some silly Craigslist scammer...

How I would learn to code (if I could start over). In this video, I give you my step by step process on how I would learn to code...

BIT BY A 20 FOOT PYTHON 🐍. Well this big pied girl has never really liked...

Monty Python Royal Society For Putting Things On Top of Other Things. When I put this clip...

Mastering Python - Everything You Need To Know To Become a Python Master...

What is the BEST Ball Python Enclosure?. Let's face it- our old "How to Care for Ball Pythons"...

Being attacked by a python - Try to protect the ducklings| Off-Grid Living...

Ball Pythons for Sale! Selling Some of my Holdbacks!. In this video I'll show you the rest of my 2021 ball pythons...

FIGURE 11.3 spaCy word embeddings method: top 8 content recommendations.

Approach 3: Transformer-based model

Testing the state-of-the-art transformers for our application, we'll use Bidirectional Encoder Representations from Transformers (BERT) which is a transformer-based machine learning technique for NLP pre-training developed by Google. A simple way to leverage BERT is via the sentence-transformers library. This library uses Hugging Face's `transformers` behind the scenes.

We'll be using the `bert-base-nli-mean-tokens` model. The resultant will be vector representations of our input text. We can then use cosine similarity to get similar content. Here's the code implementation.

```
! pip install sentence-transformers

from sentence_transformers import (
```

```
  SentenceTransformer, util
)

bert_model = SentenceTransformer(
  "bert-base-nli-mean-tokens"
)

document_embeddings = bert_model.encode(yt_text)

selected_itm = bert_model.encode(sample_doc)

# Similarity between sample doc & the rest of the corpus
bert_sim = [
  util.pytorch_cos_sim(selected_itm, itm).item()
  for itm in document_embeddings
]

# index of top 8 matches
indx_top8 = sorted(
  range(len(bert_sim)),
  key=lambda i: bert_sim[i],
  reverse=True
)[:8]
```

The top 8 recommendations can be seen in Figure 11.4.

Python Machine Learning Tutorial (Data Science). Python Machine Learning Tutorial - Learn how to predict the kind of music people like. Subscribe for more Python tutorials like ...

 Python: Create your own Music Player! (Part 1) - Set-up, Stop, Play, Songname...

 Machine Learning Tutorial Python - 8: Logistic Regression (Binary Classification). Logistic regression ...

 Keras with TensorFlow Course - Python Deep Learning and Neural Networks for Beginners Tutorial...

 Calorie Tracker in Python - Data Visualization Project. In this video we learn how to visualize...

 NumPy and Pandas Tutorial | Data Analysis With Python | Python Tutorial for Beginners |...

 Python Requests Tutorial: Request Web Pages, Download Images, POST Data, Read JSON,...

 Python Tutorial for Absolute Beginners #1 - What Are Variables?. Learn Python programming...

 Project 1: Iron Man Jarvis AI Desktop Voice Assistant | Python Tutorials For Absolute Beginners #120. This python AI project...

Ball python bite I decided to grab a snake out of its tank without asking, this was totally my fault. But now I can say I've been bit by a snake.

 Hyena Steal Python's Prey! Python Bite Hyena Mouth Off Because Of Its Brazenness - Python Vs Hyena...

 Residents of Baringo shocked as python appears after the burial of a snake charmer. Residents of Kampi Samaki...

 All Better — Sick Python Needs A Special Bubble Bath | Dodo Kids. This lost snake...

 Hunting Massive Pythons in the Glades | Swamp People: Serpent Invasion (S1, E1)...

 Snake eats chicken| python eats chicken| THE NITS. snakevsanimal rescued this python from a residential area and released...

 15 Amazing And Scary Python Battles Caught On Camera. Pythons are constrictors...

 LARVA - PYTHON | Cartoon Movie | Cartoons | Comics | Larva Cartoon | LARVA Official. Scary snake appears in the drain! ...

 African Rock Python tries to Enter Home--Eats Rabbit Instead (Time Lapse X5). Large hungry snake escaped. Distracted by eating a rabbit...

FIGURE 11.4 BERT method: top 8 content recommendations.

11.1.3   Conclusion and closing thoughts

In our results from the three models, we saw that the TF-IDF based method was fairly comparable to the BERT method, and the spaCy method had a few irrelevant items in the result set of ball python.

A more state-of-the-art solution would be the transformer model, however it would require more resources and compute power to run it at scale compared to the other approaches. In our case, TF-IDF works just as well and is a smaller and simpler model, thus it is a reasonable choice.

TIP

A common approach is to deploy a simple model and collect feedback on how many irrelevant items the user came across while browsing through the application. This data can be used further to iterate your model. For instance, user clicks on the recommended videos, or a vote button when added next to the recommended videos to thumbs up or down a recommendation can be used to further test this recommendation model, evaluate between different models, fine-tuning models, and/or data cleaning impact.

11.2   NEXT-WORD PREDICTION

Next-word prediction refers to the task of predicting what a user's next word might be while typing. Next word prediction can increase writing fluency, reduce the number of needed keystrokes, and provide auditory support to confirm word selection. Applications are found in many industry verticals. You may have noticed such applications on your email and mobile phone. Additionally, some companies employ such models to save their employees on documentation time.

Next-word prediction model can be built on any dataset available. Hence, if your use case is domain-specific, just pass in data belonging to the domain.

11.2.1   Building a next-word prediction for the data science topic

Figure 11.5 represents an example of why such analysis is of interest to a company.

Action plan

The goal for this application is to build a model that predicts next words based on the current words that the user has written. This tool will be used by a data science team to write documentations.

Concepts

In this demonstration, we'll build a next word prediction model for a corpus constructed from Wikipedia pages on the topic data science. In a practical scenario,

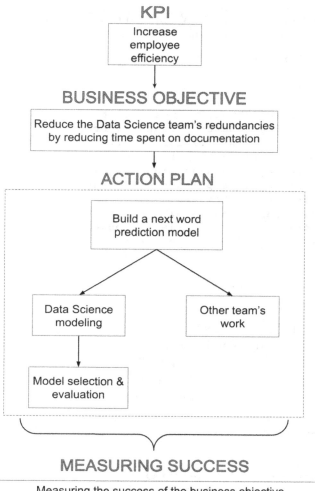

FIGURE 11.5 Building next word prediction models from a company KPI perspective.

using existing documentation as the training data will be beneficial. Here, we are assuming such a dataset does not already exist. Hence, we leverage public data sources to build this model.

We discussed the BiLSTM (Bidirectional Long Short-Term Memory) model in Chapter 4 (Section 4.2.2.4). BiLSTMs work very well on sequential data and are a good choice for a task like this. We will use BiLSTM to construct a model that predicts the next n words based on an input word.

Dataset

To curate our corpus, we use the Wikipedia crawler wrapper for Python[1] and get data for a few pages associated with data science.

```
! pip install wikipedia

import wikipedia

data = wikipedia.page("Data Science").content
data += wikipedia.page("Natural Language Processing").content
data += wikipedia.page("Artificial Intelligence").content
data += wikipedia.page("Machine Learning (ML)").content
data += wikipedia.page("Machine Translation").content
data += wikipedia.page("Deep Learning").content
data += wikipedia.page("Chatterbot").content
data += wikipedia.page("Data Analysis").content
data += wikipedia.page("Time Series").content
data += wikipedia.page("Supervised Learning").content
```

11.2.1.1   *Training a BiLSTM model*

Solution

We'll train a BiLSTM model which is a popular choice for applications where the sequence/ordering of words is important.

Now that we have curated the Wikipedia data, let's clean the data and pass it through `Keras Tokenizer`. We will remove any lines less than five characters long without considering trailing or leading spaces.

```
from nltk import tokenize
from tensorflow.keras.preprocessing.text import Tokenizer

# Remove small sentences
lines = tokenize.sent_tokenize(data)
lines = [i for i in lines if len(i.strip())>5]

# for words not found in index
tokenizer = Tokenizer(oov_token="<oov>")
tokenizer.fit_on_texts(lines)
total_words = len(tokenizer.word_index) + 1
```

Next, let's prepare input sequences to pass into the model. From each line in the corpus, we will generate n-gram tokens to create sequences of words. For instance, 'natural language processing generates responses' to 'natural language', 'natural language processing', 'natural language processing generates', and 'natural language processing generates responses'. We don't envision the model needing to predict anything more than the next 5-6 words. So while curating sequences for training, we will limit the length of the sequence to be less than 10 to keep some buffer in case the expectation evolves.

```
import numpy as np
from tensorflow.keras.utils import to_categorical
```

---

[1]https://pypi.org/project/wikipedia/

```
from tensorflow.keras.preprocessing.sequence import pad_sequences

max_seq_len = 10
input_sequences = []

for line in lines:
  tokens = tokenizer.texts_to_sequences([line])[0]
  for i in range(1, min(max_seq_len, len(tokens))):
    ngram_seq = tokens[: i+1]
    input_sequences.append(ngram_seq)
print(f"{len(input_sequences)=}")
# >> len(input_sequences)=17729

input_sequences = np.array(
  pad_sequences(
    input_sequences, maxlen=max_seq_len, padding="pre"
  )
)

xs = input_sequences[:,:-1]
labels = input_sequences[:,-1]
ys = to_categorical(
  labels, num_classes=total_words
)
```

We see the number of sequences for training the model is 17729. Next, we set up the model and begin training.

```
from tensorflow.keras.layers import (
  Embedding, LSTM, Dense, Bidirectional
)
from tensorflow.keras.models import Sequential
from tensorflow.keras.optimizers import Adam

model = Sequential()
model.add(
  Embedding(
    total_words, 100, input_length=max_len-1
  )
)
model.add(Bidirectional(LSTM(64)))
model.add(Dense(total_words, activation="softmax"))
adam = Adam(learning_rate=0.01)
model.compile(
  loss="categorical_crossentropy",
  optimizer=adam, metrics=["accuracy"]
)
history = model.fit(xs, ys, epochs=10, verbose=1)
```

To plot model accuracy and loss, we use the following code.

```
import matplotlib.pyplot as plt

plt.plot(history.history["accuracy"])
plt.xlabel("Epochs")
plt.ylabel("accuracy")
plt.show()
```

```
plt.plot(history.history["loss"])
plt.xlabel("Epochs")
plt.ylabel("loss")
plt.show()
```

As we discussed in Chapter 4 (Section 3.2.2), an epoch in machine learning means one complete pass of the training dataset through the algorithm. The accuracy should ideally increase with epochs, and the loss should decrease with epochs. The loss value implies how poorly a model behaves after each epoch on a single sample.

We first train the model with 10 epochs. We notice the accuracy increase (and loss decrease) did not settle down in 10 epochs as seen in Figure 11.6.

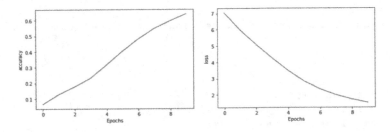

FIGURE 11.6 Next word prediction BiLSTM model accuracy and loss at 10 epochs.

We increase the epochs a few times and re-train to find a good number for this model.

```
history = model.fit(xs, ys, epochs=20, verbose=1)
```

```
history = model.fit(xs, ys, epochs=40, verbose=1)
```

We plot accuracy and loss again for each re-train, and the results can be seen in Figure 11.7. We can see that increasing the epochs further is unlikely to make our model accuracy higher / loss lower. We can use KerasTuner as demonstrated in Chapter 4 for tuning the number of epochs. Here, we end up with a model accuracy of 79%.

The full code can be found in section6/next-word-pred-bilstm.ipynb.

The other parameters of the model can be altered as well to notice changes in the model training metrics.

To generate next-word predictions, we write a function as below and call it with test samples as input.

```
def predict_nw(text, next_words=2):
    """
    For the input `text`, predict the next n words,
    where n=`next_words`
    """
    words = [text]
    for _ in range(next_words):
        full_text = " ".join(words)
        token_list = tokenizer.texts_to_sequences(
            [full_text]
```

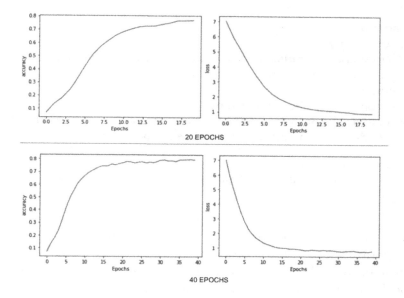

20 EPOCHS

40 EPOCHS

FIGURE 11.7 Next word prediction BiLSTM model accuracy and loss at 20 and 40 epochs.

```
) [0]
token_list = pad_sequences(
  [token_list], maxlen=max_len-1, padding="pre"
)
predicted = np.argmax(model.predict(
  token_list, verbose=0
), axis=-1)
next_word = ""
for word, inx in tokenizer.word_index.items():
  if inx == predicted:
    next_word = word
    break
words.append(next_word)

return " ".join(
  [words[0]] + [
    "".join(["\033[1m", w, "\033[0m"])
    for w in words[1:]
  ]
)

print(predict_nw("neural", next_words=1))
print(predict_nw("machine", next_words=1))
print(predict_nw("language", next_words=9))
print(predict_nw("natural", next_words=2))
print(predict_nw("deep", next_words=1))
print(predict_nw("language model is", next_words=2))
print(predict_nw("nlp", next_words=7))
print(predict_nw("processing data to", next_words=4))
```

```
neural networks
machine learning
language models learned from data to context results in contain
natural language processing
deep learning
language model is the continuous
nlp powered document ai enables non linear classification
processing data to rank when analysts perform
```

FIGURE 11.8 Next word prediction output from the BiLSTM model with the predicted words in bold.

The outcome of the above can be seen in Figure 11.8.

Other algorithms can also be used to train a next-word prediction model. Using LSTM instead of BiLSTM can result in a model that trains faster but can cause some loss in model accuracy. Fill-mask transformers can be explored for this problem as well (see notebook section3/transformers.ipynb for an example of fill-mask).

Furthermore, we are using one word as input to get a prediction for the next words. Further iterations of this model can include considering more than just one input word for the prediction of the next words.

> *TIP*
>
> In an industrial setting, adding new and recent training data and updating the model helps in keeping the model's output up-to-date with current needs. As documents are created by the team, add them to the training dataset to update the model with more relevant and current data.

The way to measure the impact of this model on the writing efficiencies of data scientists includes calculating the average time taken per page before and after the model is deployed. Such models can also reduce typing errors in writing, which can also be measured before and after the model is used.

More Real-World Scenarios and Tips

Throughout this book, we have shared tips and the consideration factors that influence the path of implementing NLP applications. Here we go over some common scenarios, key takeaways, final thoughts, and tips for building successful NLP solutions in the real world.

Let's divide the text modeling problem into three phases as seen in Figure 12.1 and discuss common scenarios for each phase.

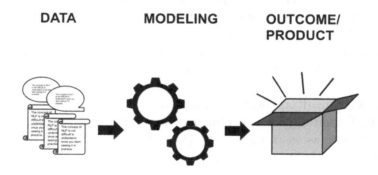

FIGURE 12.1 Phases of creating NLP projects.

12.1   DATA SCENARIOS

We will discuss some commonly observed scenarios related to data. See Figure 12.2.

DOI: 10.1201/9781003264774-12

Starting with unlabeled data is common

We have seen examples of starting with unlabeled datasets and how to approach them by labeling data manually, using topic modeling, or other pragmatic ways in the previous chapters.

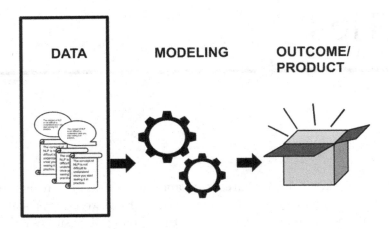

FIGURE 12.2 Phases of creating NLP projects - data.

Getting started without the data

Often, there is a vision of a data-driven product involving NLP applications but no labeled or unlabeled data to support it. The default answer should not be 'this can't be done!'. Creative thinking can help kick off a project without any data. Look for public datasets or other similar datasets that can work. If those don't exist, think of ways to manually curate data. Data augmentation techniques from Chapter 3 (Section 3.3) can further help increase data size.

Starting with limited data is common

Starting with limited data is common as well, for which using practical ways to self-create new data (as we discussed in the chatbots section) or using data augmentation techniques can help.

Noisy data is common

Another common scenario is having noisy data. Depending on the noise, data-cleaning techniques should be applied to the data. If the sentences are extra long, truncating to retain partial information for a more efficient training time is one solution.

Data preprocessing is an iterative process

Typically, passing your data through preprocessing steps is not a one-time job. It is an iterative process. You may lowercase and remove stop words first, but then notice that your data contains many URLs. You'll go back to your cleaning function to remove URLs as a step. This process is experimental and continues until you have the desired state of your data. Visualizing your data can help understand its contents.

12.2   MODELING SCENARIOS

The scenarios discussed here represent the *Modeling* phase of building an NLP project as seen in Figure 12.3.

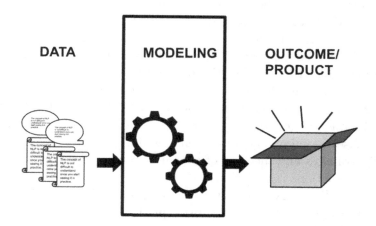

FIGURE 12.3   Phases of creating NLP projects - modeling.

Model creation is an iterative process

Creating your model is typically never about running the training code one time. Selecting the hyperparameter values or tuning methods you use is an experimental process. For instance, we built a model using different epochs for next-word prediction based on initial results and visited tools to perform hyperparameter tuning in Chapter 4.

Understanding model results on real-world data can be a manual process

It is vital to test your model on the right data. The ideal data to use for testing is random samples of the real data the model will be used on. If this is a different source than your training data, spend some time curating test samples. It is common to have to manually look at data and label data. It is also common to look at results from individual test samples to understand the model.

Retiring old categories and adding new ones

When you create a category classification model, there can be times when certain categories are no longer valid or new categories get more relevant with time. For example, COVID-19-related content on social media emerged only after December 2019. In such cases, there should be a mechanism to retire old categories and add new ones into your model. Monitoring how the data changes over time is important. If you notice less and less content being classified into a category compared to before, it may make sense to consider it for retirement. This process can be manual.

When does your model need re-training?

Re-training your model with fresh data helps keep it up-to-date as your data changes. The frequency of re-training a model is experimental and often dependent on the application that uses your model. Setting up logs to continuously monitor the performance of the model on new data can help gauge when your model results start drifting. Concept drift (also called model drift) occurs when the underlying concept being learned by the model changes over time, leading to a decline in performance. For example, if your model categorizes social media content into the health category but was trained before the onset of the pandemic, the model may miss accurately detecting the changed health landscape. The underlying assumptions of what the health category includes have changed. Another type of drift is data drift, where the distribution of data changes with time. For example, if a model is trained to predict customer purchases based on age and income, and if there are significant changes in the distribution of ages and incomes of the customers over time, then the accuracy of the model's predictions may decrease.

For models needing very frequent re-training, online learning might be a good alternative. An example includes stock price prediction, where the algorithm needs to dynamically adapt to new trends. Online learning updates the model as new data arrives without having to re-train the model on the entire dataset. It is also explored when re-training repeatedly on the entire dataset becomes computationally expensive. Rotational Labs, a US-based startup specializing in event-driven globally distributed systems, develops tools and open-source libraries to help data scientists with online learning. Another example is Vowpal Wabbit, which is a machine learning system for online learning.

Too many classes

Let's consider an example. You have a corpus containing descriptions of movies. You want to classify the text into 100s of movie genres, such as *murder mystery, legal thriller, physiological thriller, theft mystery, romantic comedy, mockumentary, silent comedy*, etc.

Often, building one classifier with 100s of classes is a complex solution with accuracy losses into a large number of other classes. The results might suffer even more if the size of the dataset is not large enough. In such cases, a practical approach is to first create a classifier with high-level ategories, such as *thriller* or *comedy*, and then create separate classification models for subcategories under each. For example, only the data classified as *thriller* from the first model will pass through the thriller classifier for getting a subclassification into *murder mystery, legal thriller, psychological thriller*, and *theft mystery* categories.

This will result in multiple models. Since the number of classes is controlled in each model, maintaining and tuning the per-class behavior becomes easier. This is also called hierarchical modeling, i.e., creating a multiclass/binary classification model first, followed by another multiclass or binary classification model under one or more of the classes. Another approach for such problems is resorting to a keywords-based model that classifies based on the keywords present in the text. These can be hand-curated or collected using clustering models. Labeling a few samples followed by using text similarity can also help kick-start the process.

Class imbalance

Class imbalance is a common problem. Solutions include getting more labeled data, using data augmentation to increase the size of the smaller class, or reducing the size of the larger class by getting rid of some samples. Libraries like `imblearn`[1] provide tools when dealing with classification with imbalanced classes.

What if you have 8 classes, of which 5 are well represented, but 3 don't have as much data? If no other technique applies, you can combine the 3 classes into one before creating the model, and then create a sub-classifier if needed.

Not every problem needs an ML model

The default thinking of a data scientist is often around ways ML can help a problem. While that is not wrong thinking, some solution options may exist that are simple, explainable, computationally cheap, and serve the purpose. For instance, your clients want you to find all social media free-form text documents available in your corpus related to a specific movie. The movie they ask for is different each time. In this case, the categories you need to find are not fixed. It would not be practical to build ML models each time. Let's say you want to find all documents associated with the Ghostbusters movie. Searching with a select set of keywords such as 'ghostbusters', 'ecto-1' (the name of the vehicle in the movie), etc. can be a great first solution. Would it include all Ghostbusters documents? Likely not, but it would include a lot of them and that can be desirable versus spending weeks or months in the development of a different solution. Opting for ML should either make an existing process better or create a new process that could not be easily solved without ML.

Don't build a solution if it already exists

It is advisable to look at existing services and open-source tools before building something from scratch. Often, available tools can help with all or a part of the problem.

100% accuracy is not the goal

In an academic setting, it is a common goal to build models with the best accuracy

---

[1]`https://imbalanced-learn.org/stable/`

and/or precision. These advancements help research efforts in finding the better and the best solutions. On the contrary, working in an enterprise, the goal is not to have a model that is best in accuracy. Factors like model complexity, compute resource cost/availability, and model explainability are also important. It would be reasonable to choose a Logistic Regression over a Random Forest classifier with a 2% accuracy loss because of the simplicity of Logistic Regression.

> *TIP*
>
> Understanding how your model results will be used can have a great impact on how you tune, test, and select your models. Let's say you have built two sentiment classification models. One of the models results in an 82% accuracy for positive sentiment and a 71% accuracy for negative sentiment. The other results in 70% accuracy for positive sentiment and 80% accuracy for negative sentiment. Which one would you select? It may seem obvious to select the first model that has an overall better accuracy. However, if one of the primary use cases of this model's result is to curate negative sentiment samples for further analysis, then your answer may change to picking the second model.
> This perspective also helps in strategizing and prioritizing data science tasks in a project/company.

What to do when your models are taking a long time to train?

- Reduce the number of parameters of your training job.

- Opt for simpler models.

- Use multi-processing where applicable.

    - using `multiprocessing` Python library[2]
    - using `spark`[3]

- Give your machine more compute resources - Memory, CPUs, and GPUs if needed.

---

[2]https://docs.python.org/3/library/multiprocessing.html
[3]https://spark.apache.org/docs/latest/api/python/

Writing better code

For ease of walking through, most of our code is not structured in an object-oriented style. In an enterprise setting,
writing production-quality code as a data scientist is an uncommon quality, but it can make you stand out, upskill you,
and open several other career avenues. Use Black[a] formatting
for more readable code, use informative variable names, put
blocks of code into functions where applicable, and create
classes and objects where applicable.

Using pipelines in NLP is popular because your data may
need to go through certain preparation stages. You may want
to test your model using cross-validation for all the stages and
not only model training. `sklearn's pipeline`[b] is a helpful
component. You can also save pipelines to pass your raw data
through all the needed stages.

---

[a]https://black.readthedocs.io/
[b]`https://scikit-learn.org/stable/modules/generated/`
`sklearn.pipeline.Pipeline.html`

12.3 DEPLOYING YOUR MODEL

Once you have built and tested your model in isolation, it usually needs to be come a
part of a broader application or product. Thus, it needs to be made available in a way
that other applications, users, developers, and/or systems can get predictions from
it. That's when you need to deploy your model. Deploying a model is the process
of putting a model into production, i.e., a live environment so it can be used for
its intended purpose. This is a phase in between *Modeling* and *Outcome/Product* in
Figure 12.1.

Your role may or may not involve deploying models, nonetheless, it is useful to
know about different deployment options and tools.

There are a few options for deploying machine learning models.

- Batch prediction

- On-demand prediction service

- Embedded models in edge and mobile devices

Service providers are popularly used for deploying models. One way is to store
your model in a storage option, such as AWS S3 or Google Cloud storage (storage
options are specific to service providers), and have other applications load the model
from the storage when required. You can also make your model available as a web
service.

Tools: TensorFlow Serving[4], MLFlow[5], Kubeflow[6], Cortex[7], Torchserve[8], and Amazon Sagemaker[9] are some examples of model deployment tools. You can also deploy models as a web application using Python frameworks like Streamlit[10], Flask[11], and Django[12]. TensorFlow Lite[13] is an open-source software library to run Tensor-Flow models in mobile and embedded platforms. Apache Airflow[14] and Prefect[15] are other tools that can be used to schedule predictions for batch processing.

The below example deploys a `scikit-learn` model created separately (not in Sagemaker) using Amazon Sagemaker (AWS's cloud machine-learning platform) as an on-demand prediction endpoint.

Once your model is created, you can persist it and re-load it later using `pickle` or `joblib`. Here's how you would do it using `joblib`.

```
# classifier
from sklearn import svm

clf = svm.SVC()
clf.fit(X, y)
```

```
! pip install joblib

import joblib

# SAVE using joblib
joblib.dump(clf, "model.pkl")

# LOAD using joblib
clf2 = joblib.load("model.pkl")
```

Let's say your model is called *comment_classifier_v12.joblib*. Save a compressed *.tar.gz* of your model in a S3 bucket. Let's say this bucket is *s3://recommendation-models/2022*, where you have a file named *comment_classifier_v12.joblib.tar.gz*. Using Sagemaker Notebooks (compute instance running the Jupyter Notebook App), you can create a *.py* file for inference as follows.

```
%%writefile inference_script.py
import joblib
import os

def model_fn(model_dir):
  clf = joblib.load(
    os.path.join(
      model_dir, "comment_classifier_v12.joblib"
```

---

[4]https://www.tensorflow.org/tfx/guide/serving
[5]https://mlflow.org/
[6]https://www.kubeflow.org/
[7]https://www.cortex.dev/
[8]https://pytorch.org/serve/
[9]https://docs.aws.amazon.com/sagemaker/latest/dg/how-it-works-deployment.html
[10]https://streamlit.io/
[11]https://flask.palletsprojects.com/en/2.2.x/
[12]https://www.django-rest-framework.org/
[13]https://www.tensorflow.org/lite
[14]https://airflow.apache.org/
[15]https://www.prefect.io/

```
  )
 )
 return clf
```

You can then deploy your model by choosing an appropriate instance type[16]. Instance types comprise different combinations of CPU, memory, storage, and networking capacity.

```
from sagemaker.sklearn.model import SKLearnModel
from sagemaker import get_execution_role

model = SKLearnModel(
  model_data='s3://recommendation-models/2022/comment_classifier_v12.
    joblib.tar.gz',
  role=get_execution_role(),
  entry_point='inference_script.py',
  framework_version='0.23-1'
)
model_ep = model.deploy(
  instance_type='ml.m5.large', #choose the right instance type
  initial_instance_count=1
)

print(model_ep.endpoint)
```

This endpoint name that prints can now be used by other applications to get predictions from this model. The *endpoints* section under Sagemaker will show all active endpoints. By default, this creates an endpoint that is always active and has dedicated resources behind it at all times. Sometimes you may not want your model to be running at all times, you can then consider making your endpoint serverless. For serverless endpoints, resources are allocated dynamically based on calls to the endpoint. Because of that, you can expect some cost savings but the inference time may be slower.

To get predictions from your model, you can use the library boto3[17].

```
import boto3

runtime = boto3.client("sagemaker-runtime")
response = runtime.invoke_endpoint(
  EndpointName=model_ep,
  Body=newdata.to_csv(header=False, index=False).encode("utf-8"),
  ContentType="text/csv",
)
results = response["Body"].read()
```

Service providers like Google[18], Microsoft[19], etc. have equivalent options for deploying ML models. These service providers also give you the option of running

---

[16]https://docs.aws.amazon.com/sagemaker/latest/dg/notebooks-available-instance-types.html

[17]https://boto3.amazonaws.com/v1/documentation/api/latest/index.html

[18]https://cloud.google.com/ai-platform/prediction/docs/deploying-models

[19]https://learn.microsoft.com/en-us/azure/machine-learning/v1/how-to-deploy-and-where?tabs=azcli

training jobs, model testing, model monitoring, and other parts of the model-to-production pipeline, also called MLOps. Machine Learning Operations, or MLOps, is a core function of machine learning engineering. Its focus is on streamlining the process of taking machine learning models to production, including maintenance and monitoring.

12.4   MODEL AND OUTCOME EXPLAINABILITY

Being able to explain your model's output can be a challenging task. Here, we refer to the *Outcome* phase in Figure 12.4.

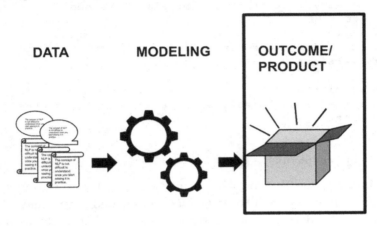

FIGURE 12.4   Phases of creating NLP projects - outcome.

It is not uncommon to opt for simpler models at the loss of some accuracy for better explainability. Often, the teams that consume the results of your models may not understand ML. While some may trust a data scientist's work completely, some need convincing material to trust and use the results of a model.

Other than open and constant communication, here are some pointers that can help a team without an ML background to trust, use, and understand your model.

- Share some high-level examples of the chosen ML model finding success in similar tasks based on published research. They may not know how great BiLSTM is but still care about understanding why you used it.

- Share examples of input -> output, including samples of both successes and failures. Showing only failures can understate the model's capabilities. Showing only successes can set false expectations.

- Share visualizations that resonate with the background of the audience. Plots of training loss of your model may not be easy to understand. Share plots that help them understand the data or model results in a way that impacts their consumption. Plots of test data errors, aggregated error/accuracy, and word clouds (with a little bit of explanation) could resonate with a wide audience.

- Communicate improvement plans for future iterations. No model is perfect and it may help others know that you see further potential to reduce issues and errors that exist or may surface upon more usage.

TIP **Understanding the impact of your work on KPIs**

Your model might be the best there is. However, if its impact on company KPIs is too small to be of significance, it may never be deployed or used in production. It does not mean you didn't do a good job. It just means that your work didn't contribute as much to what the company wanted at that point. Sometimes a simple word counts aggregation can leave a larger impact on company goals than a predictive neural network model. There also might be times when you have a clear path towards improving model accuracy by 5%, but it may not be worth four weeks of your time based on the contribution of that extra 5% to the company's goal.

As we saw from the KPI diagrams shared for each project in the previous chapters, how you test and measure the goodness of your ML models can be different from how their impact is measured from a KPI perspective.

Windup

In this section, we looked at multiple popular applications of NLP in the industry, including chatbots, customer review analysis, recommendation systems, and next-word prediction. For each application, we listed key performance indicators (KPIs), business objectives, action plans for the demonstrations, and executed implementations. Most application pipelines require integration with other systems used in the organization. We discussed model deployment tools but our aim has not been to explore all the engineering efforts required to completely deploy these applications and have focused primarily on the back-end modeling.

We used realistic datasets that help with understanding challenges in a company. We also assumed cases where datasets are not available and leveraged openly accessible data in those cases (Wikipedia data for next-word prediction). We also went through scenarios where we don't have labeled data for creating a supervised classification model (comment classification). We explored ways to generate labeled data with minimal time investment. We also made use of a conditionally available data source, i.e., YouTube API, for building a recommendation system. For chatbots, we started by manually creating labeled data. These different examples reflect a realistic state of data processes in the industry.

To begin with, we showed implementations of two types of chatbots - a simpler rule-based chatbot, and a goal-oriented chatbot. We shared code samples and popular frameworks that can help you build such chatbot applications. We shared resources and tips on creating and fine-tuning your chatbot to best serve your purpose. We also listed out multiple service providers that you can explore to deploy chatbots.

We then explored a popular NLP application surrounding customer reviews. We analyzed customer reviews by computing sentiment and looked at word clouds to understand comment themes. We then picked three popular themes to build a classification model that identifies the presence of each theme in a comment. We discussed multiple ways of approaching the problem when labeled data is not available. We built a model using one approach and also implemented alternate options to showcase different methods of achieving the goal.

Next, we looked at building recommendation systems using YouTube videos (title and description fields). For this application, we explored three modeling options and compared the results from each. There are many pre-trained and quick solutions that you can leverage for building such a model. Which one of them might be good for your data and application? This remains a popular question that practitioners often deal with. We demonstrated making a choice between different available tools, which is a common industry scenario, i.e., choosing the right tool for the job. We looked at building a model that predicts the next words. We worked under the assumption that we do not have available any existing documents that help us form a training data corpus for the task. We collected data from Wikipedia to develop the first model for this task. We shared the implementation of a BiLSTM model and shared some outcomes from the model.

Finally, we discussed some common types of modeling and data problems in the real world, model deployment, explainability, final thoughts, and tips.

Bibliography

[1] Active learning and augmentation. Khoury College of Computer Sciences, Northeastern University Khoury College of Computer Sciences, Northeastern University. https://course.ccs.neu.edu/ds4440f20/lecture-materials/ds4440-lowell-AL-augmentation.pdf. Online; accessed 2022-11-22.

[2] Ai for telecom: Automatic, adaptive, autonomous. Softengi. https://softengi.com/blog/ai-is-the-telecom-industry-trend-automatic-adaptive-autonomous/. Online; accessed 2022-01-11.

[3] Create cnn model and optimize using keras tuner – deep learning.

[4] Emerging and rare entity recognition. 2017 The 3rd Workshop on Noisy User-generated Text (W-NUT). http://noisy-text.github.io/2017/emerging-rare-entities.html. Online; accessed 2022-12-05.

[5] Insurance fraud. FBI. https://www.fbi.gov/stats-services/publications/insurance-fraud. Online; accessed 2022-01-18.

[6] istart. Adaptive Literacy Technologies . http://www.adaptiveliteracy.com/istart. Online; accessed 2022-11-02.

[7] Latest news. Financial highlights. China Mobile. https://www.chinamobileltd.com/en/global/home.php. Online; accessed 2022-01-11.

[8] Machine learning driven models in the automotive sector. reply.com. https://www.reply.com/en/topics/artificial-intelligence-and-machine-learning/nlp-across-the-automotive-value-chain Online; accessed 2022-02-05.

[9] Playmancer: A european serious gaming 3d environment. Cordis, European Commission. https://cordis.europa.eu/project/id/215839/results. Online; accessed 2022-11-08.

[10] Snorkel intro tutorial: Data augmentation. Snorkel. https://www.snorkel.org/use-cases/02-spam-data-augmentation-tutorial Online; accessed 2022-11-22.

[11] Library of Congress. Telecommunications Industry: A Research Guide. https://guides.loc.gov/telecommunications-industry. Online; accessed 2023-05-13.

[12] Telia & ultimate.ai: a new generation of customer service. `https://www.ultimate.ai/customer-stories/telia`. Online; accessed 2022-01-11.

[13] Tradeshift announces 'go,' the first virtual assistant for company spending & travel. `https://tradeshift.com/press/tradeshift-announces- go-the-first-virtual-assistant-for-company- spending-travel/`. Online; accessed 2022-11-06.

[14] Nlp in video games. Amalgam, October 2017. `http://iiitd-amalgam.blogspot.com/2017/10/nlp-in-video-games.html`.

[15] Everything you need to know about natural language processing (nlp) in real estate. `https://co-libry.com/blogs/natural- language-processing-nlp-real-estate/`, November 2020.

[16] Shift technology to support fraud detection and subrogation initiatives for central insurance. Shift Technology. `https://www.prnewswire.com/news-releases/shift-technology-to-support-fraud-detection-and-subrogation- initiatives-for-central-insurance-301121515.html`, September 2020.

[17] All about education industry: Key segments, trends, and competitve advantages. Pat Research, 2021. `https://www.predictiveanalyticstoday.com/what-is-education-industry/` Online; accessed 2022-02-13.

[18] Eliane Alhadeff. I-fleg: A serious game for second language acquisition. Serious Game Market, April 2013. `https://www.seriousgamemarket.com/2013/04/i-fleg-serious-game-for-second-language.html`.

[19] Marilisa Amoia. I-fleg a 3d-game for learning french. 07 2011.

[20] Inmaculada Arnedillo-SÃąnchez, Carlos de Aldama, and Chrysanthi Tseloudi. ressume: Employability skills social media survey. International Journal of Manpower, 39, 10 2018.

[21] Artificiallawyer. Norton rose rolls out 'parker' the legal chat bot for gdpr. Artificial Lawyer. `https://www.artificiallawyer.com/2018/05/16/norton-rose-rolls-out-parker-the-legal-chat-bot-for-gdpr/`, May 2018. Online; accessed 2022-11-07.

[22] American Speech-Language-Hearing Association (ASHA). `https://www.asha.org/practice-portal/clinical-topics/spoken-language-disorders/language-in-brief/`. Online; accessed 2021-12-10.

[23] Kevin Ashley. Applied Machine Learning for Health and Fitness. Apress, 2020.

[24] Shivam Bansal. Beginners guide to topic modeling in python. `https://www.analyticsvidhya.com/blog/2016/08/beginners-guide-to-topic-modeling-in-python/`, Aug 2016.

[25] Oliver Batey. Mining an economic news article using pre-trained language models. Towards Data Science, January 2021. `https://towardsdatascience.com/mining-an-economic-news-article-using-pre-trained-language-models-f75af041ecf0` Online; accessed 2022-05-29.

[26] Zikri Bayraktar. Natural language processing: The new frontier in oil and gas. Schlumberger-Doll Research Center. `https://www.software.slb.com/blog/natural-language-processing---the-new-frontier`. Online; accessed 2022-01-13.

[27] Pete Bell. Ten groups control 40%. of global wireless subscribers. `https://blog.telegeography.com/top-telecos-by-wireless-subscribers-global`, September 2020. Online; accessed 2022-01-11.

[28] Yoshua Bengio. Gradient-based optimization of hyperparameters. Neural Computation, 12(8):1889–1900, 08 2000. `https://doi.org/10.1162/089976600300015187`.

[29] Deepanshu Bhalla. K nearest neighbor : Step by step tutorial. Listen Data, 2018. `https://www.listendata.com/2017/12/k-nearest-neighbor-step-by-step-tutorial.html` Online; accessed 2022-11-22.

[30] Raghav Bharadwaj. Data search and discovery in oil and gas – A review of capabilities. Emerj: The AI research and advisory company. `https://emerj.com/ai-sector-overviews/data-search-discovery-oil-gas-review-capabilities/`, 11 2018. Online; accessed 2022-01-13.

[31] Raghav Bharadwaj. Using nlp for customer feedback in automotive, banking, and more. `https://emerj.com/ai-podcast-interviews/using-nlp-customer-feedback-automotive-banking/`, February 2019.

[32] Chris Biemann. Chinese whispers: An efficient graph clustering algorithm and its application to natural language processing problems. Proceedings of TextGraphs, pages 73–80, 07 2006.

[33] BigScience. Bloom: Bigscience 176b model. `https://bigscience.notion.site/BLOOM-BigScience-176B-Model-ad073ca07cdf479398d5f95d88e218c4`, 2022. Online; accessed 2022-11-22.

[34] Steven Bird, Ewan Klein, and Edward Loper. Natural language processing with Python: Analyzing text with the natural language toolkit. O'Reilly Media, Inc., 2009.

[35] David Blei, Andrew Ng, and Michael Jordan. Latent dirichlet allocation. Journal of Machine Learning Research, 3:993, 01 2013.

[36] That Data Bloke. Gesture recognition for beginners with cnn. `https://towardsdatascience.com/artificial-neural-networks-for-gesture-recognition-for-beginners-7066b7d771b5`, Apr 2020.

[37] Tom Bocklisch, Joey Faulkner, Nick Pawlowski, and Alan Nichol. Rasa: Open source language understanding and dialogue management. arXiv, 2017.

[38] Tom B. Brown, Benjamin Mann, Nick Ryder, Melanie Subbiah, Jared Kaplan, Prafulla Dhariwal, Arvind Neelakantan, Pranav Shyam, Girish Sastry, Amanda Askell, Sandhini Agarwal, Ariel Herbert-Voss, Gretchen Krueger, Tom Henighan, Rewon Child, Aditya Ramesh, Daniel M. Ziegler, Jeffrey Wu, Clemens Winter, Christopher Hesse, Mark Chen, Eric Sigler, Mateusz Litwin, Scott Gray, Benjamin Chess, Jack Clark, Christopher Berner, Sam McCandlish, Alec Radford, Ilya Sutskever, and Dario Amodei. Language models are few-shot learners. 2020.

[39] Jason Brownlee. A gentle introduction to matrix factorization for machine learning. Machine Learning Mastery, February 2018. https://machinelearningmastery.com/introduction-to-matrix-decompositions-for-machine-learning/ Online; accessed 2022-11-20.

[40] Justine Calma. Google is taking sign-ups for relate, a voice assistant that recognizes impaired speech. The verge, November 2021. https://www.theverge.com/2021/11/9/22772535/google-project-relate-euphonia-voice-recognition-command-control- assistant.

[41] Ricardo Campos, VÃ\u{n}tor Mangaravite, Arian Pasquali, AlÃ\u{n}pio Jorge, CÃ\u{i}lia Nunes, and Adam Jatowt. Yake! collection-independent automatic keyword extractor. 02 2018.

[42] CaseMine. casemine : The most granular mapping of us case law. CaseMine, Gauge Data Solutions. https://www.casemine.com/. Online; accessed 2022-11-07.

[43] Sound Relief Healing Center. https://www.soundrelief.com/hearing-loss/how-hearing-works/. Online; accessed 2021-12-10.

[44] Daniel Cer, Yinfei Yang, Sheng-yi Kong, Nan Hua, Nicole Limtiaco, Rhomni John, Noah Constant, Mario Guajardo-Cespedes, Steve Yuan, Chris Tar, Yun-Hsuan Sung, Brian Strope, and Ray Kurzweil. Universal sentence encoder. 03 2018.

[45] Sam Chapman. Sam's string metrics. https://www.coli.uni-saarland.de/courses/LT1/2011/slides/stringmetrics.pdf. Online; accessed 2022-11-24.

[46] Chartis. Ai in regtech: A quiet upheaval. IBM. https://www.ibm.com/downloads/cas/NAJXEKE6, 2019.

[47] Nagesh Singh Chauhan. Naïve bayes algorithm: Everything you need to know. KD Nuggets, April 2022. https://www.kdnuggets.com/2020/06/naive-bayes-algorithm-everything.html Online; accessed 2022-11-22.

[48] Francois Chollet et al. Keras. GitHub. `https://github.com/fchollet/keras`, 2015.

[49] Clio. Legal trends report. `https://www.clio.com/wp-content/uploads/2018/10/Legal-Trends-Report-2018.pdf`, 2018.

[50] Papers With Code. Bidirectional lstm. Meta. `https://paperswithcode.com/method/bilstm`. Online; accessed 2022-11-22.

[51] William W. Cohen.

[52] Alexis Conneau, Douwe Kiela, Holger Schwenk, Loïc Barrault, and Antoine Bordes. Supervised learning of universal sentence representations from natural language inference data. BibSonomy pages 670–680, 09 2017.

[53] ContractProbe. Contractprobe. fast. intelligent. secure. automated legal document review in less than 60 seconds. `https://www.contractprobe.com/`. Online; accessed 2022-11-07.

[54] Convoboss. Real estate chatbot live demo. `https://convoboss.com/real-estate-chatbot#live-demo-2`. Online; accessed 2022-09-30.

[55] Glen Coppersmith, Ryan Leary, Patrick Crutchley, and Alex Fine. Natural language processing of social media as screening for suicide risk. Biomedical Informatics Insights, 10:1178222618792860, 2018. PMID: 30158822.

[56] Zihang Dai, Zhilin Yang, Yiming Yang, Jaime Carbonell, Quoc V. Le, and Ruslan Salakhutdinov. Transformer-xl: Attentive language models beyond a fixed-length context. arXiv, 2019. `https://arxiv.org/abs/1901.02860`.

[57] Robert Dale. Law and word order: Nlp in legal tech. Towards Data Science `https://towardsdatascience.com/law-and-word-order-nlp-in-legal-tech-bd14257ebd06`, December 2018.

[58] Soheil Danesh, Tamara Sumner, and James Martin. Sgrank: Combining statistical and graphical methods to improve the state of the art in unsupervised keyphrase extraction. In Proceedings of the Fourth Joint Conference on Lexical and Computational Semantics pages 117–126, 01 2015.

[59] Dataflair. Kernel functions-introduction to svm kernel & examples. Dataflair, 2018. `https://data-flair.training/blogs/svm-kernel-functions/` Online; accessed 2022-11-25.

[60] Cruz E. Borges Cristina Martin Ainhoa Alonso-Vicario David Orive, Gorka Sorrosal. Evolutionary algorithms for hyperparameter tuning on neural networks models. Proceedings of the European Modeling and Simulation Symposium, 2014 978-88-97999-38-6, 2014. `http://www.msc-les.org/proceedings/emss/2014/EMSS2014_402.pdf` Online; accessed 2022-11-22.

[61] Statista Research Department. Estimated size of the legal services market worldwide from 2015 to 2025. January 2022. `https://www.statista.com/statistics/605125/size-of-the-global-legal-services-market/`.

[62] Jacob Devlin, Ming-Wei Chang, Kenton Lee, and Kristina Toutanova. BERT: pre-training of deep bidirectional transformers for language understanding. CoRR, abs/1810.04805, 2018.

[63] Jay DeYoung, Iz Beltagy, Madeleine Zuylen, Bailey Kuehl, and Lucy Wang. Ms^2: Multi-document summarization of medical studies. pages 7494–7513, 01 2021.

[64] Andrew Dickson. How we made the dyson vacuum cleaner. The Guardian. `https://www.theguardian.com/culture/2016/may/24/interview-james-dyson-vacuum-cleaner`, 2016.

[65] Kelvin Salton do Prado. How dbscan works and why should we use it? Towards Data Science, April 2017. `https://towardsdatascience.com/how-dbscan-works-and-why-should-i-use-it-443b4a191c80` Online; accessed 2022-11-20.

[66] Dr. Yiqiang Han Dr. Yannan Shen. A natural language processing model for house price forecasting. Clemson University Research Foundation. `http://curf.clemson.edu/technology/a-natural-language-processing-model-for-house-price-forecasting/`. Online; accessed 2022-11-04.

[67] Dheeru Dua and Casey Graff. UCI machine learning repository. University of California, Irvine, School of Information and Computer Sciences. `https://archive.ics.uci.edu/ml/datasets.php?format=&task=att=&area=&numAtt=&numIns=&type=text&sort=nameUp&view=table`, 2017.

[68] Swagata Duari and Vasudha Bhatnagar. scake: Semantic connectivity aware keyword extraction. Information Sciences, 477, 10 2018.

[69] University of Wisconsin-Madison (U.S.A.) Epistemic Games Group (U.S.A.). Land science. Serious Game Classification. `http://serious.gameclassification.com/EN/games/43815-Land-Science/index.html`, 2010. Online; accessed 2022-11-08.

[70] Shannon Flynn. How natural language processing (nlp) ai is used in law. Law Technology Today. `https://www.lawtechnologytoday.org/2021/06/how-natural-language-processing-nlp-ai-is-used-in-law/`, June 2021.

[71] Foresee medical. Natural language processing in healthcare. `https://www.foreseemed.com/natural-language-processing-in-healthcare`. Online; accessed 2022-01-30.

[72] Kevin Leyton-Brown Thomas Stutzle Frank Hutter, Holger H Hoos. Paramils: An automatic algorithm configuration framework. Journal of Artificial Intelligence Research 36 (2009) 267-306, October 2009. `https://arxiv.org/ftp/arxiv/papers/1401/1401.3492.pdf` Online; accessed 2022-11-22.

[73] Yan Gao. Ucsd health system provides language interpreting device to aid communication. The Guardian. `https://ucsdguardian.org/2014/04/21/ucsd-health-system-provides-language-interpreting-device-to-aid-communication/`, April 2014.

[74] William Goddard. Natural language processing in education. `https://itchronicles.com/natural-language-processing-nlp/natural-language-processing-in-education/`, September 2021.

[75] Inc. Grand View Research. Telecom services market size, share & trends analysis report by service type (mobile data services, machine-to-machine services), by transmission (wireline, wireless), by end-use, by region, and segment forecasts, 2021–2028. `https://www.grandviewresearch.com/industry-analysis/global-telecom-services-market`. Online; accessed 2022-11-07.

[76] AurÃĺlien GÃĺron. Hands-On Machine Learning with Scikit-Learn, Keras, and TensorFlow. O'Reilly Media, Inc., September 2019.

[77] Hilda Hardy, Alan Biermann, R Bryce Inouye, Ashley McKenzie, Tomek Strzalkowski, Cristian Ursu, Nick Webb, and Min Wu. The amitiés system: Data-driven techniques for automated dialogue. Speech Communication, 48(3–4):354–373, 2006.

[78] Adam Hayes. Bayes' theorem: What it is, the formula, and examples. Investopedia, March 2022. `https://www.investopedia.com/terms/b/bayes-theorem.asp` Online; accessed 2022-11-22.

[79] Brenner Heintz. Training a neural network to detect gestures with opencv in python. Towards Data Science, Dec 2018. `https://towardsdatascience.com/training-a-neural-network-to-detect-gestures-with-opencv-in-python-e09b0a12bdf1`.

[80] Matthew Honnibal and Ines Montani. spaCy 2: Natural language understanding with Bloom embeddings, convolutional neural networks and incremental parsing. To appear, 2017.

[81] Daniel Hsu. Brown clusters, linguistic context, and spectral algorithms. Columbia University. `https://www.cs.columbia.edu/~djhsu/papers/brown-talk.pdf` Online; accessed 2022-11-24.

[82] R.J. Huefner. Revenue Management: A Path to Increased Profits. Business Expert Press Managerial Accounting collection. Business Expert Press, 2011.

[83] C.J. Hutto and Eric Gilbert. Vader: A parsimonious rule-based model for sentiment analysis of social media text. 01 2015.

[84] Inc. IMDb.com. `https://developer.imdb.com/`. Online; accessed 2021-11-18.

[85] Decision Trees in Machine Learning. Decision trees in machine learning. May 2017. `https://towardsdatascience.com/decision-trees-in-machine-learning-641b9c4e8052`.

[86] Casetext Inc. casetext: Modern search technology that finds cases lexis and westlaw miss. Casetext Inc. `https://casetext.com/`. Online; accessed 2022-11-07.

[87] Ioana. Latent semantic analysis: Intuition, math, implementation. Towards Data Science, May 2020. `https://towardsdatascience.com/latent-semantic-analysis-intuition-math-implementation-` a194aff870f8 Online; accessed 2022-11-20.

[88] Ferris Jabr. The reading brain in the digital age: The science of paper versus screens. Scientific Journal. `https://www.scientificamerican.com/article/reading-paper-screens/` Online; accessed 2021-12-10.

[89] Arun Jagota. Markov clustering algorithm. Towards Data Science, December 2020. `https://towardsdatascience.com/markov-clustering-algorithm-577168dad475` Online; accessed 2022-11-20.

[90] Kipling D. Williams and Joseph P. Forgas. Social Influence: Direct and Indirect Processes. Psychology Press, May 2001.

[91] Naveen Joshi. Nlp is taking the travel and tourism industry to new places. here's how. Allerin, November 2020. `https://www.allerin.com/blog/nlp-is-taking-the-travel-and-tourism-industry-to-new-places-` heres-how.

[92] Naveen Joshi. 5 benefits of natural language processing in the travel and tourism industry. bbn times, March 2021. `https://www.bbntimes.com/technology/5-benefits-of-natural-language-processing-in-the-travel-and-tourism-industry`.

[93] Kaggle. `https://www.kaggle.com/crowdflower/twitter-airline-sentiment`. Online; accessed 2021-11-18.

[94] Dhruvil Karani. Topic modelling with plsa. Towards Data Science, October 2018. `https://towardsdatascience.com/topic-modelling-with-plsa-728b92043f41` Online; accessed 2022-11-20.

[95] Diane F. Halpern, M. Anne Britt-Joseph, P. Magliano Katja Wiemer-Hastings, Keith Millis, Arthur C. Graesser. Operation aries! Google sites, Operations Aries! `https://sites.google.com/site/ariesits/`. Online; accessed 2022-11-08.

[96] Jason S. Kessler. Scattertext: A browser-based tool for visualizing how corpora differ. 2017.

[97] Suleiman Khan. Bert technology introduced in 3-minutes. Towards Data Science, February 2019. https://towardsdatascience.com/bert-technology-introduced-in-3-minutes-2c2f9968268c.

[98] Kira. Kira. https://kirasystems.com/. Online; accessed 2022-11-07.

[99] Thomas Kluyver, Benjamin Ragan-Kelley, Fernando Pérez, Brian Granger, Matthias Bussonnier, Jonathan Frederic, Kyle Kelley, Jessica Hamrick, Jason Grout, Sylvain Corlay, Paul Ivanov, Damián Avila, Safia Abdalla, and Carol Willing. Jupyter notebooks – a publishing format for reproducible computational workflows. In F. Loizides and B. Schmidt, editors, Positioning and Power in Academic Publishing: Players, Agents and Agendas, pages 87–90. IOS Press, 2016.

[100] Kevin Knowles. How vodafone's chatbot tobi is changing the contact center. https://contact-center.cioapplicationseurope.com/cxoinsights/how-vodafone-s-chatbot-tobi-is-changing-the-contact-centre-nid-1640.html. Online; accessed 2022-01-11.

[101] Korbinian Koch. A friendly introduction to text clustering. Towards Data Science, March 2020. https://towardsdatascience.com/a-friendly-introduction-to-text-clustering-fa996bcefd04 Online; accessed 2022-11-20.

[102] John Lafferty, Andrew Mccallum, and Fernando Pereira. Conditional random fields: Probabilistic models for segmenting and labeling sequence data. pages 282–289, 01 2001.

[103] Natasia Langfelder. 3 reasons why insurers should use natural language processing technology. Data Axle, July 2021. https://www.data-axle.com/resources/blog/3-reasons-why-insurers-should-use-natural-language-processing- technology/.

[104] Encore Language Learning. What is the most spoken language in the world. Encore Language Learning. https://gurmentor.com/what-is-the-most-spoken-language-in-the-world/ Online; accessed 2021-12-14.

[105] Angelina Leigh. 10 examples of natural language processing (nlp) and how to leverage its capabilities. Hitachi. https://global.hitachi-solutions.com/blog/natural-language-processing. Online; accessed 2022-01-16.

[106] Angelina Leigh. 6 uses for natural language processing in healthcare. Hitachi Solutions. https://global.hitachi-solutions.com/blog/nlp-in-healthcare Online; accessed 2022-01-30.

[107] Jure Leskovec and Andrej Krevl. SNAP Datasets: Stanford large network dataset collection. `https://snap.stanford.edu/data/web-Amazon.html`, June 2014.

[108] Mike Lewis, Yinhan Liu, Naman Goyal, Marjan Ghazvininejad, Abdelrahman Mohamed, Omer Levy, Veselin Stoyanov, and Luke Zettlemoyer. Bart: Denoising sequence-to-sequence pre-training for natural language generation, translation, and comprehension. pages 7871–7880, 01 2020.

[109] Xuerong Li, Wei Shang, and Shouyang Wang. Text-based crude oil price forecasting: A deep learning approach. International Journal of Forecasting, 35(4):1548–1560, October 2019. `https://doi.org/10.1016/j.ijforecast.2018.07.006`.

[110] Sangrak Lim, Kyubum Lee, and Jaewoo Kang. Drug drug interaction extraction from the literature using a recursive neural network. PLOS ONE, 13(1):e0190926, January 2018. `https://doi.org/10.1371/journal.pone.0190926`.

[111] LinkedIn. `https://developer.linkedin.com/`. Online; accessed 2021-11-17.

[112] Yinhan Liu, Myle Ott, Naman Goyal, Jingfei Du, Mandar Joshi, Danqi Chen, Omer Levy, Mike Lewis, Luke Zettlemoyer, and Veselin Stoyanov. Roberta: A robustly optimized bert pretraining approach, 07 2019.

[113] Edward Ma. Data augmentation in nlp. Towards Data Science, April 2019. `https://towardsdatascience.com/data-augmentation-in-nlp-2801a34dfc28` Online; accessed 2022-11-20.

[114] Bertrand Maltaverne. Imagining the future of procurement technology. Procurement Tidbits, January 2016. `https://medium.com/procurement-tidbits/imagining-the-future-of-procurement-technology-387635ad63e8` Online; accessed 2022-11-06.

[115] Katerina Mansour. 4 ways nlp technology can be leveraged for insurance. Early Metrics. `https://earlymetrics.com/4-ways-nlp-technology-can-be-leveraged-for-insurance/`, December 2020.

[116] Chelsie May. Top 8 machine learning & ai software development companies for automotive. `https://medium.datadriveninvestor.com/top-8-machine-learning-ai-software-development-companies-for-automotive-39d33a38ff9d`, April 2020.

[117] Gretchen McCulloch. Emojineering part 1: Machine learning for emoji trends. All Things Linguistic, 2015. `https://allthingslinguistic.com/post/124609017512/emojineering-part-1-machine-learning-for-emoji` Online; accessed 2021-12-14.

[118] Merriam-Webster. Occam's razor. `https://www.merriam-webster.com/dictionary/Occam%27s%20razor`. Online; accessed 2022-11-28.

[119] Meta. `https://developers.facebook.com/docs/graph-api/`. Online; accessed 2021-11-18.

[120] Meta. Instagram api. `https://developers.facebook.com/docs/instagram-api/`. Online; accessed 2021-11-18.

[121] Andrew Stern Michael Mateas. Facade. Playabl, Inc. `https://www.playablstudios.com/facade`. Online; accessed 2022-11-02.

[122] USC Institute for Creative Technologies Mike van Lent et al. Ict mission rehearsal exercise. Soar EECS University of Michigan. `https://soar.eecs.umich.edu/workshop/22/vanLentMRE-S22.PDF` Online; accessed 2022-11-08.

[123] Libby Nelson. British desserts, explained for americans confused by the great british baking show. Vox. `https://www.vox.com/2015/11/29/9806038/great-british-baking-show-pudding-biscuit`, Nov 2015.

[124] Jordan Novet. Elon musk said 'use signal,' and confused investors sent the wrong stock up 438%. On monday. `https://www.cnbc.com/2021/01/11/signal-advance-jumps-another-438percent-after-elon-musk-fueled-buying-frenzy.html`, January 2021.

[125] Oberlo. How many people use social media in 2021?how many people use social media in 2021? `https://www.oberlo.com/statistics/how-many-people-use-social-media` Online; accessed December 31, 2021.

[126] Layla Oesper, Daniele Merico, Ruth Isserlin, and Gary D Bader. WordCloud: A cytoscape plugin to create a visual semantic summary of networks. Springer Science and Business Media LLC, 6(1), April 2011. `https://doi.org/10.1186/1751-0473-6-7`.

[127] Layla Oesper, Daniele Merico, Ruth Isserlin, and Gary D Bader. Wordcloud: A cytoscape plugin to create a visual semantic summary of networks. Source code for biology and medicine, 6(1):7, 2011.

[128] Coumbia Doctors: Department of Surgery. History of medicine: The incubator babies of coney island. Columbia Surgery. `https://columbiasurgery.org/news/2015/08/06/history-medicine-incubator-babies-coney-island`, 2015.

[129] Eirini Papagiannopoulou and Grigorios Tsoumakas. A review of keyphrase extraction. CoRR, abs/1905.05044, 2019.

[130] F. Pedregosa, G. Varoquaux, A. Gramfort, V. Michel, B. Thirion, O. Grisel, M. Blondel, P. Prettenhofer, R. Weiss, V. Dubourg, J. Vanderplas, A. Passos,

D. Cournapeau, M. Brucher, M. Perrot, and E. Duchesnay. Scikit-learn: Machine learning in Python. Journal of Machine Learning Research, 12:2825–2830, 2011.

[131] Davide Picca, Dominique Jaccard, and GÃlrald EberlÃI. Natural language processing in serious games: A state of the art. International Journal of Serious Games, 2, 09 2015.

[132] Edward Dixon Jonas Christensen Kirk Borne Leland Wilkinson Shantha Mohan Prashant Natarajan, Bob Rogers. Demystifying AI for the Enterprise. Routledge, Taylor and Francis Group, December 2021.

[133] Juliane Zeiser Prof. Dr. GÃlrald Schlemminger. Eveil-3d! Karlsruhe Institute of Technology. https://www.eveil-3d.eu/. Online; accessed 2022-11-08.

[134] Sruthi E R. Understanding random forest. Analytics Vidhya, June 2021. https://www.analyticsvidhya.com/blog/2021/06/understanding-random-forest/ Online; accessed 2022-11-22.

[135] Aparijita Ojha R. Jothi, Sraban Kumar Mohanty. Fast approximate minimum spanning tree based clustering algorithm. Science Direct, January 2018. https://www.sciencedirect.com/science/article/abs/pii/S092523121731295X Online; accessed 2022-11-22.

[136] Alec Radford, Jeffrey Wu, Rewon Child, David Luan, Dario Amodei, and Ilya Sutskever. Language models are unsupervised multitask learners. 2018. https://d4mucfpksywv.cloudfront.net/better-language-models/language-models.pdf.

[137] Colin Raffel, Noam Shazeer, Adam Roberts, Katherine Lee, Sharan Narang, Michael Matena, Yanqi Zhou, Wei Li, and Peter Liu. Exploring the limits of transfer learning with a unified text-to-text transformer, 10 2019.

[138] Raman. Ml | expectation-maximization algorithm. Geeks for Geeks, May 2019. https://www.geeksforgeeks.org/ml-expectation-maximization-algorithm/ Online; accessed 2022-11-20.

[139] Reddit. https://www.reddit.com/dev/api/. Online; accessed 2021-11-17.

[140] Radim Rehurek and Petr Sojka. Gensim–python framework for vector space modelling. NLP Centre, Faculty of Informatics, Masaryk University, Brno, Czech Republic, 3(2), 2011.

[141] Nils Reimers and Iryna Gurevych. Sentence-bert: Sentence embeddings using siamese bert-networks. In Proceedings of the 2019 Conference on Empirical Methods in Natural Language Processing. Association for Computational Linguistics, 11 2019.

[142] Nils Reimers and Iryna Gurevych. Sentence-bert: Sentence embeddings using siamese bert-networks. In Proceedings of the 2019 Conference on Empirical Methods in Natural Language Processing. Association for Computational Linguistics, 11 2019.

[143] Alberto Romero. A complete overview of gpt-3 âĂŤ the largest neural network ever created. Towards Data Science, May 2021. https://towardsdatascience.com/gpt-3-a-complete-overview-190232eb25fd Online; accessed 2022-11-20.

[144] Marla Rosner. Oil & gas and natural language processing are the perfect match no one predicted. Sparkcognition. https://www.sparkcognition.com/oil-gas-natural-language-processing-are-perfect-match-no-one-predicted/, 3 2017. Online; accessed 2022-01-13.

[145] Candida S. Punla, https://orcid.org/ 0000-0002-1094-0018, cspunla@bpsu.edu.ph, Rosemarie C. Farro, https://orcid.org/0000-0002-3571-2716, rcfarro@bpsu.edu.ph, and Bataan Peninsula State University Dinalupihan, Bataan, Philippines. Are we there yet? An analysis of the competencies of BEED graduates of BPSU-DC. International Multidisciplinary Research Journal, 4(3):50–59, September 2022.

[146] Erik Sang and Fien Meulder. Introduction to the conll-2003 shared task: Language-independent named entity recognition. Proceeding of the Computational Natural Language Learning (CoNLL), 07 2003.

[147] Victor Sanh, Lysandre Debut, Julien Chaumond, and Thomas Wolf. Distilbert, a distilled version of bert: smaller, faster, cheaper and lighter. 10 2019.

[148] Victor Sanh, Lysandre Debut, Julien Chaumond, and Thomas Wolf. Distilbert, a distilled version of bert: smaller, faster, cheaper and lighter. 10 2019.

[149] Kyriakos Schwarz, Ahmed Allam, Nicolas Andres Perez Gonzalez, and Michael Krauthammer. AttentionDDI: Siamese attention-based deep learning method for drug–drug interaction predictions. BMC Bioinformatics, 22(1), August 2021. https://doi.org/10.1186/s12859-021-04325-y.

[150] Seed Scientific. How much data is created every day? [27 staggering stats]. https://seedscientific.com/how-much-data-is-created-every-day/, October 2021.

[151] Aakanksha Chowdhery Sharan Narang. Pathways language model (palm): Scaling to 540 billion parameters for breakthrough performance. Google Research, April 2022. https://ai.googleblog.com/2022/04/pathways-language-model-palm-scaling-to.html Online; accessed 2022-11-22.

[152] Drishti Sharma. A gentle introduction to roberta. Analytics Vidhya, October 2022. https://www.analyticsvidhya.com/blog/2022/10/a-gentle-introduction-to-roberta.

[153] Alex Sherstinsky. Fundamentals of recurrent neural network (RNN) and long short-term memory (LSTM) network. Physica D: Nonlinear Phenomena, 404:132306, Mar 2020.

[154] Jyotika Singh. An introduction to audio processing and machine learning using python. opensource.com, 09 2019. https://opensource.com/article/19/9/audio-processing-machine-learning-python.

[155] Jyotika Singh. Social media analysis using natural language processing techniques. In Proceedings of the 20th Python in Science Conference, pages 74–80, 01 2021.

[156] Jyotika Singh. pyaudioprocessing: Audio processing, feature extraction, and machine learning modeling. In Proceedings of the 21st Python in Science Conference, pages 152–158, 01 2022.

[157] Jyotika Singh, Michael Avon, and Serge Matta. Media and marketing optimization with cross platform consumer and content intelligence. https://patents.google.com/patent/US20210201349A1/en, 07 2021.

[158] Jyotika Singh, Rebecca Bilbro, Michael Avon, Scott Bowen, Dan Jolicoeur, and Serge Matta. Method for optimizing media and marketing content using cross-platform video intelligence. https://patents.google.com/patent/US10949880B2/en, 03 2021.

[159] Sameer Singh, Amarnag Subramanya, Fernando Pereira, and Andrew McCallum. Wikilinks: A large-scale cross-document coreference corpus labeled via links to Wikipedia. Technical Report UM-CS-2012-015, 2012.

[160] S. Lock. Global tourism industry – statistics & facts. August. https://www.statista.com/topics/962/global-tourism/#topicHeader__wrapper.

[161] Daniel Slotta. Number of customers of china mobile limited from 2010 to 2020. Statista. https://www.statista.com/statistics/272097/customer-base-of-china-mobile/, April 2021. Online; accessed 2022-01-11.

[162] Richard Socher, Alex Perelygin, Jean Wu, Jason Chuang, Christopher D. Manning, Andrew Ng, and Christopher Potts. Recursive deep models for semantic compositionality over a sentiment treebank. In Proceedings of the 2013 Conference on Empirical Methods in Natural Language Processing, pages 1631–1642, Seattle, Washington, USA, October 2013.

[163] Bruno Stecanella. Support vector machines (svm) algorithm explained. Monkey Learn, June 2017. https://monkeylearn.com/blog/introduction-to-support-vector-machines-svm/ Online; accessed 2022-11-22.

[164] Stephanie. The current challenges of speech recognition. ONLIM. https://onlim.com/en/the-current-challenges-of-speech-recognition/, Oct 2019.

[165] Kyle Strand. Natural language processing: A keystone of knowledge management in the digital age. IDB. `https://blogs.iadb.org/conocimiento-abierto/en/natural-language-processing/`, March 2021.

[166] Elias Kalapanidas Dimitri Konstantas Todor Ganchev Otilia Kocsis Tony Lam-Juan J. SantamarÃɲa Thierry Raguin Christian Breiteneder Hannes Kaufmann Costas Davarakis Susana JimÃĺnez-Murcia, Fernando FernÃąndez-Aranda. Playmancer Project: A Serious Videogame as an Additional Therapy Tool for Eating and Impulse Control Disorders. Volume 144: Annual Review of Cybertherapy and Telemedicine 2009. Online; accessed 2022-11-08.

[167] Richard E. Susskind. Expert systems in law: A jurisprudential approach to artificial intelligence and legal reasoning. The Modern Law Review, 49(2):168–194, March 1986. `https://doi.org/10.1111/j.1468-2230.1986.tb01683.x`.

[168] Dan Symonds. Natural language processing enhances autonomous vehicles experience. `https://www.autonomousvehicleinternational.com/features/natural-language-processing-enhances-autonomous-vehicles-experience.html`, October 2019.

[169] Archisman Majumdar T. S. Krishnan. Harness natural language processing to manage supply chain risk. California Review Management, Berkley Haas School of Business. `https://cmr.berkeley.edu/2021/01/managing-supply-chain-risk/`. Online; accessed 2022-11-06.

[170] Accenture team. Malta machine learning text analyzer. Accenture `https://malta.accenture.com/`. Online; accessed 2022-11-07.

[171] Allstate team. Ask abie. Allstate. `https://www.allstate.com/static/widgets/abi/`. Online; accessed 2022-11-07.

[172] Amelia team. Amelia conversational ai. Amelia. `https://amelia.ai/conversational-ai/`. Online; accessed 2022-11-07.

[173] Chevron team. Operational excellence management system. Chevron. `https://www.chevron.com/about/operational-excellence/oems`. Online; accessed 2022-11-06.

[174] DigitalOwl team. Digitalowl. DigitalOwl. `https://www.digitalowl.com/`. Online; accessed 2022-11-07.

[175] Frase team. Free slogan generator. Frase. `https://www.frase.io/tools/slogan-generator/`. Online; accessed 2022-11-06.

[176] Lemonade team. Lemonade. Lemonade Insurance Company. `https://www.lemonade.com/`. Online; accessed 2022-11-07.

[177] Sprout.AI team. Sprout.ai. Sprout. AI `https://sprout.ai/`. Online; accessed 2022-11-07.

[178] SuperDataScience Team. The ultimate guide to convolutional neural networks (cnn). SuperDataScience, August 2018. https://www.superdatascience.com/blogs/the-ultimate-guide-to-convolutional-neural-networks-cnn Online; accessed 2022-11-22.

[179] TensorFlow Developers. Tensorflow. Zenodo. https://zenodo.org/record/5645375, 2021.

[180] Anu Thomas. How mercedes-benz is using ai & nlp to give driving a tech makeover. https://analyticsindiamag.com/how-mercedes-benz-is-using-ai-nlp-to-give-driving-a-tech- makeover/, May 2020.

[181] James Thorn. Logistic regression explained. Towards Data Science, February 2020. https://towardsdatascience.com/logistic-regression-explained-9ee73cede081 Online; accessed 2022-11-20.

[182] Sunil Gupta Svetha Venkatesh Tinu Theckel Joy, Santu Rana. Hyper-parameter tuning for big data using bayesian optimisation. In 2016 23rd International Conference on Pattern Recognition (ICPR), December 2016. https://projet.liris.cnrs.fr/imagine/pub/proceedings/ICPR-2016/media/files/0557.pdf Online; accessed 2022-11-22.

[183] Twitch. https://dev.twitch.tv/docs/api/. Online; accessed 2021-11-17.

[184] Twitter. https://developer.twitter.com/en/docs/twitter-api. Online; accessed 2021-11-17.

[185] Natalie Vannini, Sibylle Enz, Maria Sapouna, Dieter Wolke, Scott Watson, Sarah Woods, Kerstin Dautenhahn, Lynne Hall, Ana Paiva, Elizabeth AndrÃI, Ruth Aylett, and Wolfgang Schneider. "fearnot!": A computer-based anti-bullying-programme designed to foster peer intervention. European Journal of Psychology of Education, 26(1):21–44, 2011. https://doi.org/10.1007/s10212-010-0035-4.

[186] Saeed V. Vaseghi. Spectral subtraction. In Advanced Signal Processing and Digital Noise Reduction, pages 242–260. Vieweg+Teubner Verlag, 1996.

[187] Ashish Vaswani, Noam Shazeer, Niki Parmar, Jakob Uszkoreit, Llion Jones, Aidan Gomez, Lukasz Kaiser, and Illia Polosukhin. Attention is all you need. 06 2017.

[188] Vaibhav Verdhan. Computer Vision Using Deep Learning. Apress, 2021.

[189] Jo Ann Duffy Victor E. Sower and Gerald Kohers. Great ormond street hospital for children: Ferrari's formula one handovers and handovers from surgery to intensive care. American Society for Quality. https://www.gwern.net/docs/technology/2008-sower.pdf, August 2008.

[190] Alex Wang, Amanpreet Singh, Julian Michael, Felix Hill, Omer Levy, and Samuel Bowman. Glue: A multi-task benchmark and analysis platform for natural language understanding. pages 353–355, 01 2018.

[191] Jin Wang, Haiying Li, Zhiqiang Cai, Fazel Keshtkar, Art Graesser, and David Williamson Shaffer. Automentor: Artificial intelligent mentor in educational game. In H. Chad Lane, Kalina Yacef, Jack Mostow, and Philip Pavlik, editors, Artificial Intelligence in Education, pages 940–941, Berlin, Heidelberg, 2013. Springer, Berlin, Heidelberg.

[192] Jason Wei and Kai Zou. EDA: Easy data augmentation techniques for boosting performance on text classification tasks. In Proceedings of the 2019 Conference on Empirical Methods in Natural Language Processing and the 9th International Joint Conference on Natural Language Processing (EMNLP-IJCNLP), pages 6382–6388, Hong Kong, China, November 2019. Association for Computational Linguistics.

[193] Jiahao Weng. How to perform abstractive summarization with pegasus. https://towardsdatascience.com/how-to-perform-abstractive-summarization-with-pegasus-3dd74e48bafb, February 2021. Online; accessed 2022-11-20.

[194] Wikipedia. https://dumps.wikimedia.org/. Online; accessed 2021-11-18.

[195] Wikipedia contributors. Neil H. borden—Wikipedia, the free encyclopedia. https://en.wikipedia.org/w/index.php?title=Neil_H._Borden&oldid=927834229, 2019. [Online; accessed 24-January-2022].

[196] Wikipedia contributors. The blob—Wikipedia, the free encyclopedia. https://en.wikipedia.org/w/index.php?title=The_Blob&oldid=1051211531, 2021. [Online; accessed 14-December-2021].

[197] Wikipedia contributors. Optical character recognition—Wikipedia, the free encyclopedia. https://en.wikipedia.org/w/index.php?title=Optical_character_recognition&oldid=1050771946, 2021. [Online; accessed 18-November-2021].

[198] Wikipedia contributors. Pip (package manager)—Wikipedia, the free encyclopedia. https://en.wikipedia.org/w/index.php?title=Pip_(package_manager)&oldid=1039503966, 2021. [Online; accessed 18-November-2021].

[199] Wikipedia contributors. Soundex—Wikipedia, the free encyclopedia. https://en.wikipedia.org/w/index.php?title=Soundex&oldid=1080944828, 2022. [Online; accessed 21-November-2022].

[200] Adam Wilson. Natural-language-processing techniques for oil and gas drilling data. Journal of Petroleum Technology, 69(10):96–97, 10 2017. https://doi.org/10.2118/1017-0096-JPT, eprint = https://onepetro.org/JPT/article-pdf/69/10/96/2212181/spe-1017-0096-jpt.pdf.

[201] Hamed Yaghoobian, Hamid R. Arabnia, and Khaled Rasheed. Sarcasm detection: A comparative study. CoRR, abs/2107.02276, 2021. https://arxiv.org/abs/2107.02276.

[202] Hui Yang and Jonathan Garibaldi. Automatic detection of protected health information from clinic narratives. Journal of biomedical informatics, 79, 07 2015. https://www.ncbi.nlm.nih.gov/pmc/articles/PMC4989090/.

[203] Zhilin Yang, Zihang Dai, Yiming Yang, Jaime G. Carbonell, Ruslan Salakhutdinov, and Quoc V. Le. Xlnet: Generalized autoregressive pretraining for language understanding. CoRR, abs/1906.08237, 2019.

[204] YouTube. Youtube data api reference. https://developers.google.com/youtube/v3/docs. Online; accessed 2021-11-17.

[205] YouTube. Youtube data api (v3)—quota calculator. https://developers.google.com/youtube/v3/determine_quota_cost. Online; accessed 2021-11-17.

[206] Tong Yu and Hong Zhu. Hyper-parameter optimization: A review of algorithms and applications. arXiv, 2020. https://arxiv.org/abs/2003.05689.

[207] Filip Zelic and Anuj Sable. How to ocr with tesseract, opencv and python. Nanonets. https://nanonets.com/blog/ocr-with-tesseract/ Online; accessed 2022-11-19.

[208] Zelros. Zelros the recommendation engine for insurance. https://www.zelros.com/. Online; accessed 2022-11-07.

[209] Jingqing Zhang, Yao Zhao, Mohammad Saleh, and Peter Liu. Pegasus: Pretraining with extracted gap-sentences for abstractive summarization, 12 2019.

[210] Yukun Zhu, Ryan Kiros, Richard Zemel, Ruslan Salakhutdinov, Raquel Urtasun, Antonio Torralba, and Sanja Fidler. Aligning books and movies: Towards story-like visual explanations by watching movies and reading books. 06 2015.

[211] Kristijonas Å¡ibutis. Ai as a competitive advantage in the telecom industry. Medium https://medium.com/mmt-business-publishing/ai-as-a-competitive-advantage-in-telecom-industry-b4b3577e8f1f, March 2019. Online; accessed 2022-01-11.

[212] Kevin Dewalt. The coming nlp revolution in insurance. Prolego https://www.prolego.com/blog/the-coming-nlp-revolution-in-insurance, January 2022.

[213] Jay Selig. How nlp streamlines the insurance claims process. expert.ai https://www.expert.ai/blog/nlp_streamlines_insurance_claims_process/, September 2021.

[214] Iman Ghosh. Ranked: The 100 Most Spoken Languages Around the World. Visual Capitalist https://www.visualcapitalist.com/100-most-spoken-languages/, February 2020.

[215] DealerAI. DealerAI: Conversational AI Platform Designed for Dealerships. https://dealerai.com/.Online; accessed 2022-11-08.

[216] T S Krishnan and Archisman Majumdar. Harness Natural Language Processing to Manage Supply Chain Risk. https://cmr.berkeley.edu/2021/01/managing-supply-chain-risk/, January 2021.

[217] Pascal Wichmann, Alexandra Brintrup, Simon Baker, Philip Woodall, Duncan McFarlane. Towards automatically generating supply chain maps from natural language text. IFAC-PapersOnLine, Volume 51, Issue 11, Pages 1726-1731, ISSN 2405-8963. https://doi.org/10.1016/j.ifacol.2018.08.207. https://www.sciencedirect.com/science/article/pii/S2405896318313284. September 2018.

[218] Soumalya Bhattacharyya. 6 Applications of NLP in Finance. Analytics Steps https://www.analyticssteps.com/blogs/6-applications-nlp-finance, July 2022.

[219] Steve Banker. Companies Improve Their Supply Chains With Artificial Intelligence. Forbes https://www.forbes.com/sites/stevebanker/2022/02/24/companies-improve-their-supply-chains-with-artificial-intelligence/, February 2022.

[220] Sean Ashcroft. Top 10: AI firms helping minimise supply chain disruption. Supply Chain Digital https://supplychaindigital.com/digital-supply-chain/top-10-ai-firms-helping-minimise-supply-chain-disruption, October 2022.

[221] IBM. 48% Lift in Visits to Best Western Hotel and Resort Locations with IBM Watson Advertising Conversations. https://www.ibm.com/case-studies/best-western-watson-advertising. Online; accessed 2023-03-07.

[222] Collin Couey. An Overview of Artificial Intelligence in Salesforce Einstein. Software Advice https://www.softwareadvice.com/resources/salesforce-einstein-ai-primer/, December 2019.

[223] Kate Koidan. These 10 Companies Are Transforming Marketing With AI. Topbots https://www.topbots.com/ai-companies-transforming-marketing/, June 2020.

[224] StartUs Insights. 5 Top AI Solutions impacting Property & Real Estate Companies. https://www.startus-insights.com/innovators-guide/ai-solutions-property-real-estate-companies/. Accessed Online; accessed 2023-03-07.

[225] Patrick von Platen. Transformers-based Encoder-Decoder Models. Hugging Face `https://huggingface.co/blog/encoder-decoder`, October 2020.

[226] Raffel, Colin & Shazeer, Noam & Roberts, Adam & Lee, Katherine & Narang, Sharan & Matena, Michael & Zhou, Yanqi & Li, Wei & Liu, Peter. Exploring the Limits of Transfer Learning with a Unified Text-to-Text Transformer. Journal of Machine Learning Research 21, 2010.

Index

Printed in the United States
by Baker & Taylor Publisher Services